A GUIDE TO

CIVIL WAR SITES
IN MARYLAND

BLUE AND GRAY IN A BORDER STATE

BY
SUSAN COOKE SODERBERG

WHITE MANE BOOKS

This White Mane Books publication
was printed by
Beidel Printing House, Inc.
63 West Burd Street
Shippensburg, PA 17257-0152 USA

In respect for the scholarship contained herein, the acid-free paper used in this book meets the guidelines for permanence and durability of the Committee on Production Guidelines for Book Longevity of the Council on Library Resources.

For a complete list of available publications
please write
White Mane Books
Division of White Mane Publishing Company, Inc.
P.O. Box 152
Shippensburg, PA 17257-0152 USA

Library of Congress Cataloging-in-Publication Data

Soderberg, Susan Cooke, 1944-
    A guide to Civil War sites in Maryland : Blue and Gray in a border state / by Susan Cooke Soderberg.
        p.   cm. -- (A walk in time book)
    Includes bibliographical references and index.
    ISBN 1-57249-103-5 (alk. paper)
    1. Maryland--History--Civil War, 1861-1865--Monuments--Guidebooks.
2. Maryland--History--Civil War, 1861-1865--Battlefields-
-Guidebooks. 3. Maryland--History--Civil War, 1861-1865--Museums-
-Guidebooks. 4. Maryland--Tours. 5. Historic sites--Maryland-
-Guidebooks. I. Title. II. Series.
E512.S64   1998
973.7'3'09752--dc21   98-22702
                                                          CIP

PRINTED IN THE UNITED STATES OF AMERICA

CONTENTS

SITES

PREFACE

This book is a study in place and time. It can be read without visiting the sites in order to get a sense of what happened where and when. It can be used as a reference when passing through an area to see what happened along the route being traveled. Or it can be used as a guide for Civil War tours.

Whether the traveler is voyaging by armchair, by car, by foot, or on occasion by boat, the sites have been carefully selected to give a feeling of what it was like in that place during the Civil War. Nothing can compare to "being there" in discovering how geography affected strategy, what the ordinary soldier saw and felt, or how a certain childhood environment helped to forge a general.

The sites included in this tour are not only battlefields, camps and headquarters, but also places that tell stories about the people and events of the war. Certain museums and house museums have been included that will help to give a geographical and historical perspective—the lay of the land, the modes of transportation, the culture—that affected the course of the war. The traveler will also discover charming little towns like Burkittsville, Funkstown, and Vienna that lie hidden away from the main thoroughfares and retain almost the same appearance that they had during the Civil War.

Sites that are private property have not been included unless they can be viewed from a public right-of-way. Also, sites which have been destroyed, paved over, or developed are not a part of this tour unless they are important to the understanding of particular strategies or troop movements during the Civil War.

The sites are arranged in sequence within each chapter for an orderly and progressive route through the area covered in that chapter. An attempt has also been made to have the route from one chapter naturally lead into the route for the next chapter. This is true of all except Chapter 2 and Chapter 7. At the end of Chapter 2, "Circling Baltimore," the reader has the opportunity to either return southwest to the beginning of Chapter 3, "North-Central Maryland," or to proceed northeast to Elkton which is the first stop in Chapter 9, "Eastern Shore." Chapter 7 ends at the far western end of Maryland and the tour then begins again in "Southern Maryland," Chapter 8.

Sites within cities are usually not given with directions because of difficulties with one-way streets, but maps locating the sites are provided for Baltimore and Frederick, and all within walking distance of each other are grouped together.

For those who are hiking or biking on the C & O Canal there is a progressive list, starting at the southern end of the Canal, of sites along the towpath in Appendix A. These sites can then be looked up in the Table of Contents for the page with the complete description.

Short biographies of people mentioned in the text can be found in

Appendix B. These biographies are limited to people who were Marylanders before or during the Civil War, and, if military personnel, mainly to officers with the rank of major or above. Two Medal of Honor recipients are included: Sergeant Christian Fleetwood, USA; and Private Benjamin Owens, CSA. There were 42 Medals of Honor given by the Confederacy and Owens was the only Marylander to receive one. The Union gave out more than 2,000 Medals of Honor, and Fleetwood, a black man, is a representative of that number since to research all of the Maryland names in that long list would require another book. Several other black recipients of the award are included in Fleetwood's biography. References have been added to the end of this appendix if you would like to research a name that does not appear in the biographies.

In addition to the Bibliography, there is a list of "recommended reading" at the end of each chapter for those who would like to discover more about a certain area or incident.

Addresses, phone numbers and Web pages of the local tourist offices, historical societies, and major sites are given at the end of each chapter. Maryland state resources are given at the end of the Introduction.

For those who would like to follow the route of Gen. Bradley Johnson's Confederate Cavalry around Baltimore in July 1864, or Gen. Jeb Stuart's Confederate Cavalry in October 1862 or July 1863, there are maps provided in Appendix C. Each of these routes covers more area than is treated in one chapter, so the maps are provided for those who would like to follow the continuous route. Troop movement maps before or during major engagements of the opposing armies can be found in other resources.

Finally, Garrett County and Wicomico County were not formed until after the Civil War but are included in this guide for the purpose of locating sites on modern maps. References in the text to the parts of Allegany County, Somerset County, or Worcester County that are now in another county have the new county name in parentheses. West Virginia officially became a state on June 20, 1863. References in the text before that date to parts of Virginia which are now in West Virginia have "West Virginia" in parentheses.

NOTES TO THE READER

DRIVING

Those following these tours will find themselves on busy thoroughfares and limited access roads. Caution should always be exercised and the book should not be allowed to distract the driver. Some of the roads are narrow and winding and demand extreme caution and strict observation of the posted speed limit. When stopping to view a site from the road, be sure to pull off the road so as not to obstruct traffic.

HOURS OF OPERATION

Hours are listed for those sites that are open to the public only at certain times. All of these sites are closed on Thanksgiving, Christmas, and New Year's Day, and many are closed on other holidays—even if it says, "Open daily." Hours of operation may also change; so it is a good idea to telephone the site before visiting.

PRIVATE PROPERTY

Some of the sites described in this book are private property and must be observed only from a public road or street. Please do not enter the grounds of a private property or approach the owner. A property owner has the right to have anyone arrested who enters his property uninvited—whether there is a "no trespassing" sign posted or not.

RELIC HUNTING UNLAWFUL

Relic hunting is against the law on all public property, whether a national park, a local park, a national historic register property, or a property that has been nominated to be on a historic register. Buildings, structures, and grounds are protected under the National Historic Preservation Act and the Archeological Resources Protection Act. Federal Law states that an individual can be fined up to $5,000 for removing anything from a public property or defacing a public property. Maryland State Laws are even stiffer.

Please—take nothing but photographs and leave nothing but footprints!

ACKNOWLEDGMENTS

Traveling the state of Maryland in search of its Civil War past was a wonderful experience. The land of Maryland—from the tall mountains in the west in glorious fall splendor, to the rolling green hills of the Piedmont, to the marshy shores of the Chesapeake Bay—is exciting and colorful in its variety. The people of the "Middle State" are as varied as its landscape, but always a pleasure to meet and always courteous and helpful. I was truly amazed that all of these differences could be united into one state; but I was not amazed at the richness of Maryland's heritage. Maryland is an extraordinary state with an extraordinary past—which makes it all the more fascinating.

I could not have accomplished this book without the help of my husband, Bill, who carefully read everything that I put down on paper and not only edited it as a former English teacher, but discussed with me how a novice would view certain explanations in the text, and made helpful suggestions. I am also very thankful to the people who looked over the part of my manuscript that lay in their field of expertise: Charles Jacobs in Montgomery County, Roger Keller in Washington County, Donna J. Williams in Baltimore, Susan Trail of the C & O Canal National Historical Park, and Patrick J. Griffin III for the biographies. To librarians Jane Sween of the Montgomery County Historical Society and Scottie Oliver of the Talbot County Free Library, James Aguierre of the Governor's Commission on the Civil War, and historian Janet Cooke of Sotterley, I am extremely grateful for the extra effort they gave to help me find the material I needed.

In my research for this guide I contacted every visitors' bureau and historical society in the state. I visited most of these in person, as well as many of the county libraries, and, of course, the sites. I am sorry that space and memory cannot serve to allow me to express my appreciation individually to all of the many librarians, library assistants, historians, visitors' bureau workers, and volunteers with whom I communicated by mail, telephone, or in person while gathering information for this book, but I certainly could not have completed the extensive research required for a statewide guide without their help. Special thanks go out to: Marge Magruder of the Friends of Gathland, Mike Humphreys of the Potomac River Museum, Louise Ashe of the Worcester County Library, James Kerapke of the Baltimore Civil War Round Table, Scott Sheads of Fort McHenry, Sharon Kirk of the Carroll County Office of Tourism, Cliff Dowling of Harford County Tourism, John Potts on the Eastern Shore, Eunice Pogue of Pocomoke City, William R. Gardiner in southern Maryland, Doug Stone of Funkstown, John Grant of Oakland, Larry Cosner of Oakland, Don Merchant of the Dorchester Historical Society, and Natalie Chabot of the Allegany Visitors Bureau.

Thanks also to Elaine Huey, without whose help I could not have completed this manuscript.

INTRODUCTION

From the time of John Brown's raid on Harpers Ferry in October 1859 to John Wilkes Booth's escape through the southern part of the state after assassinating the President in April 1865, the state of Maryland was caught in the middle of a raging conflict in more ways than one.

Geographically, Maryland was between the Northern states wanting preservation of the Union, and the Southern states wanting separation from the Union. Because the state lay to the north of Washington, D.C., if the dispute came to war, Maryland would probably be where most of the fighting would occur—if Maryland, being a slave state and Southern by tradition, sided with her sister states in the South.

But Maryland was economically and culturally no longer a Southern state. The economic base of the state had been changing from agriculture to industry. Factories not only lined the streets of Baltimore, but also dotted the countryside wherever water power was available. Railroads now crossed the state both to the west and to the north. And all of this industry depended on commerce to the north and west.

The social makeup of the state had been changing too. Since the American Revolution people of German descent had been moving from Pennsylvania south into northern Maryland, bringing with them their German work ethic and anti-slavery views and mixing with the English/Scottish stock that had been the mainstay of Maryland from the time it was colonized. And more immigrants from Europe were flooding into Baltimore every day to supply much-needed labor for the factories and railroads. Due to industrialization and a changing economic base slavery was beginning to die out in Maryland. The value of slaves in the state had been steadily decreasing since the 1840s, and people knew that freedom for the slaves would eventually become an economic as well as a moral necessity. By 1850 Maryland had a larger free black population than any other state—84,000.

Maryland may have had a Southern tradition, but her future lay with progress and the North. Those who were looking toward the future did not want war in any form. They knew that war could only mean economic disaster for the state as well as threatening lives and property since Maryland lay between the antagonists.

But emotions were running high after the election of Abraham Lincoln as President and Southern states began to secede from the Union. During the winter of 1860-61 there was much discussion among the people of Maryland about what to do if war did raise its ugly head. Should Maryland side with the North or with the South? What would happen in either case? During the winter six states seceded from the Union and in February 1861 formed the Confederate States of America. President-elect Lincoln declared that secession from the Union was illegal, but the seceded states began to confiscate Federal property. War was imminent.

The people of Maryland were divided on the issue roughly by a line that ran from Baltimore due west—those above the line being for the North and those below the line being for the South. This was not true across the board, of course. There were many people in those northern areas who were ardent secessionists—and there was a large contingent of citizens in the southern counties who supported the Union. The residents of Caroline County, for instance, in the middle of the South-supporting southern Eastern Shore, were Union backers almost unanimously.

The Governor of Maryland, Thomas Holliday Hicks, refused to call a special session of the Maryland legislature to address the question of secession, and as winter turned into spring in 1861 temperatures and fears were rising and some of the people were turning to action. Many men who favored the Southern view left their homes and families and went across the Potomac River to Virginia where militias were being formed. The 5th Maryland State Guard dissolved because so many of its members "went South." Local militias were formed and armed all over Maryland as citizens readied themselves for a possible conflict—not knowing what to expect, but wanting to be ready to defend their families and property. These militias were later disbanded and the arms seized, sometimes by force, when the Federal government assumed military control of Maryland.

The simmering pot of mixed cultures and sentiments in Baltimore was about to boil over. The situation was so dangerous that President-elect Lincoln, instead of stopping to give speeches in Baltimore on the way to his inaugural as planned, was hastened through the city in secret. When troops from the North began marching through Baltimore on their way to Washington to answer Lincoln's call for volunteers to put down the rebellion in the South, the lid finally blew off and the troops were attacked by a frenzied mob on April 19, 1861. The situation was so volatile that city officials, with the agreement of the governor, destroyed the railroad bridges north of the city to prevent any more troops from coming through. The troops came instead by steamer, landed at Annapolis, and took the train from there to Washington.

Things started moving very quickly after the Baltimore Riot. On April 26 the Maryland legislature began meeting at Frederick. The General Assembly of Maryland did not call for secession, saying that they did not have the authority to make such a decision, but did appoint special committees to meet with the President of the United States and the President of the Confederate States to try to seek a peaceful solution. On April 27 the United States secretary of war established the Department of Annapolis, putting under military rule the countryside for twenty miles on either side of the railroad from Annapolis to Washington. On May 3 Federal troops occupied Relay, the junction point of the B & O Railroad and the Washington branch, just south of Baltimore. On May 13 Federal troops under General Butler seized Federal Hill overlooking Baltimore and trained cannons on the city. Baltimore was from that time forward under martial law for the duration of the war. On May 14, the same day that the state legislature adjourned, Governor Hicks, now a staunch Unionist, issued a call for volunteers for the U.S. Army.

Things were happening along the border too. On May 16 the new Potomac Flotilla sailed from Washington and began patrolling the Potomac River and upper Chesapeake Bay, putting a crimp in the operations of secessionists in southern Maryland who had been running a rather active smuggling trade across the river up to that time.

Once hostilities broke out, the Potomac River became the border between the warring factions. It was also the southern border of the state of Maryland. This presented a threat not only to the safety of the residents along this border, but also a threat to the commercial interests of the state. The Chesapeake and Ohio Canal, carrying coal and building stone from the mountains and produce from western Maryland, had been completed in 1850. It ran parallel to the Potomac River from Washington to Cumberland, the entire length being in Maryland. Also running parallel to the Potomac River for a good part of its distance was the Baltimore and Ohio (B & O) Railroad which ran from Baltimore, with an extension into Washington, to the Ohio River at Wheeling, Virginia (West Virginia after June 20, 1863). It had been completed in December 1852 and since that time a good deal of the commerce of Baltimore had come to depend on this railroad link with the west. Unfortunately a large part of that line lay on the southern side of the Potomac River in Virginia, which seceded from the Union in May 1861.

That railroads play an extremely important role in the conduct of a war is a fact well-known today, but this was the dawning of the railroad age, and Americans had yet to realize the full potential of this "iron horse." The B & O Railroad received little attention or protection from the Federal government at first. It didn't help that the U.S. Secretary of War, Simon Cameron, had a vested interest in the Northern Central Railroad which would benefit from the shutting down of the Railroad, or that the president of the B & O, John W. Garrett, was suspected of having Southern sympathies. Fortunately, Cameron resigned at the beginning of 1862 and the new Secretary of War, Edwin M. Stanton, from Ohio, saw the value of the railroad to the war effort and made the placing of the B & O line entirely within Federal-held territory one of his goals.

The B & O Railroad began at Camden Station in Baltimore and headed southwest to Relay where it connected with the Washington Branch. It then headed west to Ellicott Mills and Monocacy Junction, where a spur went to Frederick. It left Maryland at the bridge to Harpers Ferry and did not reenter the state, except for a brief time at the Paw Paw Tunnel, until just below Cumberland. From there it headed over the Allegheny Mountains with major stops at Piedmont, Virginia (West Virginia) and Oakland, Maryland, then into northwestern Virginia (West Virginia) to Wheeling and the Ohio River. With the many mountains, valleys, rivers and creeks that the railroad crossed it was a major feat of engineering.

Two other railroads originated in Baltimore—the Baltimore, Wilmington and Philadelphia Railroad heading northeast, and the Northern Central Railroad heading north to Harrisburg, Pennsylvania. The Northern Central line had a branch with a juncture just north of Baltimore that went to Westminster, Maryland. The Cumberland Valley Railroad connected Hagerstown, Maryland with other lines at Harrisburg.

The portion of the B & O Railroad that lay in Virginia was almost completely destroyed by the Confederate army on three separate occasions. Amazingly, the line would reopen within two to three weeks after the disputed territory was retaken by Federal troops. The speed of reconstruction was due to three factors: the protection of the military for railroad workers, the aid of the military in the reconstruction, and the foresight of John W. Garrett, a solid Union man in every respect after May 1861, in stockpiling lumber, rails, and even prefabricated trestling, to prepare for such emergencies. These factors also helped in repairing bridges within Maryland and northwestern Virginia that were continually being blown up by Confederate armies moving across the state or by small parties of raiders.

In the beginning of the war the B & O was at the mercy of the Confederates. Early in April, Virginia had placed a regiment of soldiers under the command of Colonel (later Gen. "Stonewall") Jackson at Harpers Ferry. Garrett made a deal with the Governor of Virginia that the trains could continue to run as long as they didn't carry troops or arms. And the trains kept running until May 22, the day before Virginia officially seceded from the Union. On that day Jackson managed to stop eastbound trains at Point of Rocks, Maryland and westbound trains at Martinsburg, Virginia (West Virginia) at the same time, trapping 56 locomotives and more than 300 cars in Virginia territory.

After Virginia had joined the Confederacy, the command of Harpers Ferry went to Maj. Gen. Joseph E. Johnston, who, after looking over the situation and realizing that Harpers Ferry could not be held without control of Maryland Heights on the Maryland side of the Potomac River, decided to abandon the town. He dismantled the armory, took the trains to Winchester, and destroyed the bridge over the Potomac River on June 13, 1861. By June 23 all of the bridges and most of the railroad track between Harpers Ferry and Williamsport, Maryland had been destroyed.

In order to recapture the railroad line, the Federal War Department created a new military area in October 1861—the Department of Harpers Ferry and Cumberland. First under the command of Brig. Gen. Frederick Lander, then Brig. Gen. Benjamin Franklin Kelley, the Federal troops drove the Confederates out of Romney, Virginia (West Virginia) and repairs were made on the B & O Railroad on the Virginia side of the Potomac to Hancock, Maryland. The Confederates under Jackson retaliated by damaging the C & O Canal Dam #5 in December, and removing all of the railroad track from Martinsburg to Harpers Ferry. Skirmishes occurred from Point of Rocks to Williamsport as Confederates tested the Union defenses. The Confederates fired their cannon at Hancock for two days in January 1862, until the Federal troops there were reinforced. On February 24, Federal troops under Gen. Nathaniel Banks occupied Harpers Ferry. Federal forces took Winchester, Virginia on March 12, and the rebuilding of the railroad began. The entire length of the railroad was reopened on March 29.

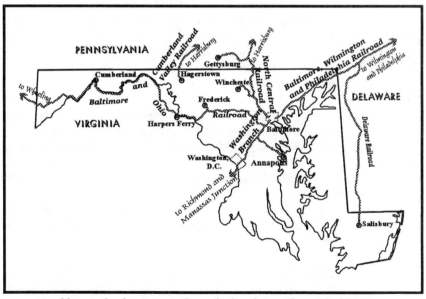

Railroads in Maryland during the Civil War

INTRODUCTION

In the fall of 1861 General Banks' Union army had been encamped near Darnestown and Poolesville, Maryland. On October 21, 1861, part of this army was led by Col. Edward Baker into the disastrous Battle of Ball's Bluff on the banks of the Potomac River. They were out to attack Leesburg, Virginia, but were stopped by a combination of geography and swift Confederate action. The steep bluffs on the Virginia side of the river proved difficult to scale. The flood-swollen waters of the river prevented any hasty retreat. And the unexpected proximity of Confederate camps allowed troops and artillery to respond quickly to the attack.

Action was also taking place on the lower Potomac River. All during the summer of 1861 the Confederates had been constructing batteries on the Virginia side of the lower Potomac River, threatening all commerce on the River. The Union Potomac Flotilla attacked many of these batteries, but some of them were just rearmed after the Federals had left, the Flotilla being just too small to be everywhere at once. Several Maryland lighthouses were disabled by the enemy, but quickly repaired. On June 30, 1861, a steam ferry was taken by Confederates on the Potomac River and then used to capture three more ships in the Chesapeake Bay. Work was begun on Fort Foote to protect Washington from any possible Confederate invasion from the Potomac River. In the fall of 1861 the Union brigades of Gen. O. O. Howard and Gen. George Sykes occupied southern Maryland and constructed small outposts along the Maryland side of the Potomac. The Eastern Shore was also being garrisoned. A Union brigade under the command of Brigadier General Lockwood cleared the Eastern Shore of Confederates all the way down to its tip at Cape Charles in November 1861.

The political scene was also changing in Maryland during 1861. The Baltimore Police Commissioners, many members of the Maryland General Assembly, and other influential citizens had been arrested by the military authority in August and September. An election had taken place creating an almost all-Unionist Maryland legislature, and making Augustus Bradford (Unionist) governor of the state. The dawning of 1862 found Maryland held fast in Union control. In March the Middle Department was established which included the eastern part of Maryland.

Also in March 1862, the Confederate batteries on the shores of the Potomac River were abandoned and artillery moved south to fight against McClellan's Peninsula Campaign, allowing ships again to sail safely to Washington.

On May 23, 1862, a battle was fought at Front Royal, Virginia that dramatically affected Marylanders back home. The 1st Maryland Infantry, CSA under the command of Frederick native Gen. Bradley T. Johnson defeated the 1st Maryland Infantry, USA, under the command of Baltimorean Gen.

John Kenly. Kenly was captured and Confederate hero Colonel Ashby was killed. There was rioting in Baltimore and several secessionists were beaten by mobs.

A major invasion of Maryland by Confederate forces began September 5-6, 1862, as Lee's army crossed the Potomac River at White's Ford and proceeded to Frederick and then Hagerstown and Harpers Ferry. They destroyed telegraph wires and railroad bridges, including the one to Harpers Ferry, all along the way, and fought minor skirmishes with small units of Union troops. The Union army under the command of Maj. Gen. George McClellan followed from the south. The two armies clashed at three gaps along South Mountain on September 14, and then fought the "Bloodiest Battle of the Civil War" around Antietam Creek at Sharpsburg, Maryland on September 17, 1862. The Confederate army retreated across the Potomac River the next day. President Lincoln issued the Emancipation Proclamation after the battle and visited the battlefield from October 1-4.

From October 10 to 12, 1862, Gen. Jeb Stuart's Confederate cavalry rode through Maryland, crossing the Potomac River near Williamsport and riding to Chambersburg, Pennsylvania, Emmitsburg, Maryland, then on to Liberty, New Market, Monrovia, Hyattstown, Barnesville, and returning to Virginia at White's Ford between two Union units closing in from Beallsville and Point of Rocks. In the approximately 90-mile ride the fast moving cavalry cut telegraph lines, destroyed railroad bridges, and captured supplies.

Many of the Maryland legislators and other civilians who had been arrested by the military in September 1861 were finally released in November 1862. But others were being arrested as General Wool tightened his restrictions in Baltimore and other parts of Maryland.

By the beginning of 1863 the people of Maryland were getting very tired of having the Civil War on their doorstep. The Confederate invasions and Union occupation had wreaked havoc on the countryside. Livestock had been stolen, fences and crops destroyed, and practically all of the good horses in the region had been commandeered. Martial law had added to tensions as people were arrested for singing Southern songs or wearing Southern colors. Some, however, turned the war to profit. The railroads and steamship lines found a lucrative market in transporting supplies and troops for the Federal government. In spite of efforts to curtail it the smuggling trade continued from southern Maryland, the Eastern Shore, and even from Baltimore. A secret Confederate Mail Line had been established through southern Maryland that carried mail from the South to all the northern regions, including Canada.

The Confederate troops under Gen. William E. Jones and John D. Imboden were creating havoc along the western portion of the B & O Railroad in late April 1863, tearing up tracks, destroying locomotives and burning bridges. Although the line was reopened by the middle of May, it was just another headache for the people of Maryland created by the war.

For this border state, however, the worst was yet to come. Another major Confederate offensive into the North began in mid-June 1863, as 75,000 Confederate soldiers crossed the Potomac mainly below Williamsport, Maryland and made their way northeast toward Hagerstown and Chambersburg, Pennsylvania. Gen. Jeb Stuart's Confederate cavalry crossed further south near Seneca, Maryland and proceeded through Rockville, Brookeville, Cooksville, and Westminster. By the end of the month the Confederate army was spread from Chambersburg to York. The Army of the Potomac, 95,000 strong, came after them, crossing the Potomac at Edward's Ferry and moving across Maryland to Frederick and Winchester. The armies would clash at Gettysburg, Pennsylvania from July 1-3, 1863, leaving behind more than 50,000 casualties. The Confederates retreated toward Williamsport, but found that recent rains had turned the quiet Potomac into a raging torrent. The Confederate army was forced to wait for nine days until the pontoon bridges they had used on their original crossing, which had been destroyed by Federal troops, could be repaired. During those nine days numerous skirmishes were fought from Hagerstown to Boonsboro.

The western area of Maryland remained well protected by Federal troops for the rest of that year, the new Department of West Virginia, named after the new state, having been created, which included western Maryland as well as eastern Ohio. After the Battle of Gettysburg, Point Lookout Prisoner of War Camp was established at the southern tip of Maryland. Two other events greatly affected the lives of Marylanders in 1863: the first draft was instigated in July, and blacks, both free and slave, began to be recruited to serve in the Union army in August. Many of these recruits for the United States Colored Troops were trained in camps on the Eastern Shore.

Raids along the border continued, but Maryland saw the last large Confederate invasion from July 5-14, 1864, as Gen. Jubal Early's Confederate army threatened Washington. The main army crossed the Potomac near Harpers Ferry and marched to Frederick. McCausland's and Johnson's cavalries crossed near Williamsport and demanded a ransom of the people of Hagerstown. A ransom was also demanded in Frederick. On July 9 the Confederates met with resistance at the bridge over the Monocacy River south of Frederick and fought a day-long battle with the forces under the command of Gen. Lew Wallace, finally driving the Federal troops toward Baltimore. The Confederates then proceeded down the Washington-Frederick Pike to stop in Silver Spring just outside Fort Stevens, one of the forts built to protect Washington from just such dangers. As a part of this thrust, the Confederate cavalry under Gen. Bradley Johnson galloped to the north, west, and south of

Baltimore, burning railroad bridges and cutting telegraph lines. Seeing that Washington was quickly being reinforced by troops from the south all of the Confederate forces retreated, crossing the Potomac near Poolesville.

In one last effort to disrupt Federal communications and retaliate for destruction by Union troops in the Shenandoah Valley General McCausland's Confederate cavalry came into Maryland on July 29, 1864, burned Chambersburg, Pennsylvania on July 30, and then fought a skirmish with Federal troops near Cumberland before returning to Virginia.

From that time on no more major encounters interfered with the lives of Marylanders, but the war had a definite effect on the way of life in the state. In October 1864 the voters of Maryland adopted a new state constitution which freed the slaves in the state effective November 1, 1864. More than 46,000 Maryland men served in the Union army or navy, and about 20 percent of these were black. About 16,000 Maryland men served in the Confederate forces, and at the end of the war these men had to be repatriated and absorbed back into Maryland society with a minimum of conflict. After the war the people of Maryland tried to heal their wounds, but the schisms between family members and friends created by the conflict were sometimes much harder to heal than the broken fences.

The assassination of President Lincoln and the escape of his murderer in April 1865 turned the whole of southern Maryland inside out as the search for the assassin proceeded. John Wilkes Booth was eventually found, as were his accomplices, but the death of the President cast a pall over the country which was just taking its first sighs of relief over the end of the war.

On April 21, 1865, the body of Abraham Lincoln took the same route back to Springfield, Illinois that the President-elect had taken to begin his career in Washington just four years earlier. Only this time the trip was not secret, and his coffin lay open in downtown Baltimore as thousands of mourners passed by to pay their respects.

INTRODUCTION

SUGGESTED READING

Brugger, Robert J. *Maryland: A Middle Temperament.* Baltimore: Johns Hopkins Univ. Press, 1988.

Manakee, Harold R. *Maryland in the Civil War.* Baltimore: Maryland Historical Society, 1961.

Mills, Eric. *Chesapeake Bay in the Civil War.* Centreville, Md.: Tidewater Publishers, 1996.

Soderberg, Susan Cooke. *Lest We Forget: A Guide to Civil War Monuments in Maryland.* Shippensburg, Pa.: White Mane Publishing Co., 1995.

Toomey, Daniel Carroll. *The Civil War in Maryland.* Baltimore, Md.: Toomey Press, 1988.

FOR INFORMATION ON MARYLAND

Maryland Office of Tourism
Maryland Dept. of Business
& Economic Development
217 East Redwood Street
Baltimore, MD 21202
410-767-3400

Maryland State Archives
350 Rowe Boulevard
Annapolis, MD 21401
800-235-4045, 410-974-3914
www.mdarchives.state.lib.md.us

Maryland Historical Society
201 West Baltimore Street
Baltimore, MD 21201
410-685-3750
  www.mdhs.org

State of Maryland home page
  www.state.md.us

SAILOR (Maryland's on-line public information)
  www.sailor.lib.md.us

North Star (Underground Railroad)
  www.ugrr.org.

National Parks and Monuments
  www.cr.nps.gov

A GUIDE TO

CIVIL WAR SITES

IN MARYLAND

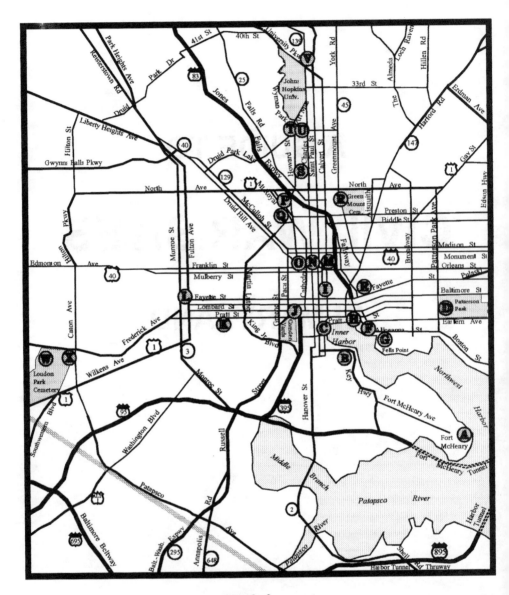

Baltimore

CHAPTER 1

BALTIMORE

At the time of the Civil War Baltimore was the largest city in Maryland. Situated on a natural harbor on the northwest branch of the Patapsco River just 14 miles from the Chesapeake Bay, the small pre-revolutionary trading port had become one of the largest centers of commerce in the nation by 1800. By 1860 there were three major railroads leading from the city west, north and south, with connections just outside the city to two other railroad lines. Steamship lines made connections with cities in both the North and the South. Ships from all over the world could be found in her harbor. Major industries such as shipbuilding, furniture making, and glass making had developed. There were distilleries, iron works, fulling mills, and major manufacturing plants in the city, which also boasted a large financial district as well as many merchant houses.

Baltimore on the eve of the Civil War was a city of multiple personalities. Stately Southern mansions of such old families as the Carrolls, the Steuarts, and the Howards topped small hills in the city, while down below along the waterfront rowdy taverns and boarding houses catered to sailors and laborers. Climbing up the hill from the harbor, one found factories and warehouses interspersed with the middle class homes of merchants, with the shanties of immigrant families and artisans lining the alleyways between the larger buildings. Baltimore also had the largest free black population of any city in America, alongside a large population of blacks who were still slaves.

Perhaps because of this motley assortment of residents Baltimore had a reputation for mob violence, especially around election times. The "Pug Uglies," "Butt Enders," "Blood Tubs," and other gangs were known to resort to cudgels, rocks, and sometimes even revolvers to make a political point. For this reason the city was referred to by some as "Mobtown." Nevertheless, the city was host to both of the split Democratic Party Conventions in the fall of 1860, as well as the convention of the short-lived Constitutional Union Party.

Baltimore was also known for its fashionable high society of a definite Southern flavor, boasting cultured gentlemen and accomplished and beautiful women. Some of these Southern-leaning young women were bold enough to defy the military authorities by wearing secessionist colors, singing Southern songs, and even harassing Federal troops, and became known as the "Monument Street Girls." Two sisters of this group, Hetty and Jennie Cary, put the poem "Maryland" to music and popularized the song with Maryland Confederates in Virginia after they were forced to flee to the South for their secessionist activities. The poem had been written by James Ryder Randall after the Baltimore Riot of April 19, 1861, and the song, "Maryland, My Maryland," later became the official state song.

The Southern heritage and slave status of the city gave it a definite Southern leaning at the beginning of the Civil War, but the large influx of immigrants, the growing industries and commerce dependent on Northern trade, and the outflow of a number of people to the South made the city increasingly mixed in sentiments as the war continued. The reversal of the allegiance of the city was demonstrated when the riot against Northern soldiers passing through the city on April 19, 1861, was followed a year later by the riots against "secessionists" after the Union 1st Maryland regiment was bested by the Confederate 1st Maryland Regiment, at Front Royal, Virginia in May, 1862. Violent mob flare-ups continued throughout the war, but were considerably reduced under military rule.

As the war progressed, citizens turned their efforts to more constructive activities such as the Union Club, and the Union Relief Association, formed in June 1861, to help feed the Union soldiers in the city and care for the sick and wounded. The Women's Auxiliary of this organization raised more than $80,000 for the cause of the Union at their Sanitary Fair (April 18-May 2, 1864).

After Gen. Benjamin Butler trained his cannon on the city from Federal Hill on May 13, 1861, military control of the bustling metropolis began. Fort McHenry, on the other side of the harbor from the city, had been garrisoned by Federal troops in early April, but it had been built to protect the city from invasion by sea. Its guns did not have the range to threaten the city.

On June 10, 1861, Maj. Gen. Nathaniel P. Banks was put in charge of the Department of Annapolis, which now included Baltimore. He had the chief of the city police and the police commissioners arrested, and turned the running and protecting of the city over to his own appointees. He appointed a provost marshal to oversee all activities in the city. Banks was replaced on July 23, 1861, as head of the area—now designated as the Maryland Department—by an even more ardent pursuer of secessionists, Maj. Gen. John Adams Dix, who passed ordinances against the wearing of secessionist colors and arrested many prominent Baltimoreans, including the mayor. Dix was succeeded in June 1862 by Gen. John Wool, and in December 1862 Gen. Robert C. Schenck took over the Department. Schenk's provost marshal, William S. Fish, who instigated the forcible exiling of secessionist women and other measures abhorrent to the people, was later indicted on fraud and corruption charges. Schenck was followed by Brig. Gen. Henry H. Lockwood in November 1863, and finally by Maj. Gen. Lew Wallace in March 1864, as the Maryland Department was expanded into the Middle Department.

Wallace, later the author of *Ben Hur: A Tale of Christ*, served until the end of the war. The provost marshal's office officially ceased to exist and the Baltimore citizens' constitutional rights were restored January 31, 1866.

Even under military rule clandestine activities continued. Levi White, for instance, established a smuggling business at the beginning of the war that sent goods from New York and elsewhere to the Confederate States Ordinance Department. He had a regular schedule and routes leading out from Baltimore via Curtis Creek or the Miles River and then down the Chesapeake Bay. He lost only one wagon-load during the whole war.

Although there were scares when Lee's army entered the North in September 1862 and June 1863, the only time Baltimore was really threatened with invasion by Confederates was in July 1864 when Gen. Jubal Early's army defeated General Wallace's much smaller force at the Monocacy River. Early marched on to menace Washington, D.C., while a large contingent of his cavalry was sent to test the resistance of Baltimore and then to free the prisoners at Point Lookout. Gen. Bradley T. Johnson's Confederate Cavalry burned railroad bridges and cut telegraph wires to the north and west of the city, and one of his companies, led by Colonel Gilmor, a native of the area, came within four miles from the city. Barricades had been set up in the streets, temporary perimeter forts manned, and citizens armed and inducted into a defensive guard. The defenses of the city were formidable, and not the primary aim of the Confederates at any rate, so the bulk of Johnson's cavalry gave Baltimore a wide berth, going on to the south of the city to damage the B & O Railroad line to Washington, D.C. Johnson had found out, however, from a spy he sent into Baltimore, that the XIX Corps and two divisions of the VI Corps, Union troops, had been brought in by steamer to defend Washington. This information was sent on to General Early, who decided to abandon the whole plan.

During the war there were 15 military camps set up in Baltimore, and at least 13 forts. Many large buildings and homes were converted into hospitals at different times during the war, including the Maryland Institute and the National Hotel. There were five large military hospitals constructed in the city, the largest of which was Jarvis Hospital, part of Camp Andrew, built on the grounds of the estate of Confederate Gen. George H. Steuart.

Baltimore's railroads were used extensively by the Union military during the war. The recent spur of the B & O Railroad to Locust Point, a shipping dock south of Fort McHenry, was expanded and used to transfer military supplies and armaments from ships to rail to be taken to Washington via the Washington Branch of the B & O. The B & O Railroad west, when it was operating, brought in coal to fuel the fires of the military steamships and the furnaces of the steel plants. The Northern Central Railroad north and the

Philadelphia, Wilmington and Baltimore Railroad northeast transported both military supplies and soldiers. All during the war the city was a beehive of military transport and manufacture.

There were eleven Union generals and one admiral from Baltimore: Generals Abercrombie, Bankhead, Blumenberg, Bowerman, Robert Buchanan, Deems, Denison, French, Kenly, Stanton, Stokes; and Admiral Ringgold. Two Confederate generals hailed from Baltimore: Robert Tyler and Lewis Henry Little; as well as Maj. Snowden Andrews of the Confederate artillery and Cmdr. Frank Chatard of the Confederate navy.

1A. FORT McHENRY

East end of Fort Avenue. This is a National Monument and open to the public free of charge daily 8 a.m. to 5 p.m. For information call 410-962-4290.

Fort McHenry was built in the late 18th century to protect the port of Baltimore. It was used for that purpose during the war of 1812 when, on the night of September 13-14, 1814, British ships anchored down the river bombarded the fort with more than 1,500 shells of varying sorts. The cannon at the fort did not have the range of the newer British models, and so the fort and its defenders lay helpless. On board one of the British ships happened to be a young Maryland lawyer, Francis Scott Key, who had come to the ship to

Fort McHenry

plead for the release of a friend. As he watched the fort being bombarded he could see the large United States flag flying from the center of the enclosure and knew that the Americans were still holding their own. He wrote a poem about this inspiring experience which was later put to music and called "The Star Spangled Banner."

During the Civil War Fort McHenry was first garrisoned by 30 U.S. Marines sent up from the Navy Yard in Washington, D.C. on January 9, 1861, who were joined by three U.S. artillery companies from Fort Leavenworth on January 12. The fort gave the Federals an important base of operations from which they could oversee both commerce in the port and activities in the city.

Throughout the war Fort McHenry was used as a prison camp for civilians arrested by military authorities in Baltimore and other parts of Maryland, along with Union soldiers guilty of misconduct, augmented by an occasional influx of captured Confederate soldiers. In July 1863, after the Battle of Gettysburg, it held 6,957 Confederate soldiers captured during and after the battle. The next month there were only 328 prisoners since all the others had been redistributed to larger institutions. The number of prisoners housed here was usually about 250-300.

Many prominent citizens were arrested and incarcerated at Fort McHenry. One of the more famous was John Merryman. On April 17, 1861, President Lincoln, using his authority as President since Congress was not scheduled to meet until July, suspended the Writ of *habeas corpus* in Maryland. This is the law that guarantees that a person who is arrested must be charged with a specific crime. Lincoln was afraid that Maryland might secede from the Union and cut the capital off from the Northern states, so he had many influential people who sympathized with the Southern cause arrested. On May 25, 1861, John Merryman was arrested at his home, "Hayfields" (see Hayfields, site #2G). Merryman had been the leader of a local militia that had burned the railroad bridges over the Gunpowder River, following Governor Hicks' orders, in order to prevent more Northern troops from entering Baltimore after the riots of April 19. Chief Justice Roger B. Taney used Merryman's case to issue an opinion, "*ex parte* Merryman," stating that the President did not have the authority to suspend the Writ of *habeas corpus* and in effect declare martial law, without the express permission of Congress. Lincoln paid no attention.

Fort McHenry continued to receive prisoners arrested by the military throughout the summer. The chief of the Baltimore Police, George Kane, was arrested June 27, 1861. In September 1861 a number of members of the Maryland legislature and other important people were arrested to prevent the legislature from meeting and to prevent protests against this military action. Those incarcerated included George William Brown (Mayor of Baltimore),

Severn Teakle Wallis, Ross Winans, Francis Key Howard (editor of the *Baltimore Exchange* and grandson of Francis Scott Key), and Thomas W. Hall (editor of *The South*). Most of these men were sent to Fort Warren in the Boston Harbor, and those who had not already been released were given their freedom on November 26, 1862, by order of the adjutant general. Francis Key Howard wrote a book about his experience, *Fourteen Months in the Bastilles of America*, which was published in 1863 and immediately banned by the Federal military authorities.

The prison camp was not located inside the bastion's walls, but in barracks approximately where the Visitor Center parking lot is today. The bodies of those who died in the prison camp were re-interred in Loudon Park National Cemetery in Irvington (formerly part of Catonsville) in 1884. The batteries outside the walls of the fort, overlooking the river, display Civil War cannon that replaced the earlier cannon used in the War of 1812.

1B. FEDERAL HILL
Key Highway and Battery Avenue

Federal Hill is a high bluff overlooking the Baltimore harbor. A traveler standing on the hill can see the old city is laid out below as it rises from the harbor to the north. Behind and to the right of the modern Aquarium complex is the tall Battle Monument. Most of the area below the Battle Monument to the harbor was burned out in the great fire of 1904 so is newer construction than the Civil War period, but the street layout is the same, and many older buildings still exist to the north of the monument.

On the evening of May 13, 1861, General Butler brought Federal troops from Annapolis on the railroad and set up cannon on Federal Hill pointed toward Baltimore. He instructed the commander of Fort McHenry, Major Morris, to also point his cannon toward the city. Among Butler's troops were 500 from the 6th Massachusetts Infantry, one of the regiments stoned by citizens in the streets of Baltimore April 19 (see Pratt Street, site #1H). Also under Butler's command that night were the 8th New York Infantry and the Boston Light Artillery. In the following weeks a fort was built which covered the entire top of the hill and included walls and barracks as well as cannon emplacements. It was garrisoned by the 5th New York Zouaves commanded by Colonel Brewerton, and stood throughout the war as a reminder to the citizens of the city that they were under military control.

a. GENERAL BUTLER'S HEADQUARTERS
337 Hamburg Street, Federal Hill. Private—not open to the public.

After the garrisoning of Federal Hill on May 13, 1861, General Butler was recalled by Secretary of War Scott on May 17 because the move on Baltimore had been unauthorized. He was reassigned to Fort Monroe and

General Cadwallader from Fort McHenry was given command of the Department of Annapolis, which now included Baltimore. So this house, known as the headquarters of General Butler, could only have been used by him for a few days. It may have been used later, however, by other commandants as local tradition holds that there are iron rings in the floor, used to shackle prisoners.

1C. THE USS *CONSTELLATION*

Inner Harbor. Open May 15 through October 15 daily from 10 a.m. to 6 p.m., October 16 through May 14 from 10 a.m. to 4 p.m. Monday through Saturday and 10 a.m. to 5 p.m. Sunday. There is an entrance fee.

The nation's oldest warship, the USS *Constellation*, saw action in the Mediterranean during the Civil War. It was built in 1797 as the first ship to be commissioned by the U.S. Navy, and soon gained a reputation as the fastest ship on the Atlantic.

1D. PATTERSON PARK

Patterson Park Avenue between Eastern Avenue & Baltimore Street

This park was the site of one of the largest military camps and hospitals in the city. The barracks built to house the sick and wounded could accommodate 1,200 patients. To the east of the park on Smoke Hill was Fort Marshall, the main fort in Baltimore that protected the Baltimore, Wilmington and Philadelphia Railroad.

1E. SHOT TOWER

Fayette and Front Streets. Open daily 10 a.m. to 4 p.m.

Built in 1828, the 215 feet tall brick tower was one of three such towers in Baltimore. The tower was used to make ammunition in the form of round lead balls. The molten metal was poured through a sieve at the top and the droplets became round as they fell down the tower to land in a vat of water at the bottom. About 500,000 25-pound bags of shot were produced annually during the Civil War. The tower continued operation until 1892, and was made into a museum in 1977.

1F. FELLS POINT

South of Eastern Avenue, east of East Falls Avenue.

The main piers of the Baltimore harbor lay to the west of Fells Point during the war. Just before the war more than 30 steamships from various lines docked here on their way to New York, Philadelphia, Washington, D.C., Norfolk, Virginia, and other places up and down the Atlantic coast. The first steamship to ply the Chesapeake Bay, the *Chesapeake*, was built in 1813, and the idea of a boat that could run against the wind and tide and keep to a schedule took hold quickly. The steamships carried mail and freight as well as passengers and many made connections with railroad lines. At the beginning of the war the B & O Railroad had just bought their own steamship line. During the war many steamships were taken over, either by leasing or direct purchase, by the military to deliver troops and supplies. These military steamships usually used the Locust Point dock below Fort McHenry.

A historic marker at Aliceanna and Durham Streets locates the area where Frederick Douglass was brought when he was seven years old as a slave to work for his master's brother, Hugh Auld. Douglass escaped to Massachusetts from the Eastern Shore in 1838 and later became an outspoken advocate for abolition, a writer and an orator. He wrote an autobiography, *The Life and Times of Frederick Douglass*, and became U.S. minister to Haiti after the Civil War.

1G. PRESIDENT STREET STATION/CIVIL WAR MUSEUM
601 President Street. Open daily 10 a.m. to 5 p.m. There is an admission charge. 410-385-5188. www.civilwarinbaltimore.org.

The brick President Street Station was the terminus for the Baltimore, Wilmington and Philadelphia Railroad. Rails running along Pratt Street connected this station with Camden Station. Cars could be uncoupled from the train engine and hauled by horses along this rail to be re-coupled to a new engine at Camden Station or emptied and returned. City regulations

President Street Station

prohibited the running of a locomotive through the streets of the city.

This is the station where a sleeping car carrying Abraham Lincoln arrived from Philadelphia in the early morning hours of February 23, 1861. Lincoln was accompanied by his bodyguard Ward Hill Lamon and detective Alan Pinkerton on this secretive trip through Baltimore on the way to his March 4th inauguration. Lincoln had been forced to deviate from his scheduled stop in Baltimore the next day because of threats of kidnapping, assassination, or, at the very least, rioting. The car was hauled through the quiet darkened streets and coupled to a waiting train at Camden Station and went on without incident to Washington, D.C.

This is also the station where volunteers from the North, responding to President Lincoln's call for troops, arrived on the morning of April 19, 1861, and ran into problems with rioting citizens.

The station now houses the Baltimore Civil War Museum with displays of the Civil War in Baltimore and the "Underground Railroad" for escaping slaves before the Civil War.

1H. PRATT STREET—SITE OF THE APRIL 19, 1861 RIOT
Pratt Street between Sharp Street and President Street.

At 11 a.m. on April 19, 1861 a train arrived at President Street Station with 35 cars carrying about 2,000 soldiers from the North headed for Washington, D.C. The main body was made up of the 6th Massachusetts Regiment with Col. Edward Jones in command. The rest of the soldiers came from six companies of the 1st Pennsylvania Regiment, four companies of the 2nd Pennsylvania Regiment, and half of the "Washington Brigade" from Philadelphia.

Neither Mayor Brown nor Police Chief Kane had been notified of the troop transport until an hour before the soldiers arrived. The troops had to be taken from the President Street Station, by horse-drawn rail cars, several blocks west on Pratt Street to Camden Station where they boarded the B & O train for Washington, D.C. The first nine cars passed without incident as the crowd gathered. The tenth car had to stop because of mechanical difficulties, and the crowd, which was growing larger as the time passed, began to throw stones. The driver of that car reversed the team and took the car back to the President Street Station. The mob, which was about 800 people by that time, blocked the track with stones and anchors so that no more cars could pass. As the crowd swelled to 2,000 or more around the President Street Station, jeering and waving secessionist flags, the police came to restore order. But as the troops began to march down Pratt Street, led by Mayor Brown, the crowd tried to block their way and, after the mayor left, threw stones at the troops and beat some of the stragglers. It was all the police could do to protect the rear of the line of soldiers. When the march was stopped by rioters blocking the way there was an order to "fire" and several people fell, others ran, and some fired back. When the soldiers reached Camden Station they continued to fire their rifles from the windows of the railroad cars as the train pulled out, and some innocent bystanders, outside the riot area, were shot. Twelve citizens and four soldiers were killed in this riot, and a number wounded.

James Ryder Randall, a native of Baltimore who was living in Louisiana at the time, heard about the riot and wrote a poem about it called "Maryland." The poem was published by the Baltimore journal *The South*. The young Baltimore sisters Hetty and Jennie Cary read the poem and set it to the music of the popular college song "Lauringer Horatius." The song became a big hit at home, its popularity probably even encouraged by its being outlawed. When the two Cary sisters charmed the Confederate soldiers at a camp near Fredericksburg, Virginia with their rendition of "Maryland, My Maryland" it became a favorite hymn of the Maryland Confederates away from home. After the war it was sung at so many public ceremonies that it was made the official state song in 1939. The words were changed in 1995.

1I. BATTLE MONUMENT
Calvert and Fayette Streets.
This is the oldest

Battle Monument

American monument, having been built in 1815 to commemorate the Battle of Baltimore, September 12-13, 1814, during the war of 1812. As a major city landmark it was a gathering place for soldiers during the Civil War and for political speeches during election time. Political factions would gather here and march to meet rival factions gathered at the Washington Monument (site #1Na), with fights and riots erupting along the way, especially during the "Know-Nothing" campaign of 1856 and the presidential election of 1860. Governor Hicks and Mayor Brown spoke at a rally here the night of the April 19, 1861, riot to try to calm the citizens.

1J. CAMDEN STATION
Camden and Howard Streets.

This brick railroad station was built in 1851 as the station for the Baltimore and Ohio (B & O) Railroad going west to Wheeling with later connections to Washington, D. C. and Annapolis. Besides being the destination of the Federal troops attacked by mobs in the April 19, 1861, riot, it was the station used by Abraham Lincoln on his secretive trip to his first inauguration in February 1861 (see President Street Station, site #1G), and also on his way to give the Gettysburg Address in 1863, and to the Baltimore Sanitary Fair in April 1864. On April 21, 1865, Lincoln's funeral train stopped here and his body was viewed by the public at the rotunda of the "Exchange" before continuing the trip to Springfield, Illinois.

1K. B & O RAILROAD MUSEUM
901 West Pratt Street.
Open Wednesday through Sunday from 10 a.m. to 4 p.m. There is an admission charge. 410-752-2490.www.borail.org.

The museum is on the site of the original Mount Clare Station for the Baltimore and Ohio Railroad. The roundhouse and machine shops of the B & O stretched for several blocks around the station. The first train in America made its first

Civil War–Era Locomotive

run from this station to Ellicott Mills (Ellicott City) on August 24, 1830. The B & O Railroad line, completed to Wheeling, Virginia (now West Virginia) and the Ohio River on December 24, 1852, was essential to the Union army for transporting troops and supplies quickly. It was continually repaired after Confederate damage and used throughout the war.

In 1858 John W. Garrett took over as president of the B & O Railroad. At that time the B & O had 519 miles of track, and 85 freight and passenger cars. The line ran west from Baltimore with a spur to the docks at Locust Point, just south of Fort McHenry. At Relay, south of the city, the main line connected with a line to Washington, D.C., and this line connected at Annapolis Junction with a line to Annapolis. The main line ran due west from Relay with major stops at Ellicott Mills, Monocacy Junction where there was a spur to Frederick, Brunswick and across the Potomac River to Harpers Ferry, Virginia (now West Virginia). The line then ran on the Virginia side of the Potomac River to Martinsburg where there was a roundhouse and repair shops. From Martinsburg the line continued on the Virginia (West Virginia) side of the river, with a brief re-entry into Maryland at the Paw Paw Tunnel, until recrossing the Potomac River at Cumberland, Maryland. Continuing through Maryland across the mountains to the state line just west of Oakland, it re-entered Virginia (West Virginia) and continued on to Wheeling.

The Virginia side of the line was under Confederate control from May through October 1861; from May to June 1862; from September to November 1862; and June and July 1863. During those times many miles of rail were destroyed, many bridges burned, the Martinsburg shops burned, and more than 48 locomotives and 386 cars destroyed or stolen. In addition, many Confederate forays into Federal-held territory throughout the war damaged many additional miles of track and bridges. Some bridges were destroyed as many as four times during the war. In spite of all these setbacks the tracks continued to be repaired within days or weeks, locomotives and cars were replaced, and the trains kept running. Armored cars were made to protect workers so that they could continue to make repairs even under enemy fire. Parts of iron bridge trestling were pre-fabricated at the Mt. Clare shops so that they could be moved to needed areas immediately. A large stockpile of lumber for cross-ties and bridges was kept near Relay. It seemed that no matter what the Confederates did to it the B & O Railroad just kept coming back.

There are several Civil War vintage trains and railroad cars on display in the museum. The model train setup on the second floor shows the Paw Paw Tunnel section of the railroad as it passes briefly back into Maryland, and demonstrates the terrain that the train had to pass through as it crossed the mountains.

14

1L. CAMP ANDREW AND JARVIS HOSPITAL SITE

North of Baltimore Street between Fulton and Monroe.

Early in the war the Federal government confiscated the Baltimore home and grounds of Confederate Capt. (later Gen.) George H. Steuart, called Steuart's Grove. The military camp on the grounds was named Camp Andrew. A large hospital was built at the camp and named Jarvis Hospital after the surgeon Nathan S. Jarvis, Medical Director of the Middle Department, who died May 15, 1862. The head of the hospital was Dr. J. Russell.

1M. CENTRE STREET RAILROAD STATION SITE

In the block bounded by Centre Street to the north, Calvert Street to the west and Orleans Street to the south, opposite the Franklin Street intersection with Calvert Street.

This was the terminus for the Northern Central Railroad to Harrisburg, Pennsylvania. At Harrisburg it connected with the Pennsylvania Central Railroad running west from Philadelphia, and the Cumberland Valley Railroad to Chambersburg, Pennsylvania and Hagerstown, Maryland. Just north of Baltimore a connecting line of the Western Maryland Railroad had just been built as far as Westminster, Maryland. All of these railroad lines were vital supply links for the Union army—especially during the Battle of Gettysburg.

On February 23, 1861, the train that was supposed to be carrying Abraham Lincoln to his inauguration arrived here about noon, and Mrs. Lincoln and the rest of the future President's company were greeted by a mob that harassed them all the way to Camden Station, Lincoln himself having passed through Baltimore on another train during the early morning hours (see President Street Station, site #1G).

1N. MOUNT VERNON PARK

Bounded by Cathedral Street, St. Paul Street Madison Street, and Centre Street.

Extending one block in each direction from the Washington Monument, Mount Vernon Park is a National Historic Landmark and is considered one of the most elegant parks in America. Its Old-World flavor is reflected in its late 19th-century townhouses and numerous statues.

a. WASHINGTON MONUMENT

Open Wednesday through Sunday 10 a.m. to 4 p.m. 410-396-7837.

The 1829 Washington Monument was designed by Robert Mills, who also designed the Washington Monument in Washington, D.C. The statue was sculpted by Henrico Causci. The 178-feet-tall monument was a rallying point for political factions before and during the Civil War and many inflammatory speeches were given at this commanding site.

b. STATUE OF CHIEF JUSTICE TANEY
On the north side of Mount Vernon Place is a statue of Chief Justice Roger Brook Taney that was cast from the same mold as the statue, created by William Henry Rinehart, on the State Capitol grounds in Annapolis. It was donated by W. T. Walters in 1887. A native of Maryland, Taney is most remembered for his "Dred Scott decision" and *ex-parte* Merryman case (see Fort McHenry, site #1A).

c. STATUE OF SEVERN TEACKLE WALLIS
At the end of the park to the east is a statue of Severn Teackle Wallis sculpted by Laurent Marqueste in 1906. Wallis was a Baltimore writer and lawyer who was very influential in Maryland politics before, during and after the war. He was a delegate to the special session of the Maryland General Assembly in Frederick in 1861 and was one of those arrested. He was incarcerated at Fort McHenry from September 13, 1861, later taken to Fort Warren in Boston Harbor, and released November 27, 1862. He was the principal orator at the unveiling of the Taney monument in Annapolis (original of the one just described) in 1872. He is buried at Green Mount Cemetery.

10. MARYLAND HISTORICAL SOCIETY
201 West Monument Street. Open 10 a.m. to 5 p.m. Tuesday through Saturday and 1 to 5 p.m. Sunday. There is an admission charge. 410-685-3750.

The Historical Society has a large museum in a 19th–century house and modern annex. The museum features Maryland cultural history and includes a Civil War Room that contains exhibits describing the division between Marylanders during the war. The library is comprehensive and contains many rare manuscripts, including prints from the Civil War showing various hospitals and military camps in Baltimore.

1P. 5TH REGIMENT ARMORY
Howard Street, 29th Division Street, and Preston Street. The museum is open by appointment.

Although this building was not constructed until 1935 (replacing one on the same site that burned down in 1933) the 5th Regiment, National Guard itself was greatly influential in the reconciliation of Northern– and Southern–leaning Marylanders after the war.

After the Civil War the 5th Regiment State Guard was re-formed, having broken up when the war began. It was made up at that time mainly of Confederate veterans and was often referred to as "The Rebel Brigade," or the "Dandy Fifth." The men of the 5th Regiment tried actively to heal the wounds of the war by participating in all ceremonies, both Union and Confederate, holding its summer camps in Northern states, and adopting a flag that combined the symbol of the Southern Marylanders—the red and white cross bottony—and the symbol of the Northern Marylanders—the black and gold checkers. Although both of these symbols had come from the Calvert shield on the State Seal, they had come to be embraced by the opposing factions during the war since Maryland did not have an official state flag at the time. The flag of the 5th Regiment was adopted as the state flag in 1904. In World War I the 5th Regiment became part of the 29th (Blue and Gray) Division.

1Q.   CONFEDERATE MONUMENT

Old Mount Royal Avenue and Mosher Street (west of the armory)

"Gloria Victis" ("Glory to the Vanquished") is the title of this monument to Confederate soldiers and sailors that was erected by the United Daughters of the Confederacy in 1903 amid great fanfare and thousands of spectators. The bronze statue was sculpted by F. Wellington Ruckstuhl. The winged figure represents "Glory," and she holds aloft the laurel wreath of honor as she supports a mortally wounded Confederate soldier who grasps a drooping furled flag. According to the organization that built it the statue is an "allegorical representation of the glory of the South in her defeat," and is meant to honor those who died in battle fighting for a cause in which they believed.

Confederate Monument

1R. GREEN MOUNT CEMETERY
Greenmount Avenue and Oliver Street.

Founded in 1837 on the estate of Robert Oliver on a high hill overlooking Baltimore, the large park cemetery was very fashionable after the Civil War and more than 20 generals and notable personages from the war are buried here, including: Maj. Gen. John Reese Kenly, USA, leader of the 1st Maryland Regiment, USA and protector of Baltimore; Brig. Gen. George Steuart, CSA; Maj. Gen. Isaac Trimble, CSA; Admiral Ringgold, USN; Governor Bradford; and John Wilkes Booth. A directory to the cemetery is available at the cemetery office at the entrance.

1S. CAMP BRADFORD SITE
Charles and 25th Streets.

Established in 1861 on the fairgrounds of the Baltimore Agricultural Society Camp Bradford was sometimes referred to as the "Cattle Grounds." It is named for Governor of Maryland Augustus Bradford, elected October 1861. On October 15, 1862, the first Maryland draft began and Camp Bradford was the place where draftees were to report. All during the month the camp was rife with those buying and selling substitutes for those drafted, a legal transaction which went for up to $300.

1T. LEE/JACKSON MONUMENT
Howard Avenue and Art Museum Drive.

Baltimore banker J. Henry Fergusen left a large amount of money in his will to construct a monument to his boyhood heroes, General Lee and General Jackson. The artist, Laura Garden Fraser, chose to depict the generals at their last meeting just before the Battle of Chancellorsville where Jackson was killed. This beautifully executed monument was known worldwide as the first life-size, double-equestrian statue cast all in one piece.

The monument was dedicated May 1, 1948, and every year there is a re-enactment ceremony at the monument on a Saturday in January near the anniversary of both generals' birthdates, put on by the Sons of Confederate Veterans.

1U. UNION SOLDIERS AND SAILORS MONUMENT

Charles Street and 29th Street, just below Art Museum Drive.

This monument by Adolph Weinman was unveiled November 6, 1909. It was financed by the State of Maryland to honor those Marylanders who fought to preserve their nation. The two angels represent "War" and "Victory" and are pushing a farmer away from his plow and anvil as he dons a uniform and buckles his sword belt. A large crowd gathered for the unveiling ceremony at which both the Governor of Maryland, Austin Crothers, and the Mayor of Baltimore, Barry Mahool, spoke. The monument was originally at the entrance to Druid Hill Park.

Union Monument

1V. MONUMENT TO CONFEDERATE WOMEN

University Parkway and Charles Street.

After a delegation from the United Daughters of the Confederacy appealed to the Maryland General Assembly for funds for this monument in 1914, the State of Maryland appropriated funds and appointed a commission to construct this statue. J. Maxwell Miller, a student at the Rhinehart School of Sculpture at the time, was the artist who won the competition to design the monument. It is a heroic-size grouping of three bronze figures representing a young woman standing and looking off into the distance and a mother kneeling, holding a dying soldier.

The monument was dedicated on November 2, 1918, with a large crowd in attendance. The main speaker, Judge James Trippe, son of Gen. Andrew C. Trippe, praised the virtues of the Confederate women of Maryland who suffered under the hardships of military rule for four years. The inscription reads: "In difficulty and danger, regardless of self, they fed the hungry, clothed the needy, nursed the wounded, and comforted the dying."

1W. LOUDON PARK CEMETERY
3801 Frederick Avenue, Irvington. Return to I-95 going south from Baltimore and take the Caton Avenue exit. Travel north on Caton Avenue about 1 mile, keep left at the "Y" and turn left onto Frederick Avenue. Go 3 blocks and to the left.

This popular park cemetery, located outside the limits of the city of Baltimore when it was built in 1852, is the resting place of many Confederates in an area of the park called "Confederate Hill." There, a statue of Gen. "Stonewall" Jackson by Frederick Volk watches over the headstones which stand in long rows or are clustered around smaller monuments on the Hill. Here lies the body of the dashing Col. Harry Gilmor, who almost invaded Baltimore with his Confederate cavalry, but who later became police chief of that same city. Also here are Major James Herbert, leader of the Independent Grays, CSA; Brig. Gen. Bradley T. Johnson, who led the 1st Maryland Regiment, CSA, and his wife, Jane Claudia Johnson, who provided uniforms and arms for that same regiment. The first monument erected to a woman in Maryland was put over the grave of Mrs. Johnson by the Confederate veterans in 1901. There is also a monument to Confederate widows in the Bethel Section on the east side of the cemetery.

1X. LOUDON PARK NATIONAL CEMETERY
Adjoining Loudon Park Cemetery to the east, but with a separate entrance off Frederick Avenue.

The U.S. government bought this section of Loudon Park Cemetery in 1874 to make it into a national cemetery. There are several monuments on the grounds including one erected by the Union Daughters, one to the Unknown Dead, and a Navy monument. Buried here are more than 2,300 Union veterans, and about 700 Confederates who died in Baltimore hospitals or prisons. Two Union generals are laid to rest here: Brig. Gen. Adam E. King and Brig. Gen. David Leroy Stanton.

SUGGESTED READING

Beirne, Francis F. *Amiable Baltimoreans.* New York: Dutton, 1951.

Gilmor, Harry. *Four Years in the Saddle.* New York: Harper & Brothers, 1866.

Holly, David C. *Tidewater by Steamboat: A Saga of the Chesapeake.* Baltimore: Johns Hopkins University Press, 1991.

Jacobs, Timothy, ed. *The History of the Baltimore and Ohio: America's First Railroad.* New York: Crescent Books, 1989.

Scharf, J. Thomas. *History of Baltimore City and County.* Baltimore: Regional Publishing Co., 1971 (reprint of 1881).

Sheads, Scott S. *Fort McHenry.* Baltimore: Nautical and Aviation Publishing Co. of America, 1995.

Shriver, Frank R. *Walking in Baltimore: An Intimate Guide to the Old City.* Baltimore: Johns Hopkins University Press, 1995.

Soderberg, Susan Cooke. *Lest We Forget: A Guide to Civil War Monuments in Maryland.* Shippensburg, Pa.: White Mane Publishing Co., 1995.

Summers, Festus P. *The Baltimore and Ohio In The Civil War.* Gettysburg, Pa.: Stan Clarke Military Books, 1993 (reprint of 1939).

Wilson, Jane B. *The Very Quiet Baltimoreans.* Shippensburg, Pa.: White Mane Publishing Co., 1991.

FOR INFORMATION ON OTHER SITES, ACCOMMODATIONS, ETC.

Baltimore Area Convention and Visitors Association
100 Light Street, 12th floor
Baltimore, MD 21202
800-282-6632, 410-659-7300
www.baltimore.org

Maryland Historical Society
201 West Baltimore Street
Baltimore, MD 21201
410-685-3750
www.mdhs.org

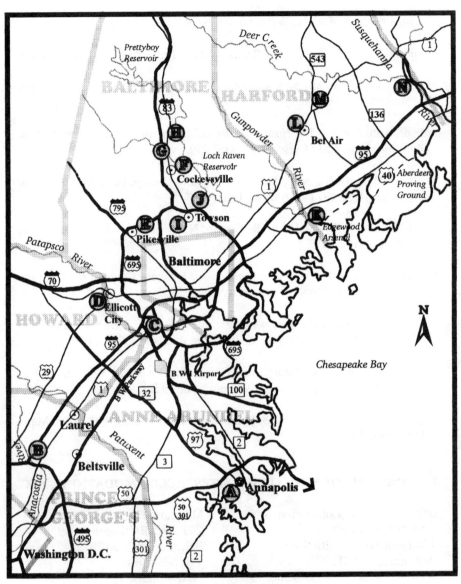

Circling Baltimore

CHAPTER 2

CIRCLING BALTIMORE

BALTIMORE COUNTY, HARFORD COUNTY, ANNE ARUNDEL COUNTY, NORTHERN PRINCE GEORGE'S, AND EASTERN HOWARD COUNTIES

Baltimore was a much smaller city in the 19th century than it is today, reaching not even a mile beyond the harbor. Beyond the limits of the city the area was rural with a few small towns at the main crossroads. Much of this farmland has now been developed into suburbs or even become part of the expanding city itself. Some of the old roads and houses have been preserved, but the environment that they exist in today is much different from the slow and easy-paced days of the past.

To the south and west of Baltimore there were many slave-holding plantations and consequently many Southern-leaning residents. Some of these residents were involved in sabotage activities in the beginning of the war. After the Federal military presence in the area, however, these "secesh" mainly kept their opinions to themselves and faded into the background—or underground. The area north of Baltimore had a scattering of plantations, but was mainly made up of small farming communities and fishing villages. The closer to the border of Pennsylvania, the more residents who had family ties across the state line to the north. Except for a few renegades, most of whom "went South" soon after the war began, the people who lived north of Baltimore were strongly in support of the Union.

The area surrounding the city of Baltimore was directly affected by two events during the Civil War: the Baltimore Riot and the subsequent taking over of the city by the Federal army in the spring of 1861, and the invasion by the Confederate cavalry of Gen. Bradley Johnson in the summer of 1864.

After the Baltimore Riot on April 19, 1861, the Mayor of Baltimore and the Governor of Maryland ordered that the railroad bridges to the east and north of Baltimore be destroyed to prevent any more troops from the North from entering the city and creating further disturbances. The action was carried out by the Baltimore police and the local units of volunteer militia. On hearing of this impediment to troop movement Gen. Benjamin Butler, who was in command of troops in the North, arranged to transport the troops by way of steamship to Annapolis. From there they were sent by rail to Washington. Units from the Union army were then stationed for the duration of the war in Annapolis, Baltimore, Relay, and other strategic points along the railroad lines. Martial law was declared in Baltimore and was tacitly in effect in other parts of the state. The heavy concentration of Federal troops south of Baltimore and the strong Northern sentiments north of the city kept the area fairly quiet during the war—until the invasion in the summer of the last year of the war.

On the morning of July 9, 1864, Gen. Bradley T. Johnson was dispatched by Gen. Jubal Early from Frederick to take the 1st Maryland Cavalry, CSA, along with the Jones Cavalry Brigade, to destroy railroad and telegraph lines to the north and west of Baltimore and between Baltimore and Washington, D.C. and then go down to Point Lookout at the southern tip of Maryland and free the Confederate prisoners there. The cavalry consisted of about 1,500 riders and 5 cannon of the Baltimore Light Artillery. By daybreak of July 10 they arrived at Reisterstown, then went on to Cockeysville where Colonel Gilmor's company was detached to ride east and destroy the railroad bridges over the Gunpowder River. The night of July 10 Johnson's cavalry rested at the home of John Carroll, "The Caves," in Green Spring Valley. On July 11 they were heading back southwest and crossed the B & O Railroad at Woodstock. General Johnson lunched at the home, "Doughgren Manor," of John Lee Carroll. The cavalry then went on to Triadelphia where they spent a few hours of the night resting. On the morning of July 12 they rode to Laurel and then as far as Beltsville, where they were ordered to turn back. They retreated toward Rockville and recrossed the Potomac River on July 14 (see map in Appendix C).

The Civil War produced several officers from the Annapolis area.: Brig. Gen. and Surgeon General William Alexander Hammond, USA; Commodore James Ward, USA; as well as Commander Hunter Davidson, CSN; Captain James Waddell, CSN; and Col. John Taylor Wood, CSA.

The Confederates held sway to the west of Baltimore whence came Brig. Gen. George Hume Steuart, CSA; Col. William Norris, CSA; Col. Harry Gilmor, CSA; Gen. James Herbert, CSA; and Brig. Gen. Allen Thomas, CSA.

To the north of the city Brig. Gen James Archer, CSA, was from near Bel Air (see site #2L), as was John Wilkes Booth (see site #2M). Also from the northern part of the state, Havre de Grace, was Com. John Rodgers, USN.

24

2A. ANNAPOLIS

Gen. Benjamin Butler arrived in Annapolis with the 8th Massachusetts Regiment of Volunteers aboard the Susquehanna River ferryboat *Maryland* late on the night of April 20, 1861. The troops camped on the grounds of the Naval Academy, and were soon joined by Col. Marshall Lefferts and the 7th New York Regiment coming in on the steamer *Baltimore* around Cape Charles and up the Chesapeake. Finding that rebellious Marylanders had destroyed much of the track of the Annapolis to Elkridge spur of the B & O Railroad the troops were directed to repair the line. The soldiers repaired a locomotive and put together some railroad cars, along with a small cannon mounted on a flatbed, in order to protect themselves from enemy fire as they rebuilt the track. The repair was finally completed on April 25 and the New York troops were the first to enter Washington via train. The Massachusetts troops went on to garrison Relay, Maryland (site #2C). The 20-mile line became very important throughout the war as it was used to transport troops, armaments, and later supplies, from Annapolis into Washington.

During the war Annapolis served as a training area for Northern troops and a major hospital center for wounded brought in on ships. It also provided prisoner exchange facilities, and Camp Parole was established west of town in 1863 to house and care for the growing number of Union soldiers brought in from Confederate prisoner of war camps.

a. MARYLAND STATE HOUSE

Take Rowe Boulevard (Rt. 70) from Rt. 50 to the historic area. The Maryland State House is in the Center of Annapolis at the end of Rowe Boulevard and has a Visitor Center inside the building which offers guided tours. Open daily 9 a.m. to 5 p.m. Admission is free. 410-974-3400. This is a National Historic Landmark. Parking on the street is limited to two to three hours but there are parking garages. All of the Annapolis sites are within walking distance of the State House.

The original part of the State House was built in 1772. During the Civil War the Maryland General Assembly met at Kemp Hall in Frederick, Maryland from April through September 1861, but returned to the State House in Annapolis for the duration of the war.

From April 25 to September 6, 1864, a convention was held at the State House to formulate a new constitution for the state of Maryland. This constitution, which passed in the state referendum in October 1864, freed the slaves in the state, making Maryland the first state to free her own slaves.

The statue of Chief Justice Roger Brook Taney in front of the State House was unveiled in 1872. The chief justice was a native of Maryland and is known for his delivery of the Dred Scott decision of the Supreme Court which declared that a slave could not escape his condition by moving to free

Statue of Taney at the Maryland State House

territory. In May 1861, in his capacity as judge on the federal circuit court, Taney issued a writ of *habeas corpus* on behalf of John Merryman who had been arrested without charges (see Fort McHenry, site #1A).

On the other side of the State House from the Taney statue is St. Anne's Church, built in 1859. Inside the church is a brass eagle lectern in honor of Captain James I. Waddell, CSA, donated by his wife after his death.

b. BANNAKER-DOUGLASS MUSEUM

84 Franklin Street. From the State House take School Street west one block to Church Circle and on the other side of the circle go down Franklin Street a half block to the museum. Open Tuesday through Friday 10 a.m. to 3 p.m., and Saturday 12 noon to 4 p.m. Admission is a donation. 410-974-2893. (www2.ari.net/mdshpo)

The museum has displays of African American life in Maryland, and famous African Americans from Maryland such as Frederick Douglass (see Tuckahoe, site #9C). Rotating exhibits often depict artifacts demonstrating slave life, or the livelihood of free blacks in Maryland both before and after emancipation at the end of 1864. The museum is the official state repository for materials on African American heritage and thus is under the Maryland Historical Trust.

c. ST. JOHN'S COLLEGE

From the Bannaker-Douglass Museum return to Church Circle and take College Avenue two blocks. The college is on the left.

St. John's College was used as a hospital during the Civil War, designated USA General Hospital Division #2. At first it was also where exchanged prisoners of war waited to recuperate and be paroled to return home. The hospital beds were kept full with exchanged prisoners brought by steamers coming up from the James River. Many of these former prisoners of war were in serious need of medical care due to starvation, disease, and exposure. When there became too many of these parolees for this hospital to handle, Camp Parole was established three miles west of Annapolis in 1863. On the grounds of St. John's College McDowell Hall, Humphries Hall and other buildings served as hospital buildings during the war.

St. John's College

d. UNITED STATES NAVAL ACADEMY

From St. John's College follow College Avenue northeast to turn right on King George Street and follow this street three blocks until it ends at Gate #1. The Armel-Leftwich Visitor Center is one block on the right. Parking is available. The Visitor Center offers guided tours of the Academy. Open daily March through November from 9 a.m. to 5 p.m. and December through February 9 a.m. to 4 p.m. Admission is free. 410-263-6933. This is a National Historic Landmark.

The Naval Academy opened in 1845, founded by Navy Secretary George Bancroft with Commander Franklin Buchanan as its first superintendent. Buchanan was head of the Navy Yard in Washington, D.C. when the war broke out and resigned his commission to serve a memorable career in the Confederate navy.

The superintendent of the Academy in 1861 was Captain George Blake. All during the winter of 1860-61 cadets from the seceding states had been leaving the Academy with sad farewells to their comrades, so only about half the students were in attendance when the 8th Massachusetts and Gen. Benjamin Butler arrived on April 21, 1861. The student training ship, the USS *Constitution*, or "Old Ironsides," was towed out to sea to prevent its being captured by secessionists, and soon it along with the remaining students and staff of the Academy were transferred to Newport, Rhode Island for the duration of the war. Today the USS *Constitution*, the oldest ship in the U.S. Navy, is permanently docked at Boston Harbor.

During the Civil War the Academy grounds were used for a hospital designated USA General Hospital Division #1. Long rows of hospital ward buildings and tents were constructed on the grounds.

The Naval Academy Museum in Preeble Hall inside Gate #3 at Maryland Avenue has displays from the Civil War period including memorabilia of Admiral Franklin Buchanan, CSA and Commodore John Rodgers, USA, models of the USS *Monitor*, the *CSS Virginia*, the CSS *Shenandoah*, and items crafted from pieces of Civil War ships. It even has the spur of John Wilkes Booth that got caught in the drapery of the President's Box at Ford's Theatre as the assassin leaped to the stage after having shot President Lincoln. The museum also has a model of the Naval Academy as it looked in the 1850s.

There are no buildings left at the Academy from before the Civil War. The Academy grounds were much smaller then, comprising less than 10 acres—roughly the area from and including Brancroft Hall to the marble tablet in front of Mahan Hall that commemorates the opening of the Academy, to the wall on Hanover Street. Most of the land south of Bancroft Hall and east of Michelson Hall have been added by filling in part of the harbor.

There are, however, several tributes to people and events from the war on the grounds. A historical marker outside Luce Hall on Holloway Road near the sailboat basin describes the takeover of Annapolis by General Butler and the arrival of Union troops. Worden Field is named for Adm. John Worden; Ward Hall is named for Lt. James Harwood Ward; the superintendent's house and the road on which it lies are named for the first superintendent, Franklin Buchanan; and there are windows in the chapel dedicated to Admirals Porter and Farragut.

Northwest of the main campus of the Academy across Dorsey Creek is the Academy Cemetery which contains the graves of several Civil War heroes.

e. U.S. NATIONAL MILITARY CEMETERY AT CAMP PAROLE

From Church Circle follow West Street about five blocks west to the intersection with Taylor Avenue. The cemetery is just northwest of the intersection.

This cemetery was established in 1862 and contains many graves from the Civil War as well as many buried there since. A flagpole sits in the center of the neat rows of about 3,000 graves.

The cemetery lies at the eastern end of what was Camp Parole, established in 1863 to house and care for former prisoners of war until they were able to be paroled and return home, or go back to their military unit. The camp covered a large area from the intersection of Spa Road and West Street west to Annapolis Mall. There is nothing left today of Camp Parole except the cemetery—which houses those paroled to a higher existence.

2B. BROWN'S TAVERN

From the Capital Beltway take the Rt. 1 exit north toward Beltsville. The tavern is about .3 mile on the left. At the time of this writing the tavern is being restored and will be open to the public in the future.

Brown's Tavern, also known as White House Tavern, was built in 1834 on the Baltimore Turnpike by John W. Brown. It was the overnight stop for Gen. Bradley T. Johnson's Confederate cavalry on July 12, 1864. They were part of the Confederate advance on Washington, D.C. led by Gen. Jubal Early, and were on their way to free the Confederate prisoners of war at Point Lookout after having cut telegraph wires and destroyed railroad track around Baltimore.

As the Confederate cavalry regiment approached from the north, having just burned some railroad cars at Laurel, they ran into a company of Union cavalry who had just raided the larder, corn crib, and hay barns belonging to the widow Brown. The advance force of the Confederate cavalry, led by Maj. George Emack, drove off the Federals with a blaze of gunfire. One Union soldier who was wounded was taken to the nearby home of Major Emack's father, "Locust Grove" (no longer standing). The Confederates rested around Brown's Tavern and watered their horses, drinking three wells dry according to local tradition, then resumed their march down the Baltimore Road toward the Agricultural College (University of Maryland). But they had hardly gone a mile before General Johnson received the message from General Early to abandon the plan to attack Point Lookout and return to Virginia by way of Rockville instead (see Appendix C, Sites #4A, #4F).

2C. THOMAS VIADUCT AND RELAY HOUSE AT ELKRIDGE

Traveling north on Rt. 1 toward Laurel will take you along the route that Gen. Bradley Johnson's Confederate cavalry took south from Laurel. Annapolis Junction is 1 mile east of Rt. 1 just below Rt. 32. This is where the Annapolis and Elkridge spur of the B & O Railroad joined the main branch at the time of the Civil War. To reach the south side of the Thomas Viaduct, turn left (west) on Levering Avenue from Rt. 1 just south of the Patapsco River. The viaduct can be viewed from below from Patapsco Valley State Park (open 10 a.m. to sunset) which is on the north side of the Patapsco River. The entrance is one block north of Rt. 1 on Rolling Road. The site of Relay House, on the hill above, is no longer accessible. This is a National Historic Landmark.

The first section of railroad track in the United States opened between Baltimore and Ellicott Mills (Ellicott City) May 24, 1830—a distance of 13 miles. The first trains were drawn by horses along wooden tracks, and Relay House was the station where a fresh team of horses was hitched to the train. The emphasis was on speed, so changing teams every six or seven miles was necessary. Relay remained a station after the trains changed to steam locomotives, and it became the switching point for the connection of the new railroad line to Washington, D.C. with the B & O Railroad west from Baltimore.

The stone viaduct carrying the track across the gorge of the Patapsco River was designed by Benjamin Latrobe and completed in 1835. The eight-arch, 612-feet-long curved bridge was considered a major feat of engineering at the time. It was named for Philip Thomas, the first president of the Baltimore and Ohio Railroad.

After General Butler took the 8th New York, the 6th Massachusetts Regiments, and Cook's Boston Battery and occupied Relay House on May 5, 1861. These soldiers had been busy repairing the tracks of the Annapolis spur of the railroad since they landed in Annapolis on April 21 and 23. A number of different Federal units occupied the Relay throughout the war and a fort was built on either side of the viaduct. The fort on the Baltimore County side was Fort Dix. The primary objective of the troops was to protect the railroad line from sabotage or direct attack, and their secondary objective was to stop the smuggling of goods and people to the South on the railroad.

Union troops patrolled the line from Ellicott Mills to Baltimore and south to the Annapolis Junction. Except for railroad accidents there were no major incidents at Relay during the war.

Ellicott City Railroad Station

2D. ELLICOTT CITY

From the Patapsco Valley State Park take Rolling Road west 3.5 miles and turn left (west) on Rt. 144. Follow Rt. 144 west 3 miles to Ellicott City. After crossing the bridge over the Patapsco River continue up the hill and turn left on Hamilton Street just before the Post Office where there is a large parking lot. There is a Visitor Center in the Post Office open 9 a.m. to 5 p.m. Monday through Friday. 800-288-8747 (24 hours).

By the 1850s a prosperous city had grown up around the grist mills and iron works established by the Ellicott family in the 1770s. Ellicott Mills, so named until chartered as a city in 1867, had a population of more than 2,000 at the beginning of the war. A mill still operates on the south side of the river. Although devastated by several floods over the years, the steep main street of the town still is lined with pre-war stone, brick, and frame stores, hotels and homes, and retains the look of a late 19th-century railroad town. The steep streets and houses built in stair-step fashion up the bluffs of the river add to the charm of the town.

The Colonial Inn and Opera House on Main Street opposite the railroad station is reported to be the place where John Wilkes Booth made his acting debut. The building now houses a shop, but the second floor, with the natural stone wall of the cliff forming its back wall, is open to the public.

George Gaither organized a Confederate cavalry unit from this area known as the "Howard Dragoons"—which was first Company K of the 1st Virginia Cavalry, then Company M of the 1st Maryland Cavalry and finally Company K of the 2nd Maryland Cavalry. There is a monument, erected in 1848, honoring this unit in front of the Howard County Courthouse on Courthouse Road overlooking the town.

a. B & O RAILROAD STATION MUSEUM

2711 Maryland Avenue. From the Visitor Center walk two blocks down Main Street and the station is on the right. Open daily year-round 10 a.m. to 3:30 p.m. 410-461-1944. This is a National Historic Landmark.

This first railroad station in the United States was built in 1831. It has been restored and contains a museum that includes a remarkable miniature railroad display of that first railroad line between Baltimore and Ellicott Mills.

In 1830 the first railroad track in the country reached Ellicott Mills from Baltimore. This wooden track with cars drawn by horses soon evolved into a thriving steel rail, steam locomotive railroad which reached all the way to Wheeling, Virginia (now West Virginia) by 1853. The Baltimore and Ohio Railroad was an important supply link for the Federal army (see site #1K).

Early in May of 1861 Gen. Benjamin Butler, USA, learned of the secret transport of a unique steam-powered cannon—the Winans Steam Gun—aboard a train from Baltimore headed toward Cumberland where it would be transported to the Confederate side. The steam gun, supposed to be able to shoot 200 rounds a minute at a range of up to two miles, was disguised as a piece of farm machinery. It was manufactured at the locomotive shop of Ross Winans in Baltimore. Butler sent a detachment from the 6th Massachusetts Regiment to Ellicott Mills where the unit intercepted the train and captured the gun. The inventor of the steam gun, Charles Dickenson, escaped with some essential machinery components, making the Winans Steam Gun inoperable. The gun was never used and another one was never made.

2E. PIKESVILLE — CONFEDERATE SOLDIERS HOME

From Ellicott City take I-70 east. Go north on the Baltimore Beltway (I-695) to exit #20 east, Reisterstown Road, Pikesville, and travel 1 mile to the armory on the left (north) side of the road. There is a museum inside the walls of the armory which is open Tuesdays from 10 a.m. to 1 p.m., or by appointment by calling 410-653-4238.

Currently the state police headquarters, the armory at Pikesville was built in 1812. No longer being used after the Civil War, the buildings were donated by the state, along with $5,000 a year toward maintenance, to the Association of the Maryland Line in 1888 to house Confederate veterans. The Association was founded in 1880 by the Society of the Army and Navy of the Confederacy in Maryland specifically to care for the aging Confederate veterans since they had no pensions. The home was run by the Women's Auxiliary of the Association and admitted 139 residents between 1888 and 1893. It closed in 1932 with only three residents remaining, and the property reverted to the state.

After Colonel Gilmor's Confederate cavalry captured Gen. William B. Franklin and others from the train at the Gunpowder River Bridge (Site #2K) on July 11, 1864, a detachment was sent west with the prisoners. This detachment stopped to rest near the Cradock House just west of Pikesville on Greenspring Valley Road just east of the intersection with Reisterstown Road. As the exhausted cavalrymen slept General Franklin escaped near dawn, July 12. When Colonel Gilmor and the rest of the cavalry caught up with them the colonel and several of his men rode down the Pike within four miles of Baltimore in search of the escapees, but came back empty-handed.

2F. COCKEYSVILLE

Return to the Baltimore Beltway (I-695) and travel north to exit #26, north (Rt. 45). Take Rt. 45 five miles north to Cockeysville.

On the morning of July 10, 1864, the day after the Battle of Monocacy, Gen. Bradley T. Johnson's Confederate cavalry reached Cockeysville and here he detached a company under the command of Col. Harry Gilmor to travel east to destroy railroad bridges and telegraph wires. Along the way Gilmor visited his parents at their home, Glen Ellen (no longer standing) near Timonium.

As the unit passed through Dulaney Valley it passed the house of Ishmael Day who had a Union flag flying in front of the house. When one of the Confederate cavalrymen tried to take the flag down, Day shot him and he later died. Day and his family ran to hide in the woods as the rest of the cavalry arrived. Not finding Day, the Confederates burned down his house. Although Day's house was soon rebuilt, there is no house on the site now.

2G. HAYFIELDS

Travel 2 miles northwest of Cockeysville on Rt. 45 and turn left on Rt. 145. After crossing I-83 the house is on the right. The house and grounds are private and not open to the public.

Hayfields, the Merryman estate, was built in 1824 by Col. Nicholas Merryman Bosley. John Merryman, who inherited the plantation from his great-uncle in 1847, was a lieutenant in the Maryland Horse Guards, formed in January 1861 to protect the state. Following the orders of Governor Hicks and Mayor Brown after the Baltimore Riot of April 19, 1861, Merryman directed the men under his command to destroy the railroad bridge over the Gunpowder River near Parkton to prevent more Federal troops from entering the seething city. For this action Merryman was arrested on May 25, 1861, and taken to Fort McHenry where he was imprisoned without trial (see Fort McHenry, site #1A).

Gen. Bradley T. Johnson with his Confederate cavalry lunched here on July 11, 1864, after sending detachments to destroy the railroad bridges and cut telegraph wires to the east. After leaving Hayfields General Johnson and his men moved down the Green Spring Valley and, nearing the country house of Maryland Governor Augustus Bradford, sent a detail under the command of Lt. Henry Blackistone to burn down the mansion in retaliation for the burning of Virginia Governor Letcher's home by General Hunter. The mansion was burned after allowing some time for the residents to remove valuables. It was on Charles Street just north of the Baltimore city boundary—now the site of the Elkridge Country Club.

2H. GUNPOWDER RIVER BRIDGE OF THE NORTH CENTRAL RAILROAD

The bridge was north of Rt. 145 one mile east of Hunt Valley. The old railroad line is now a recreation trail, the Northern Central Railroad Trail (call 410-592-2897 for a map of the trail).

This bridge was burned by the Baltimore Guard on April 20, 1861 as a part of the aftermath of the Baltimore Riot. It was burned again by Gen. Bradley Johnson's Confederate cavalry on July 11, 1864, as a part of the Confederate invasion led by Gen. Jubal Early.

2I. TOWSON

Return Rt. 45 and go south, past the Baltimore Beltway (Rt. 695) 1 mile.

Returning from burning the railroad bridges (the long bridge over the Gunpowder River, and the bridges over Stemmer's Run, Mud Creek, Bush River and Back River) of the Baltimore, Wilmington and Philadelphia Railroad (see site #2K), Col. Harry Gilmor's company of cavalry stopped for refreshment at Ady's Tavern in Towson and presented the owner of the tavern with a fine horse in return for his hospitality. They sent a detachment with the prisoners they had captured from the trains toward Pikesville. On hearing that there was a Union cavalry unit approaching on the York Road, they rode out to meet the enemy. Charging with sabers aloft and rebel yells splitting the air, the Confederates routed the Union cavalry under the command of Maj. E. R. Petherbridge and chased them down the York Road as far as Govanstown. From Towson Gilmor's cavalry rode west, catching up with the prisoner detachment just west of Pikesville.

Hampton

2J. HAMPTON

From the Baltimore Beltway (I-695) take the Dulaney Valley Road Exit (#27) north to an immediate right (after the Beltway ramp) onto Hampton Lane. Or from Towson take Dulaney Valley Road north 1 mile to Hampton Lane. The estate is 1 mile east on Hampton Lane, to the right. Hampton is a National Historic Site, administered by the National Park Service, and is open to the public free of charge daily year-round 9 a.m. to 5 p.m. 410-823-1309.

Hampton was built by Capt. Charles Ridgely between 1783 and 1790. It is a showpiece of Georgian architecture and has been restored to reflect its early 19th-century appearance. The estate is complete with English gardens, orangery, and stone outbuildings including barns, stables, a dairy, and slave quarters. The rooms are decorated in the several different styles of the generations that lived there. Hampton is an example of the opulent plantation—a showcase of wealth and fashion. This type of plantation was dependent on slave labor to care for the vast grounds and provide the labor for the farming and mining activities. The family went bankrupt soon after the war.

In January 1861 a local guard, the Baltimore County Horse Guard, was raised in Towson to protect local citizens and property in the times of unrest. Charles Ridgely, the son of the owner of Hampton, was elected captain. The Guard was armed by the state of Maryland and trained weekly by Captain Switzer of the U.S. Army. On April 20 Ridgely's men were ordered to patrol the York Road north to Cockeysville and prevent any troops coming from the north from entering Baltimore, and on April 22 they were ordered to burn the railroad bridge near Parkton, which order was carried out by a detachment under Lieutenant Merryman. The Horse Guards ceased to exist after the military takeover of the state. Hampton was searched several times by Federal officers, but Charles Ridgely was never arrested, and took no more part in the war.

2K. GUNPOWDER RIVER BRIDGE OF THE BALTIMORE, WILMINGTON & PHILADELPHIA RAILROAD

From the Baltimore Beltway (Rt. 695) take Rt. 40 (exit #35) north 9 miles to Gunpowder Falls State Park at the mouth of the Gunpowder River.

On July 11, 1864, Confederate cavalry under the command of Col. Harry Gilmor captured a train near the bridge and burned it after unloading passengers and cargo. They also captured the next train, a freight train arriving about an hour after the first, set it on fire and rolled it onto the bridge. The Confederates were being fired upon from across the river by local volunteer troops under the command of Capt. Thomas Hugh Sterling and Company F of the 109th Regiment Ohio National Guard. The Union troops were able to uncouple two of the cars before the rest of the burning train fell through the bridge destroying the draw span.

The passengers from the train, including several Union officers, were released by the Confederates—with the exception of Major General Franklin and several others, who were headed for Southern prisons. Franklin later escaped from his captors near Pikesville (see Pikesville, site #2E).

2L. BEL AIR COURTHOUSE

Take I-95 north to Rt. 24 (exit #77) and follow Rt. 24 for 5 miles to Bel Air. The courthouse is in the center of the old town.

The second-floor hallway and courtroom of the 19th-century courthouse display portraits of Civil War generals and naval officers from the area, including Gen. James Archer, CSA; Commodore John Rodgers, USN; Governor Augustus Bradford; Dr. David Harlan, USN; and Edwin Booth.

Tudor Hall

2M. TUDOR HALL

Take Rt. 22 for 3 miles northeast of Bel Air and turn left on Tudor Hall Road. It is open to the public on Sundays June through September from 1 to 3 p.m.

This simple frame house was built in about 1822 by the actor Junius Brutus Booth after he immigrated from England in 1821 where he had been a prominent Shakespearean actor. John Wilkes Booth was born here in 1838 and followed in the footsteps of his acting brothers Edwin and Junius. He made his acting debut in 1855, three years after the death of his father. John Wilkes Booth would gain infamy as the assassin of President Abraham Lincoln. John's mother, father, and siblings all supported the Union during the war (for more about Booth see sites #8D, E, F G, J, K).

Rock Run

2N. ROCK RUN

From Bel Air take Rt. 924 north .5 mile to Rt. 1. Turn right (north) and travel 13 miles to turn right on Rt. 161, then left into Susquehanna State Park, following the signs to the park. Rock Run is at the bottom of the park overlooking the river and is open to the public Saturdays and Sundays May through September. 410-557-7994.

Rock Run is the birthplace and home of Brig. Gen. James J. Archer, CSA. Wounded and captured at the Battle of Gettysburg, Archer was exchanged and returned to service in August 1864. He died in Richmond in October 1864 from debilitation caused by his imprisonment and is buried there. He had been a lawyer in Baltimore before the war.

The house contains memorabilia and furniture of Archer and his family. It is in a state park, but is run by a private non-profit organization.

SUGGESTED READING

Brooks, Neal A. *A History of Baltimore County*. Towson, Md.: Friends of the Towson Library, 1979.

Edsall, Margaret Horton. *A Place Called the Yard: Guide to the U.S. Naval Academy*. Annapolis: DWE & Associates, 1992.

Jacobs, Timothy, ed. *The History of the Baltimore and Ohio: America's First Railroad*. New York: Crescent Books, 1989.

Mills, Eric. *Chesapeake Bay in the Civil War*. Centreville, Md.: Tidewater Publishers, 1996, pp. 35-38.

Smith, Gene. *American Gothic: The Story of America's Legendary Theatrical Family—Junius, Edwin and John Wilkes Booth*. New York: Simon & Schuster, 1992.

Toomey, Daniel Carroll. *A History of Relay, Maryland and the Thomas Viaduct*. Baltimore, Md.: Toomey Press, 1984.

FOR INFORMATION ON OTHER SITES, ACCOMMODATIONS, ETC.

Annapolis/Anne Arundel County
Conference and Visitors Bureau
26 West Street
Annapolis, MD 21401
410-280-0445
www.visit-annapolis.org.

Baltimore County Convention and
Visitors Bureau
435 York Road
Towson, MD 21204
800-570-2836, 410-583-7313
www.visitbacomd.com

Prince George's County Conference
and Visitors Bureau
9200 Basil Court, Suite 101
Largo, MD 20774
301-925-8300
www.princegeorges.com

Prince George's County Historical
Society
P.O. Box 14
Riverdale, MD 20738
301-464-0590

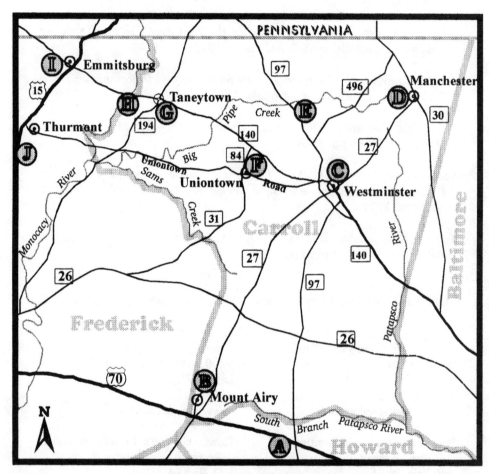

North-Central Maryland

CHAPTER 3

NORTH-CENTRAL MARYLAND

CARROLL, WESTERN HOWARD, AND NORTHERN FREDERICK COUNTIES

Carroll County and northwestern Howard County were very similar in the rolling terrain of their landscape dotted with small farms and grist mills. The B & O Railroad line ran along the Patapsco River which divides the two counties. In addition the Western Maryland Railroad had just completed a line from Baltimore that ran as far as Westminster. Although the residents were mixed in their sympathies during the Civil War, the closer one got to the Pennsylvania state line, the more people there were in support of the Union.

The Civil War directly affected the residents of these two counties three times during the war. Confederate Gen. Jeb Stuart's cavalry had briefly touched some of the towns in southwestern Carroll County as the unit moved south in the October 1862 raid. In July 1864 Gen. Bradley Johnson's cavalry came through Carroll County from Frederick on the way to Baltimore and stopped to rest in Westminster. The biggest shock to the area came before the Battle at Gettysburg when massive divisions of the Union army tramped through Carroll and northern Frederick counties in late June 1863. At the same time Gen. Jeb Stuart and his cavalry brigade again visited the county, moving north to find Lee's army and barely missing running into the masses of Union troops, sometimes skirmishing with scouting Union cavalry parties (see Appendix C for maps of both routes).

The command of the Union forces moving north from Washington and Virginia had transferred from Maj. Gen. Joseph Hooker to Maj. Gen. George Gordon Meade on June 28, 1863. Instead of trailing the Confederate army, General Meade devised a plan that anticipated the enemy's movements and was designed to confront the Confederate army in order to prevent it from proceeding further into Northern territory. This was called the "Pipe Creek Plan" and would have formed the Union battle lines along Big Pipe Creek with the center at Union Mills, Maryland, north of Westminster. The Pipe Creek Plan has been lauded by historians as an ingenious and well-thought-out plan, but unfortunately General Meade was not able to carry it out. Before all the corps were in place the advance unit, the Union I Corps under Gen. John Reynolds, ran into a major part of the Confederate army at the little town of Gettysburg and an escalating battle broke out. Under the

Pipe Creek Plan the I Corps would have withdrawn toward Union Mills, drawing the Confederate army to the chosen battleground, but General Reynolds was moving so fast that he probably never received the order to withdraw.

On June 30 the Union army started to move into positions for the Pipe Creek Plan—the III Corps (Maj. Gen. Daniel Sickles) moving from Taneytown to Bridgeport, the V Corps (Maj. Gen. George Sykes) moving from Liberty (Frederick County) to Union Mills, the VI Corps (Maj. Gen. John Sedgwick) moving from Westminster to Manchester, the XII Corps (Maj. Gen. Henry W. Slocum) moving from Taneytown to Littlestown, Pennsylvania, and the Union II Corps (Maj. Gen. Winfield Scott Hancock) remaining in Uniontown. The Union cavalry under Brig. Gen. David McD. Gregg moved from Westminster to Manchester along the Hanover Pike. Also involved in the Battle of Gettysburg, but not moving through Carroll County, were the XI Corps (Maj. Gen. Oliver O. Howard) moving from Middletown (west of Frederick) to Emmitsburg, and the I Corps (Maj. Gen. John Reynolds) which was already in Emmitsburg on June 30. When the battle broke out at Gettysburg, Pennsylvania on July 1, all of the units were redirected toward that town.

Western Howard County and northern Frederick County have been included in this chapter in order to better demonstrate these troop movements.

3A. COOKSVILLE

Junction of Rt. 97 and Rt. 144. From Brookeville go north on Rt. 97 eleven miles.

As they were traveling north to catch up with the main body of Lee's army before the Battle of Gettysburg, part of Gen. Jeb Stuart's 6,000 Confederate cavalry (the cavalry had been divided in Rockville) ran into part of the 1st Eastern Shore Infantry Union Regiment at Cooksville on June 29, 1863. The Confederates gave chase to the fleeing infantrymen and managed to capture several of them who identified themselves as members of "the Seven Hundred Loyal Eastern Shoremen."

After leaving Cooksville the Confederate cavalry headed toward Westminster, sending a detachment east to destroy the railroad bridge and telegraph line at Piney Run near Sykesville. The rest of the unit crossed the B & O Railroad and the South Branch of the Susquehanna River at Hood's Mill (where Rt. 97 crosses).

3B. MT. AIRY (RIDGEVILLE)

From Cooksville take I-70 west to the Mt. Airy exit. At the end of the off-ramp go straight at the traffic light into Mt. Airy and travel about 1 mile to Pine Grove Chapel on the right.

Before the Battle of Gettysburg the Union VI Corps under the command of General Sedgwick, moved through Mt. Airy, then called Ridgeville, from New Market heading north toward Westminster. They were followed by two brigades of Gregg's 2nd Division of Union cavalry. There were a total of 18,000 men and the columns were ten miles long. Finding a supply train at the railroad station they camped in the area on June 29, moving out on June 30, 1863. There was a brief confrontation on June 29 with advance scouts from Gen. Jeb Stuart's Confederate cavalry.

a. PINE GROVE CHAPEL

Company K of the New Jersey Militia was stationed at Mt. Airy to guard the railroad. The officers were housed in the chapel, which was called the Ridge Presbyterian Church at the time of the war. The men camped in the churchyard and there was a mess tent behind the church. An unknown soldier who fell ill and died in Ridgeville (Mt. Airy) was the first person to be buried in the cemetery now surrounding the church.

3C. WESTMINSTER

From Mt. Airy travel north on Rt. 27 twenty miles.

A bustling industrial town at the crossroads of four major roads, Westminster had 2,500 inhabitants at the beginning of the war. It lay at the junction of the main route north from Washington, D.C. (Rt. 27) and the turnpike from Baltimore to Pittsburgh. The Western Maryland Railroad had completed its line west to Westminster from Baltimore by 1861. This railroad was to be an important supply line for the Union army during the three-day Battle of Gettysburg, but was overlooked by Gen. Jeb Stuart's Confederate cavalry.

The town saw Confederate cavalry pass through three times during the war. On September 11, 1862, the town was occupied by the 5th Virginia Cavalry, CSA, under Col. T. L. Rosser as a part of the screening movement of General Lee's army as it moved into Pennsylvania. On June 29, 1863, Gen. Jeb Stuart's cavalry moved through on the way to join with Lee's army before the Battle of Gettysburg. The final invasion occurred July 9, 1864, when Gen. Bradley Johnson's Confederate cavalry, as a part of Gen. Jubal Early's plan to take Washington, stopped for a while in town for a rest.

From June 28 to July 1, 1863, a large number of Union troops tramped the streets of Westminster on the way to find their destiny on the battlefield at Gettysburg, just 26 miles to the northwest. The Union VI Corps came through twice (see site #3D).

a. ROSSER'S CHOICE
70 West Main Street. From Rt. 27 turn left on West Main Street and go about a block to the house on the left.

The home of John Brooke Boyle was used as headquarters on the night of September 11, 1862 by Col. Thomas Lafayette Rosser, commander of the 5th Virginia Cavalry, CSA. Rosser's cavalry was part of a screening movement for General Lee's army invading the North from the Poolesville area and headed for Pennsylvania, but later stopped on the bloody fields of Antietam.

Rosser's Choice

b. ASCENSION EPISCOPAL CHURCH
24 North Court Street. Turn around and travel east on Main Street about .5 mile to Court Street on the left.

Two officers from the 4th Virginia Cavalry killed in the skirmish on the east side of town on June 29, 1863 (Corbit's Charge, site # 3Cd) are buried here. They were: Lt. St. Pierre Gibson and Lt. William M. Murray.

Gibson's body has been removed and reinterred elsewhere by his family.

c. SHELLMAN HOUSE

206 East Main Street, across from Court Street. The house is open to the public. For hours of operation call 410-848-6494. Next door is the Carroll County Office of Tourism which is open Tuesday through Saturday 9 a.m. to 5 p.m., and Sunday 10 a.m. to 2 p.m. 800-272-1933.

On July 9, 1864, Gen. Bradley T. Johnson, CSA, made his headquarters at this house for a brief time as he rested his cavalry which had just arrived from Frederick. Johnson was under orders from Gen. Jubal Early to destroy the railroad bridges and telegraph wires around Baltimore.

A local tale tells that when Gen. Jeb Stuart's cavalry was passing by on June 29, 1863, a bold young girl from this house by the name of Mary Shellman called him a "Johnny Red Coat." The general stopped his horse and spoke to the youngster, telling her that her punishment for her loyalty to the Union would be a kiss. The kiss delivered, the general moved on.

d. CORBIT'S CHARGE

Intersection of Old Washington Road (Rt. 97) and Main Street. Travel east on Main Street from Court Square about .5 mile.

On June 28, 1863, two companies of the 1st Delaware Union Cavalry under Maj. Napoleon B. Knight entered Westminster and camped where the Western Maryland College is now, joining a provost guard from the 150th New York Infantry commanded by Lt. P. Bowman. The next afternoon (June 29) they received a report that Confederate cavalry were coming up from the south.

Crest-Trumbo House

Capt. Charles Corbit of Company C ordered Lt. D. W. Clark to take 12 men to reconnoiter. Clark and his men ran smack into the front of Gen. Jeb Stuart's 6,000 cavalry and were pushed back. Corbit ordered a charge toward the enemy. After a few minutes of fighting, 67 of Major Knight's force of 95 were captured or killed.

The Crest-Trumbo House (297 East Main Street) stands next to the road and was right in the line of fire during the skirmish. Bullet holes can be seen in the north wall.

3D. MANCHESTER

Return west on Main Street to the intersection with Rt. 27. Turn right on Rt. 27 and travel 8 miles. The camp was about 1 mile west of Main Street (Rt. 30) on the old Westminster Road, now called Old Fort Schoolhouse Road. There is a shopping center there now. The small brick building nearby is a reconstruction of the schoolhouse where General Sedgwick had his headquarters.

The VI Corps of the Army of the Potomac under Maj. Gen. John Sedgwick camped just south of town on the evening of June 30, 1863, ready to form the eastern edge of the Union front in the Pipe Creek Plan. Learning on the evening of July 1 that they were needed at Gettysburg, they marched through the night to Westminster and turned left (east) on Main Street instead of right. The entire corps of approximately 10,000 men had to reverse direction and go back in order to take the road north (Rt. 97). There they ran into miles of supply wagons heading north which further impeded their progress. Nevertheless they made the march of 37 miles in a remarkable 17 hours, arriving at Little Roundtop at Gettysburg on the afternoon of July 2. The 2nd Cavalry Division, USA, headed by Gen. David McM. Gregg, passed through the town on their way from Westminster to Hanover on June 30, 1863.

3E. UNION MILLS

From Manchester travel 2 miles north on Rt. 30. Turn left on Rt. 496 and travel 7 miles. Turn right on Rt. 97 and travel four miles to the Homestead on the right. Open June through August, Tuesday through Friday 10 a.m. to 4 p.m., Saturday and Sunday 12 noon to 4 p.m. May, September and October open weekends only. There is an admission fee. 410-848-2288.

Union Mills

The brothers Andrew and David Shriver established a mill on this site in 1797 and called it Union Mills to demonstrate their union in business. In the 1820s their children divided the property and one of the original brother's family built a house on the other side of the road (Rt. 97) from the original homestead. Those living at the "Homestead" were loyal to the North although owning slaves, and those living across the road, although against slavery, were loyal to the South. Sons from both families fought on either side during the war. Unlike some families that were permanently divided by the war, the two branches of the Shriver family remained friendly during and after the war. Gen. Jeb Stuart's Confederate cavalry, on their way to join up with Lee's army to the north, were fed from the huge kitchens at the Homestead on the evening of June 29, 1863, as they camped around the mills. The Confederates left early on the morning of June 30, after General Stuart had a sumptuous breakfast and song-fest at the Shriver house on the west side of the road. Sixteen-year-old Herbert Shriver led the cavalry to Hanover and General

Stuart in return helped him to enroll in the Virginia Military Institute. Herbert was wounded in the Battle of New Market where the cadets participated in heroic action.

Just a few hours after the Confederate cavalry had left, the Union V Corps under the command of Maj. Gen. George Sykes camped on the same ground around Union Mills, Gen. James Barnes staying at the Homestead. The Corps broke camp the next morning, July 1, and headed toward Hanover. They would be at Gettysburg on July 2.

3F. UNIONTOWN

From Union Mills return to Westminster on Rt. 97 and turn right on Main Street. After about 1 mile turn left on Rt. 31, then turn right on Uniontown Road at the traffic light. Travel 6 miles to the town.

Uniontown is a small town gem with streets lined by ancient trees, many houses dating back to the 18th century, and an original general store/post office. It has not been encroached upon by modern buildings and so a walk down the main street is like a walk into the past.

On the night of June 29, 1863, the Union II Corps, Maj. Gen. Winfield Scott Hancock commanding, camped east of town, having marched 32 miles from Monocacy Junction. The Corps consisted of about 10 brigades. General Hancock's headquarters were located on the John Babylon Farm about 1.5 mile east of town. The II Corps stayed in camp until July 1 when they marched to Gettysburg. The Union III Corps also passed through the town on June 29 on the way to Taneytown, and the V Corps came through on June 30 on the way to Union Mills.

Uniontown Post Office

a. WEAVER HOUSE
3406 Uniontown Road.

General Hancock rested for the night here at the home of Dr. Jacob Weaver on June 29, 1863. The one-story wing on the left was the office of Dr. Weaver. He had built this house around an older log house in 1859.

b. POST OFFICE
3444 Uniontown Road.

June 29 and 30, 1863, many Union soldiers camped nearby mailed letters from this post office. For some it would be their last letter home. The current post office and general store is the same building that existed in the Civil War, operated at that time by Harrison H. Weaver.

c. UNIONTOWN HOTEL
3477 Uniontown Road.

General Hancock met with his staff here on June 29, 1863, before going on to spend the night at the Weaver home. The hotel was built in 1802, making it one of the oldest buildings in town.

3G. TANEYTOWN

From Uniontown turn right on Rt. 84. Travel 3 miles and turn left on Rt. 140. Travel 5 miles to Taneytown.

On June 29, June 30, and July 1, 1863, the Union II Corps, III Corps, and XII Corps marched through the town on the way to Gettysburg.

a. ANTRIM

30 Trevanian Road. From Rt. 140 the entrance is on the left just before the intersection with Rt. 194.

Now an inn, the 1844 mansion was host to Union troops on June 30, 1863, and it is said that the widow's walk on the roof was used as a look-out by the soldiers.

b. GENERAL MEADE'S HEADQUARTERS SITE

Turn right on Rt. 194 and travel north .9 mile to the historical marker on right.

Maj. Gen. George Gordon Meade moved his headquarters here on the nearby Shunk Farm on June 30, 1863, and remained here until July 1, directing the Army of the Potomac in movements.

c. TRINITY LUTHERAN CHURCH

Return to Rt. 140 and turn right. The church is a half block on the right side of the street.

The Union Signal Corps established a signal station on the church tower on June 30, 1863. Signals were passed to and from Gettysburg using flags or flares. The steeple has been replaced twice since that time.

d. CAMP OF UNION XII CORPS

Continue west on Rt. 140 to just west of town where you will see a town park with the historical markers on the left (south) side of the road.

The Union XII Corps camped in this vicinity on June 29-30, 1863, and then headed north to Littlestown, Pennsylvania on Rt. 194. The III Corps moved through on June 30 heading west to Bridgeport along Rt. 140. Both Corps were taking their places for the Pipe Creek Plan.

e. SWOPE'S PLACE

Just a little further west on Rt. 140 is Harney Road on the right (north) side of the road. The house is at the intersection.

Maj. Gen. Winfield Scott Hancock was resting his Union II Corps here on July 1, 1863, when he received word of General Reynolds' death and the order to go immediately to Gettysburg and take command of the forces in the field. He rode to Gettysburg along the Harney Road, known by historians as the "backdoor to Gettysburg."

The farm was owned at the time by Dr. Swope who treated many wounded after the Battle of Gettysburg.

3H. BRIDGEPORT

Travel west on Rt. 140 for 3 miles and the historical marker is on the left.

On June 30, 1863, Gen. Daniel Sickles' Union III Corps camped here before moving on to Emmitsburg. It was to form the left flank of the Union "Pipe Creek" plan before the confrontation at Gettysburg moved front.

Elizabeth Elliot House

3I. EMMITSBURG

From Bridgeport travel west on Rt. 140 for 5 miles to turn left on South Seton Avenue. Historical markers are next to the post office on the left (east) side of the road.

Emmitsburg lay right in the path of Union troops traveling from Frederick and Taneytown to check the invading Confederate army at Gettysburg on July 1-3, 1863. The I Corps and the XI Corps camped here on June 30, 1863. The I Corps was under the command of Maj. Gen. John Fulton Reynolds. They marched to Gettysburg in the early morning hours of July 1, and ran into part of the Confederate army there. A battle erupted and quickly escalated as more troops from both sides joined in the melee. General Reynolds was killed. Maj. Gen. Daniel Edgar Sickles' III Corps marched through here on July 1, 1863.

a. ELIZABETH ELLIOT HOUSE

103-107 South Seton Avenue, next to the post office on the east side (now the Chronicle building).

The widow Elizabeth Elliot was a strong supporter of the Confederacy and during the war her home was used as a refuge for Confederate spies on several occasions.

b. SISTERS OF CHARITY CONVENT

Now the National Emergency Training Center on east Seton Avenue near Rt. 15.

The convent provided 231 sisters to work as nurses after the Battle of Gettysburg and other nearby battles. The dedicated work of the Sisters of Charity is described in *Angels of the Battlefield* by George Barton, written in 1897.

3J. CATOCTIN FURNACE AND HARRIET EPISCOPAL CHURCH

From Emmitsburg travel south on Rt. 15 eight miles to Rt. 806 south. The furnace is on the right side of the road and the chapel is .5 mile further on the left.

From 1844 to 1853 the future Brig. Gen. William Nelson Pendleton, CSA, was pastor to the Harriet Episcopal Chapel as well as to All Saints Episcopal Church in Frederick (see site #5Fg).

Catoctin Furnace was constructed in 1774 by the Thomas Johnson family. It produced iron for the patriot cause during the Revolutionary War and was in continuous operation through the Civil War and produced weaponry for the Union.

SUGGESTED READING

Klein, Fredrick S. *Just South of Gettysburg*. Westminster, Md.: Historical Society of Carroll County, 1963.

Klein, Fredrick S. "Meade's Pipe Creek Plan," Maryland Historical Magazine, 57 (1962): 133-49.

Warren, Nancy M., et al. *Carroll County, Maryland: A History*. Westminster: Carroll County Bicentennial Committee, 1976.

FOR INFORMATION ON OTHER SITES, ACCOMMODATIONS, ETC.

Carroll County Office of Tourism
224 North Center Street
Westminster, MD 21157
800-272-1933, 410-857-2983
www.carr.org

Howard County Tourism Council
P.O. Box 9
Ellicott City, MD 21041
800-288-TRIP, 410-313-1900
www.howardcountymdtour.com

Historical Society of Carroll County
210 E. Main Street
Westminster, MD 21157
410-848-6494

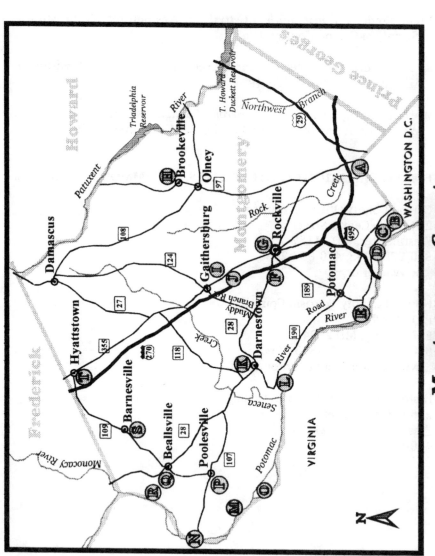

Montgomery County

CHAPTER 4

MONTGOMERY COUNTY

Montgomery County, with the Potomac River as its western border, was like a revolving door for Union and Confederate troops during the Civil War. Although no major battles were fought in the county, skirmishes between Confederate raiding parties and Union units camped in the area and between the rear guards and front guards of the closely passing enemy armies left a sprinkling of graves scattered around the county. Citizens of the county suffered the damaging effects from encampments of large numbers of troops, as well as the loss of goods stolen by Confederate raiders and roaming gangs of scavengers from both sides.

The majority of the citizens of the county were pro-Southern, many people having family ties across the Potomac River in Virginia. As evidence of this Southern leaning Montgomery County had only 50 (out of more than 2,000) votes for Lincoln in the 1860 election, and gave only seven volunteers for the Union army before the December 1862 draft. The Union also had its supporters in the county, as some citizens held a mass meeting at Rockville on New Year's Day 1861 and passed a resolution supporting the Union, and expressing an "abhorrence of the unconstitutional assaults upon our domestic institutions." The Quaker settlement in the Sandy Spring area on the eastern edge of the county favored the Union and the abolition of slavery, but did not agree with the aggressive action of the Federal government. During the war spies from both sides, some local and some from the outside, were scattered throughout the county.

This mixture of allegiances created tensions among the citizens of the county, and some animosities that were created by the war separated families and friends forever. During the military rule suspected secessionists were arrested and held without trial while their houses were searched. Pro-Southern elected officials were arrested and held until after a new election had ousted them from office. The editor of the *Montgomery County Sentinel*, the county's principal weekly newspaper, was arrested several times and his newspaper suppressed. Union supporters, on the other hand, could expect rough treatment at the hands of Confederate troops when they passed through.

At the beginning of the war Federal authorities in Washington, D.C. knew that Confederate troops were massing in Leesburg and Harpers Ferry, Virginia. It was essential to protect the border between Maryland and Virginia, formed by the Potomac River, and a large part of that border was in

Montgomery County, Maryland. The first Union troops started arriving in the county in early June 1861. They were concentrated around Darnestown and Poolesville, but were actually spread from the Muddy Branch Creek on the south to the Monocacy River to the north. The bulk of these Federal troops left for winter quarters elsewhere in November; permanent garrisons were situated at the major river crossings.

In September of 1862 General Lee's Confederate army invaded the North by way of White's Ford to the north of Poolesville and headed for Frederick, leaving a screen of cavalry to protect his rear. McClellan's Union army followed from Washington, D.C. to finally clash at South Mountain and Antietam. Advance Union cavalry skirmished with Confederate rear guard cavalry at Beallsville, Barnesville, and Hyattstown. Gen. Jeb Stuart's Confederate cavalry returned to the area in October of the same year, passing through Hyattstown and Barnesville on the way back to Virginia via White's Ford after having circled the Union army a second time (see Appendix C for map of route).

As a part of the second Confederate invasion of the North in June 1863, Gen. Jeb Stuart brought three brigades of cavalry across the Potomac River at Rowser's Ford, near Violette's Lock on the C & O Canal, heading on to Rockville. Before Stuart's trek, many corps of the Union army had pa ed through the county traveling north to counter the invasion which would culminate at Gettysburg (see Appendix C for map of route). Four corps that were in Virginia crossed the Potomac River into Maryland on pontoon bridges constructed at Edward's Ferry.

The last major movement of troops through the county occurred in July 1864 when Gen. Jubal Early brought his Confederate army of 12,570 men down the Frederick/Georgetown Pike (Rt. 355) and Georgia Avenue to menace the capital city from Silver Spring. He then retreated through Rockville, Darnestown, and Poolesville to return to Virginia at White's Ford, followed closely by several Union brigades. Thus the last Confederate invasion of Maryland left by the same door through which the first invasion had entered the State in September 1862 (see Appendix C for map of route).

Col. Elijah "Lige" White, CSA; Col. Ridgely Brown, CSA; Lieut. Gip Peter, CSA; and Confederate spy Rose O'Neale Greenhow were from Montgomery County. On the Union side Commodore Samuel Phillips Lee, USN, and Montgomery Blair, Postmaster under President Lincoln, made their homes in the county before and after the Civil War.

4A. SILVER SPRING

Travel 1.5 miles south of the Capital Beltway on Georgia Avenue. To reach the spring turn right on East West Highway and the spring is one block on the left. Turn left here onto Newell Street and travel one block to the post office, which is on the site of the Blair house, "Silver Spring." The sites of the Confederate action (the grounds of Walter Reed Army Medical Center), and Union action at Fort Stevens (13th Street and Quackenbros Street) are all in Washington, D.C.

The large French chateau-style house, named "Silver Spring" after the spring on the property, had been built in 1845 by Francis Preston Blair, editor of the *Globe* newspaper and advisor to President Andrew Jackson. Blair had retired there in the 1850s. The house was unoccupied, however, when Gen. Jubal Early marched in with his Confederate army on July 11, 1864, and made the house his headquarters. The soldiers camped on the grounds. From here General Early sent out Gen. Robert E. Rodes with his cavalry to test the defenses of Fort Stevens about one mile to the south.

After learning of the arrival of the Union VI Corps in Washington, General Early decided not to attack Washington D.C., but remained in the area throughout the day on July 12, leading his army toward Rockville and the Potomac River crossings to the west that evening. All through the day the Union cannon fired missiles at the Confederates, but most fell short of their marks and did more damage to local houses. Rifle fire was also exchanged periodically during the day, and at one point President Lincoln, viewing the position of the Confederates from atop the wall of Fort Stevens, was narrowly missed by the bullet of a Confederate sharpshooter firing from what is now the grounds of the Walter Reed Army Medical Center. Toward evening skirmishers were sent out from the fort and engaged Rodes' troops. Both sides lost about twenty men who were killed in this skirmish. The Confederates are buried in the churchyard of Grace Episcopal Church on Georgia Avenue, and the Union are buried in the Battleground National Cemetery, 6625 Georgia Avenue, in Washington, D.C. (for the Confederate retreat route see Sites #4F and #4N).

After the Confederates had left, "Falkland," the nearby home of Montgomery Blair, son of Francis Preston Blair, burned to the ground. General Early said that the house was not burned intentionally by his troops, and may have caught fire from a stray cannonball.

4B. BATTERY BAILEY

From Silver Spring go west on East-West Highway to turn left on Wisconsin Avenue, then right on Western Avenue to Westmoreland Circle. Turn right onto Massachusetts Avenue and go two blocks west to turn left onto Jamestown Drive. Take the first right onto Elliott Road and follow until it ends in Little Falls Park. The battery remains are beyond the end of the parking area.

Battery Bailey was an arm of Fort Mansfield and Fort Sumner to the west of the city and overlooked the Powder Mill Branch valley. There were platforms for six siege guns, but the battery was never armed. It was named for Capt. Guilford D. Bailey of the 2nd U.S. Artillery who was killed at Seven Pines (Fair Oaks), Virginia, May 31, 1862. Descriptive markers were placed at the battery in 1994.

4C. CLARA BARTON HOUSE

From Battery Bailey return to Massachusetts Avenue and travel west 2 miles to turn left onto Goldsboro Road, then right on MacArthur Boulevard and an immediate left onto Oxford Road. From the Capital Beltway (I-495) take the Exit for the Cabin John Parkway and travel east to take a left onto MacArthur Boulevard, then left on Oxford Road (Canal mile 7). The house is operated by the National Park Service and is open daily. Call 301-492-6245 for information.

This house was built in 1891 by Clara Barton as a residence and headquarters for the American Red Cross, which she founded. Clara Barton was known as the "Angel of the Battlefield" for her tending to wounded soldiers in the battlefields during the Civil War—including Antietam Battlefield. The house contains memorabilia of Barton and the Red Cross.

4D. CABIN JOHN BRIDGE (UNION ARCH)

From the Clara Barton House turn left onto MacArthur Boulevard and travel .5 mile to the one-lane bridge.

This bridge is part of the aqueduct built to carry water from the Potomac River at Great Falls into Washington, D.C. It was constructed between 1853 and 1861 by the Army Corps of Engineers. It was the longest single-arch span in the world when it was built. The chief engineer for the project was Lt. Montgomery C. Meigs and the resident engineer was Alfred Rives. As soon as the project was completed Meigs became a brigadier general in the Union army and Rives joined the Confederate army. Meigs had a plaque placed on the side of the aqueduct that said, "Washington Aqueduct, begun A.D. 1853, President of the U.S., Franklin Pierce, Secretary of War, Jefferson Davis; building completed A.D. 1861, President of the U.S., Abraham Lincoln, Secretary of War, Simon Cameron." The Secretary of the Interior under Lincoln, Caleb Smith, had Jefferson Davis' name removed, but it was replaced by order of Congress in 1909. The plaque is on the south side of the bridge on the west pier.

Great Falls Tavern

4E. GREAT FALLS TAVERN (CROMMELIN)
Continue west about 5 miles to the end of MacArthur Boulevard to the entrance to the Great Falls National Park. There is an entrance fee. 301-299-3613 (Canal mile 14.3).

Thinking that the Confederates might try to destroy the aqueduct dam or ford the river to the north, the Federals garrisoned troops nearby from the beginning of the war. No such attempt was ever made by the Confederates, but there was an across-the-river skirmish by snipers on July 7, 1861, which resulted in two Union deaths.

The north and south parts of the tavern were built in 1831, but the central part was constructed as a lockhouse in 1828. Known as Crommelin House this tavern was in continual use during the war and was known to have been used on occasion by Confederate spies. There is a museum of the C & O Canal's history, operated by the National Park Service, in the tavern.

4F. WATTS BRANCH SKIRMISH

From Great Falls take Falls Road toward Rockville. After 6 miles turn left on Wooton Parkway and take to the intersection with Darnestown Road (Rt. 28). Turn right and go 1 mile to Hurley Avenue. Rt. 28 crosses Watts Branch just ahead.

As Gen. Jubal Early led his Confederate army of 14,000 in retreat from Silver Spring (Site #4A) on July 13, 1864, the route taken was north on Viers Mill Road and then northwest on Darnestown Road (Rt. 28) toward Poolesville and the Potomac River. A Confederate artillery unit under the command of Col. William B. Jackson was set up on the hill at the intersection of Muddy Branch Road with Darnestown Road to protect the retreat. As Gen. Bradley Johnson's 1st Maryland Cavalry, CSA, bringing up the rear of the retreat, reached this point on the morning of July 13, the artillery was being threatened by the 2nd Massachusetts Cavalry, USA, under the command of Col. Charles R. Lowell, massed just beyond the range of the artillery at Watts Branch. General Johnson sent out a squadron of the 1st Maryland Cavalry under Capt. Wilson G. Nicholas and Lt. Thomas Green to push the enemy back. The two forces fought fiercely at Watts Branch, but the Union cavalry was soon forced into Rockville along Montgomery Avenue where they dismounted and fired from behind houses and trees. In the dust and confusion both Nicholas and Green had their horses shot from under them and were captured. General Johnson made another charge with his cavalry and was able to recapture Green, but Nicholas had been taken off by the retreating Federals. There were several casualties on both sides from this skirmish. The Union lost 5 killed, 20 wounded and 60 captured. No information was located on the number of Confederate casualties.

The Confederates resumed their trek to Poolesville and were able to cross the Potomac River at several fords and ferries on July 14 without further incident, the Union VI Corps not following until the next day (see Sites #4P, #4R).

4G. ROCKVILLE

Continue on Rt. 28 (becomes Montgomery Avenue) into Rockville. Turn left at the intersection with Rt. 189. Then turn left at the next corner onto Adams Street and then left again onto Middle Lane. The parking lot for the Beall-Dawson House is on the left.

The newly incorporated (1860) county seat had less than 500 residents at the beginning of the war. It was occupied by Federal forces in June 1861, and then off and on throughout the war. The fairgrounds (present site of Richard Montgomery High School) was a transitory camp for these soldiers. During occupation many pro-Southern citizens were arrested and their houses searched. They were incarcerated in the Old Capital Prison in Washington, D.C. and most were released after a short time.

From September 7-11, 1862, part of Gen. George McClellan's Union army, consisting of the II, VI, and XII Corps, passed through the city on the way to meet the Confederate army at South Mountain and Antietam. McClellan had his headquarters on Falls Road just outside Rockville.

On Sunday morning, June 28, 1863, Gen. Jeb Stuart's Confederate cavalry corps invaded Rockville coming from Rowser's Ford (see site #4L). They stopped to capture a Union wagon train of 120 wagons, and take into custody several stray Union soldiers in the area as well as many pro-Union citizens, including the town commissioner, county judge, town postmaster, and local provost. The Confederates were greeted gaily by the young women at the Female Seminary and many other citizens of a pro-Southern bent. General Stuart with two brigades of the cavalry, and wagon train, moved out down the Old Baltimore Road (Rt. 28) and then north on the Brookeville Pike (Rt. 97). Most of the approximately 400 prisoners were released at Brookeville that evening, and the rest at Cooksville the next day. The delay to the cavalry caused by the encumbrance of the wagon train contributed to Stuart's failure to rejoin Lee's army before the Battle of Gettysburg. A third brigade of Confederate cavalry had been sent by Stuart from Rockville to Sykesville to destroy telegraph lines and railroad bridges.

In July 1864 the city again experienced troop movements through its streets, this time with considerably more gunfire. After meeting Federal forces violently at the Monocacy River, Gen. Jubal Early's Confederate army moved through Rockville on July 10 and 11. The advance cavalry under General McCausland drove out some 500 Union defense cavalry from Derwood, north of Rockville, along Rockville Pike, through the city and to the south. The Confederate cavalry camped at the fairgrounds the evening of July 10. They continued down the Rockville Pike on the eleventh. The bulk of the 8,000 infantry marched through town and down the 7th Street Pike (Viers Mill Road and Georgia Avenue) on July 11, heading for Silver Spring. They returned through Rockville on July 13 heading towards Poolesville by way of the Darnestown Road (Rt. 28). A rear guard of cavalry set up a defensive line along Watts Branch a mile west of town, and when approached by pursuing Union cavalry, attacked and chased the Federals in a running battle through Rockville.

The Beall-Dawson House and Dr. Stonestreet's Office are two of the very few pre-war structures that remain in the city.

Beall-Dawson House

a. BEALL-DAWSON HOUSE AND DR. STONESTREET OFFICE

Open Tuesday through Saturday 12 noon to 4 p.m. and the first Sunday of each month from 2 to 5 p.m. Call 301-762-1492 for information.

      This Federal-style brick house was built in 1815 by Upton Beall. At the time of the Civil War it was occupied by his three unmarried daughters, Margaret, Matilda, and Jane Beall (Jane died in 1863 at age 47). Situated on the Darnestown Road (Rt. 28) and only three blocks from the courthouse and Rockville Pike, the ladies saw the passing of many troops from both sides during the war. Gen. George McClellan spent the night of September 7, 1862, at the house. After the skirmish at Watts Branch on July 13, 1864, the Misses Beall nursed a wounded Union soldier, Private James Hill, at their home.

      The house is decorated in mid-19th-century style and operated by the Montgomery County Historical Society which also has a fine research library on the grounds.

      Dr. Stonestreet's Office has been moved to the museum grounds from a few blocks away. Dr. Edward Elisha Stonestreet used the office from 1852 to 1903, and during the Civil War he was employed by the U.S. Army as both an examining surgeon and a contract surgeon. Both duties he fulfilled from his office in Rockville, attending the emergency hospital set up in Rockville after the Battle of Antietam in the fall of 1862. The office houses an extensive collection of 19th-century medical equipment.

b. CONFEDERATE MONUMENT

The monument is on the east side of the Old Red Brick Courthouse at Jefferson Street and Maryland Avenue, just three blocks from the Beall-Dawson House.

The monument is a life-size bronze of a cavalry private, arms folded and looking into the distance. The model for the statue was reportedly Spencer C. Jones who had been a private in Company A, 1st Maryland Cavalry, and had gone on to become a prominent politician in Montgomery County. The monument was erected by the E. V. White Chapter of the United Daughters of the Confederacy (UDC), the Ridgely Brown Chapter, UDC, and the Ridgely Brown Camp of the United Confederate Veterans. It was constructed by Michael J. Falvey of the Falvey Granite Company in Washington, D.C. and the inscription reads: "To our heroes of Montgomery Co., Maryland, that we through life may not forget to love the thin gray line. CSA 1861-1865."

The monument was placed in front of the county courthouse, facing south, and was unveiled on June 3, 1913. In 1971 it was moved to the side of the courthouse to make way for an urban renewal project.

4H. BROOKEVILLE

From Rockville travel east on Rt. 28 four miles to turn left onto Georgia Avenue (Rt. 97). Travel north 9 miles to Brookeville.

This 18th-century National Register town was the site of the headquarters of Gen. Ambrose Burnside, in command of General McClellan's right wing as he moved his Union army north to eventually meet Lee's army on the fields of Antietam. The headquarters were established on September 8, 1862, and the next day the Union I Corps under Gen. Joseph Hooker arrived, leaving for Cooksville on the eleventh. The IX Corps also moved through heading northwest toward Damascus.

On June 28, 1863, Gen. Jeb Stuart released the bulk of his captives here as he moved his corps of cavalry from Rockville toward Westminster, with the remainder being released at Cooksville.

4I. RICKETTS RUN

From Brookeville take Brookeville Road west from Rt. 97. Turn right on Rt. 108, then immediately left onto Muncaster Road. At the traffic light at Redland continue straight on Redland Road for 2 miles and after crossing the bridge over the railroad and Metro tracks turn left onto Sommerville Drive and then right into the McDonald's restaurant parking lot. The site of the fight is downhill on the other side of Sommerville Drive at the small creek.

On October 6, 1864, a small band of about ten of Mosby's rangers under the command of Walter Bowie, a local lad from the Ashton area, was riding west toward the Potomac River having come up through southern Maryland on a raid. Late that evening they stopped at the Bently and Gilpin store at Sandy Spring, tied up the five men whom they found there, took what they wanted from the store, and continued west. The five men, who were Quakers, roused the town and contacted the county sheriff who formed a posse to chase the rebels and regain their property. The posse of 17 villagers found the Confederates in the dark of the early morning of October 7 camped and sleeping near a creek on the Rickett's farm. They opened fire and the rudely awakened and confused Confederates returned fire until the civilians retreated. Capt. Walter "Watt" Bowie had been mortally wounded in the fight and his comrades left him in the care of his brother, Brune, as they continued west to cross the Potomac River near the mouth of the Monocacy. Two Union cavalry units were dispatched to chase the rebel band, but they escaped. The men of the posse who were members of the Society of Friends were charged by the local Quaker counsel with "imprudence" but were allowed to continue worship at the church.

Two months earlier, during the Confederate march on Washington, D.C., General McCausland's Confederate cavalry, heading south on Rt. 355, was confronted by about 500 Union cavalry near here and pushed them toward Rockville with no casualties on either side.

4J. SUMMIT HALL FARM

From Redland Road turn right onto Rt. 355 and travel north for 2 miles to turn left onto Education Boulevard. You will have just passed the Summit Hall Farm on the left, which has been made into a city park. Follow the park signs to the house, which is <u>not</u> open to the public, but you may walk around the grounds.

After the Battle of Monocacy on July 9, 1864, Gen. Jubal Early's army camped on the farm on the evening of July 10. General Early and his staff were the unwelcome guests of John T. DeSellum of Summit Hall. Mr. DeSellum describes the experience and his conversations with General Early in a letter which can be viewed at the Montgomery County Historical Society Library (see site #4Ga).

64

4K. DARNESTOWN

Rt. 28, eight miles west of Rockville on Rt. 28. From Gaithersburg (Summit Hall Farm) go north on Rt. 355 to turn west on West Diamond Avenue. Turn left on Muddy Branch Road. Travel 2 miles to turn right on Rt. 28 (the hill at this intersection was where the Confederate artillery protected the retreat of General Early's army in July, 1864—see Site #4F), and go 6 miles to Darnestown.

The area around Darnestown became the holding point and training ground for Union forces gathering in the summer and fall of 1861, then for the troops responsible for guarding the Potomac River crossings. As many as 20,000 soldiers camped along the road to Beallsville (Rt. 28) and Seneca Road leading to the River. They were first under the jurisdiction of Col. Charles P. Stone, then under the command of Maj. Gen. Nathaniel Banks. Most of the troops left for winter quarters near Frederick in November 1861.

Nearby is the home of the prominent Peter family, Montanverd. One of the sons of the family, Gip Peter, joined the Confederate army and was hanged as a spy in Tennessee, though whether he was actually a spy is one of the mysteries left by the war (see biographies in Appendix A).

a. MAGRUDER FARM

14800 Seneca Road. Travel west on Seneca Road from Darnestown for 1.5 miles and the house is on the left (south) side of the road just past Deakins Lane (on left).

Magruder Farm

Situated on a hill overlooking the Potomac River to the west, the property served as division headquarters for Union Gen. Nathaniel Banks in the fall of 1861. Banks and his staff resided in the house, the middle section of which was built in the 1830s and the main section in 1858. The Union troops camped on the surrounding fields. A signal station was set up near the house at the top of a large old chestnut tree. The signal station connected Washington, D.C. with stations on Sugarloaf Mountain, Maryland Heights (Harpers Ferry), and as far north as Fairview Mountain, overlooking the Potomac River north of Williamsport. They remained in operation through the fall of 1862. The owner of the house, Samuel Thomas Magruder, and his family retreated to live in the attic of the house during the occupation.

In May 1864, Lt. Nicholas Dorsey of the 35th Virginia Cavalry, CSA, a cousin of the Magruders, arrived at the house having escaped from prison at Fort McHenry. He had been captured in September 1863 while looking for some horses that Col. E. V. White had left behind during a raid. When he arrived at the house he had on the remnants of a Confederate uniform. The family fed him and gave him rest for the night. The next morning a company of Union troops had arrived on the farm, so Mr. Magruder gave Dorsey one of his suits and he walked out the front door, waving and smiling to the Union sentries, and got a ride on a wagon traveling down the road in front of the house to Seneca, where he was rowed across the river to Virginia.

4L. ROWSER'S FORD
Seneca Road joins River Road about 2 miles west of Darnestown. Coming from Darnestown turn left on River Road and travel .2 mile to turn right on Violette's Lock Rd. Go .7 mile to parking area (Canal mile 22.12). The ford was immediately below the dam.

On crossing the Potomac as a part of Lee's invasion of the North in June 1863, before the Battle of Gettysburg, Gen. Jeb Stuart found the river high and most of the crossings too difficult. He finally managed to cross his three brigades of cavalry here on June 27, and continued on to Rockville. His men breached the canal in several places and damaged the lock.

John Mosby's Confederate raiders had used this ford two weeks before as they crossed from Virginia to attack the 6th Michigan Cavalry at Seneca on June 10, 1863. Four Union and two Confederate soldiers were killed in the skirmish. The Union cavalry retreated to Poolesville and set up barricades, but Mosby never attacked.

Just to the east of this ford is the mouth of Muddy Branch Creek where there was a small Union camp and blockhouse that was destroyed by Colonel Mosby's Confederate cavalry as they detached from the main army during the retreat of General Early's forces on July 13, 1864. Gen. Horatio

Wright's VI Corps moved from Tenleytown in pursuit of the Confederates and camped overnight at Potomac. They were followed the next day by the XIX Corps in crossing the Potomac to Virginia.

4M. EDWARD'S FERRY

From Violette's Lock return to turn left on River Road and turn left at the T intersection to continue on River Road. After about 8 miles (road narrows after 5 miles and becomes Mt. Nebo road after about 6 miles), turn left on West Offutt Road and then left onto Edward's Ferry Road for 1 mile to the park. The parking area is on the west side of the canal (Canal mile 31).

This major crossing of the Potomac River had a pivot bridge over the canal that allowed traffic to cross the canal after crossing the river. This has now been replaced by a permanent bridge. Once a little town surrounded the lock-keeper's white house next to the canal. The ruins of a large brick store are all that remains of a once active commercial enterprise.

Union troops were posted here throughout the war and their camps were raided twice by Col. "Lige" White's Confederate cavalry. In December 1861 Thaddeus Lowe made several tethered ascensions in his balloon from here to observe enemy positions across the Potomac River.

In June 1863 twin pontoon bridges were constructed at the ferry to allow General Hooker's Army of the Potomac, then in Fredericksburg, Virginia, to cross the Potomac River into Maryland in pursuit of Lee's army invading northern Maryland and Pennsylvania before the Battle of Gettysburg. The

Edward's Ferry Lockhouse

Union I, III, and XI Corps crossed on June 25; the Union II, V, and XII Corps crossed on the twenty-sixth; and the Union VI Corps crossed on the twenty-seventh.

The following summer McCausland's Confederate cavalry destroyed the lock gates and canal bridge, after threatening Washington, D.C. at Fort Reno as part of Gen. Jubal Early's Confederate invasion in July 1864.

White's Ferry

4N. WHITE'S (CONRAD'S) FERRY

From Edward's Ferry continue on Edward's Ferry Road for about 4 miles to turn left onto White's Ferry Road and go 4 miles to the ferry. You can turn left onto River Road from Edward's Ferry, but this is 5 miles of gravel road and can be impassable during or after a heavy rain.

This major crossing of the Potomac River was known as Conrad's Ferry during the Civil War. After the war the ferry was named for Col. Elijah (Lige) White of the 35th Virginia Cavalry who was a native of Poolesville, and owned a warehouse here after the war.

The ferry was usually well-protected by Union forces during the war, and the ford associated with the ferry was too deep for troops. It was, however, used by Confederate cavalry raiders several times when the Union guard units were elsewhere. Small raiding bands from Col. Lige White's 35th Virginia Cavalry would cross either here or at White's Ford to the north and return at the other. Confederate spies on the Maryland side of the river would get the message to the other side when Union troops were scarce in the area, sometimes by a light in a certain window, sometimes by a colored curtain.

Colonel Mosby brought his Rangers across here from Virginia during General Early's attack on Washington in July 1864; and General McCausland's Confederate cavalry crossed back into Virginia here during the retreat of General Early's forces a few days later.

4O. HARRISON'S ISLAND

About .5 mile south of White's Ferry on the C & O Canal.

It was here that Col. Edward Baker, brigade commander in Gen. Charles Stone's division, ferried four Union regiments across the Potomac River in an ill-fated attack headed toward Leesburg on October 21, 1861. Baker was responding to an order by General McClellan to make a "slight demonstration" near Leesburg, Virginia. The Union troops met with an increasing number of Confederate forces on the Virginia side in the Battle of Ball's Bluff. With the river running high and not enough boats to get them back in a large group, the Union soldiers at the foot of the bluff on the Virginia side were cut to pieces by the Confederates.

The Union casualties were 48 killed, 158 wounded, and 714 captured or missing. Bodies were turning up for days after the battle as far south as Georgetown. The Confederates fared somewhat better in the battle with 33 killed, 115 wounded, and one missing. Lige White from Poolesville, acting as a courier for the Confederate army that night, captured about 300 Union soldiers with a small band of men. Lt. Oliver Wendell Holmes, Jr., USA, was wounded in the fight, and Colonel Baker was killed. Baker had been a senator from Oregon and a personal friend of President Lincoln.

There is a National Cemetery—with some of the victims of the disastrous fight—on the Virginia side of the river. It is about two miles south of White's Ferry off Rt. 15.

4P. POOLESVILLE

From White's Ferry take Whites Ferry Road 6 miles to Poolesville. From Rt. 28, three miles north of Darnestown take Whites Ferry Road (Rt. 107) west 3 miles to Poolesville.

Poolesville was one of the largest towns in the county, but most of its citizens held allegiance to the South, many having close relatives across the Potomac River in Virginia. Several fords and ferries crossed the river near the town, so it was strategically important to the Union. Early in June 1861 Union troops started coming into town and camping on the outskirts or on nearby farms. By August 1861 there were about 12,000 troops from infantry, cavalry, and artillery in the vicinity of the town. Most left for winter quarters near Frederick by the end of that year, but there were Union training camps in the area on and off throughout the war. The presence of Union troops did not keep Confederate raiders, who seemed to have an uncanny knowledge of when the main body of Union troops had left the area, from coming in on occasion. On September 8, 1862, Gen. Jeb Stuart's Confederate cavalry skirmished with the 8th Illinois and 3rd Indiana Cavalry in Poolesville, then went on toward Frederick. On November 25, 1862, Confederate Capt. George Chiswell, a native of Poolesville, raided Federal camps in the area with a small band of men, capturing men and supplies. Another band of Confederate cavalry under Col. Lige White, born and raised near Poolesville, came into town on Sunday, December 14, 1862, capturing a number of Union soldiers, arms and horses. The soldiers were released before they re-crossed the river. After these incidents the 11th New York Cavalry (Scott's 900) was reinforced by an entire Union brigade and an artillery battery.

In late June 1863 the town became the headquarters of the Army of the Potomac as it moved north toward Frederick and Gettysburg.

On July 14, 1864, Gen. Jubal Early's Confederate army retreated through Poolesville on its way to cross the Potomac River at White's Ford.

Although two major fires have ravaged the town since the war, many of the fine old brick houses still line the streets of Poolesville. The Presbyterian Church on the west side of Elgin Road, St. Peter's Episcopal Church, 20100 Fisher Avenue, and the old Methodist Church on the north side of Willard Road existed at the time of the Civil War, as did many of the houses on the east side of Fisher Avenue south of Elgin Road and the west side of Fisher Avenue north of Elgin Road. Many ante-bellum plantation houses can be found in the countryside surrounding the town.

a. JOHN POOLE STORE

Behind the 1910 Town Hall in the middle of Poolesville. It is operated by the Historic Medley District, a local historic preservation group, and is open on weekends from April through October. Call 301-972-8588 for information.

The 1 1/2-story log house had been built as a store and residence in 1793. Although it was not being operated as a store in 1861-65, there were five stores in Poolesville at the time, all of which are now gone—so the restored John Poole Store now represents these stores of the past. In the rear section of the building is a display of Civil War artifacts from the area and a hand-drawn map showing the troop encampments in the town in December 1863.

Monocacy Chapel

4Q. BEALLSVILLE AND MONOCACY CHAPEL
From Poolesville take Elgin Road (Rt. 109) north 2 miles to Rt. 28.

Beallsville sits on the crossroads of two roads leading to Potomac River crossings, so Union guards were stationed here periodically. The soldiers, thinking that the small wooden chapel at the top of the hill was abandoned, used it to stable their horses and burned the pews for firewood. The building was the Monocacy Chapel, a 1748 original Anglican Chapel-of-Ease. The destroyed chapel was replaced by the United Daughters of the Confederacy in 1915. The Daughters also placed a memorial tablet next to the chapel bearing the names of local Confederate soldiers.

On September 9, 1862, the 8th Illinois Cavalry and two companies of the 3rd Indiana Cavalry, under the command of Col. John Farnsworth, clashed here with the 12th Virginia Cavalry, forming the rear guard of Lee's army in Frederick. The outnumbered Confederates fell back, losing their flag in the encounter. On October 12, 1862, at the end of their second ride around the Union army, Gen. Jeb Stuart's cavalry, coming from Barnesville, crossed the Beallsville-Monocacy Road (Rt. 28) about 1.5 miles north of Beallsville, heading for White's Ford. Union forces from Beallsville to the south of him, and from the Mouth of the Monocacy River to the north of him, tried to attack, but were held off by John Pelham's light artillery until the cavalry had safely crossed the Potomac River into Virginia (see Appendix C for map).

71

4R. WHITE'S FORD

From Beallsville travel north on Rt. 28 for 2 miles to turn left on Martinsburg Road. Follow the road for 2 miles (avoiding the PEPCO plant) to the Dickerson Park. Follow the C & O Canal south for about .5 mile to the tip of Mason's Island. (Canal mile 39.5) The Monocacy Aqueduct and Sugarloaf Mountain are easily accessed from this point although they are listed in the Frederick County tour (#5A and #5B).

Located at the northern tip of Mason's Island, but not directly connected with a road, this obscure ford was a favorite crossing spot for Confederate raiders. Although picketed by small Union units intermittently during the war, it was never fully protected by a blockhouse or heavy artillery.

On September 5 and 6, 1861, 35,000 Confederates from Longstreet's and Jackson's commands crossed here from Virginia into Maryland and moved up the canal, crossing the Monocacy River at the aqueduct, then on to Frederick before the Battle of Antietam. The Confederate cavalry moved directly east from the crossing, forming a screen for the army from Beallsville to Mt. Airy. Jeb Stuart's cavalry crossed from Maryland back into Virginia here on October 12, 1861, completing their second "Ride Around McClellan."

The ford was used a third time by a large body of Confederate troops when the major part of Gen. Jubal Early's army crossed back into Virginia on July 14, 1864, after threatening Washington, D.C. Gen. Horatio Wright's VI Corps crossed here two days later in pursuit of Early.

4S. BARNESVILLE

From Dickerson take Mt. Ephraim Road east 1 mile to turn right onto Barnesville Road and follow for 2 miles to the town.

After crossing the Potomac River into Maryland with Lee's army on September 5, 1862, Gen. Jeb Stuart's cavalry moved eastward to form a protective screen for the main body of the army which had moved northeast toward Frederick. Leonard Hays in Barnesville, whose son was in the Confederate army, offered General Stuart and brigade commanders Gen. Fitz Lee, Gen. Wade Hampton, and Col. Thomas Munford food and drink as they passed through. Stuart left a company in Barnesville. On September 9, the 12th Virginia Cavalry, driven back from Beallsville by the 8th Illinois and part of the 3rd Indiana, joined this company in fighting a running battle with the Union cavalry advancing from the southwest along Beallsville Road (Rt. 109), through the town and continuing toward Hyattstown on Old Hundred Road.

4T. HYATTSTOWN

From Barnesville take Old Hundred Road (Rt. 109) northeast 5 miles until it intersects with Rt. 355.

Besides seeing the masses of troops marching through town on Rt. 355 before and after the battles of Antietam, Gettysburg, and Monocacy, Hyattstown was the site of the small skirmish that drew Gen. Jeb Stuart and his officers away from the Ball at Urbana (see site #5C) on the night of September 11, 1862, as pickets in Gen. Wade Hampton's Confederate cavalry brigade clashed with advance units of Union cavalry from the II Corps. The skirmish ended when both units pulled back to await the light of morning.

Gen. Jeb Stuart's cavalry visited the town again on the morning of October 12, 1862, as they came from Monrovia heading for White's Ford after having ridden around the Union army.

SUGGESTED READING

Coleman, Margaret. *Montgomery County: A Pictorial History*, Norfolk, Va.: The Dorning Co., 1984.

Cooling, Benjamin Franklin. *Jubal Early's Raid on Washington*. Baltimore: The Nautical and Aviation Publishing Company of America, 1989.

Cooling, Benjamin Franklin. *Mr. Lincoln's Forts: A Guide to the Civil War Defenses of Washington*. Shippensburg, Pa.: White Mane Publishing Co., 1988.

Forman, Stephen. *A Guide to Civil War Washington*. Washington, D.C.: Elliott & Clark Publishing, 1995.

Hahn, Thomas F. *Towpath Guide to the C & O Canal*. Freemansburg, Pa.: Am   ⸏n Canal and Transportation Center, 1993.

Hiebert, Ray Eldon, and Richard K. MacMaster, *A Grateful Remembrance: The Story of Montgomery County, Maryland*. Rockville: Montgomery County Historical Society, 1976.

Holien, Kim Bernard. *Battle at Ball's Bluff*. Self-published, 1985.

Jacobs, Charles T. *Civil War Guide to Montgomery County*. Rockville: Montgomery County Historical Society, 1996.

Laas, Virginia Jeans, ed. *Wartime Washington: The Civil War Letters of Elizabeth Blair Lee*. Chicago: University of Illinois Press, 1991.

Sween, Jane. *Montgomery County: Two Centuries of Change*, Woodland Hills, Calif.: Windsor Publications, Inc., 1984.

INFORMATION ON OTHER SITES, ACCOMMODATIONS, ETC.

Conference and Visitors Bureau
  of Montgomery County
12900 Middlebrook Rd.
  Suite 1400
Germantown, MD 20874
800-925-0880, 301-428-9702

Montgomery County Historical
  Society
111 West Montgomery Avenue
Rockville, MD 20850
301-762-1492
  www.montgomeryhistory.org

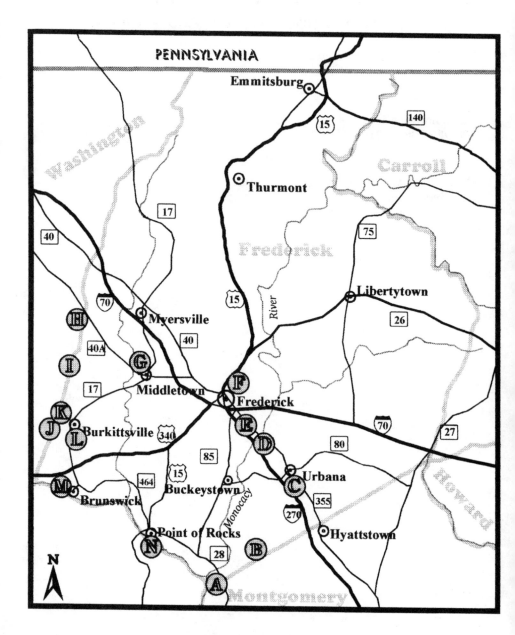

Frederick County

CHAPTER 5

FREDERICK CITY AND COUNTY

Frederick County was quite literally in the middle during the Civil War. With the Mason-Dixon Line forming its northern border and the Potomac River part of its southern border, the county was situated between enemy factions. The residents of the county were divided in their loyalties, some descended from old Southern families, and many from fairly new German families who had moved south from Pennsylvania. Frederick County had contributed more than 1,000 volunteers for the Union army by 1863, falling just short of its quota. About equidistant from both Baltimore and Washington, D.C., the main roads west from those major cities passed through the county and actually crossed in Frederick City. The first railroad in the country, the Baltimore and Ohio (B & O), had been completed to Point of Rocks in 1832, with a spur going into Frederick from Monocacy Junction, and by the time of the Civil War reached all the way to the Ohio River. The City of Frederick was a large and prosperous town of more than 8,000 people who, like the rest of the county residents, were about equally divided in their allegiances during the war.

Because of the major arteries passing through it, the county saw the comings and goings of major armies of both the Union and Confederacy during the war years. Lee's army crossed the Potomac River into Maryland near Poolesville on September 5, 1862, and went on to camp around Frederick before dividing—part of the army going west to attack Harpers Ferry, and the remainder heading north. McClellan's Union army followed close behind the Confederates, camping at many of the same places, and clashing with the Confederates at South Mountain on September 14, 1862. The ridge of South Mountain forms the border between Frederick and Washington Counties, so most of this battle, fought on the eastern side of the mountain as the Confederates defended the passes from the attack of the Union forces coming from the east, occurred in Frederick County. The opposing armies would face each other three days later at the Battle of Antietam.

Less than a month after the Battle of Antietam General Lee sent a unit of Confederate cavalry under Gen. Jeb Stuart to raid Chambersburg, Pennsylvania and wreak havoc on telegraph lines and railroad bridges in lower Pennsylvania and northern Maryland. About 1,800 cavalrymen supported by four light cannon crossed into Maryland near Williamsport on October 10, 1862, heading for Chambersburg. By October 11 Stuart's fast-moving cavalry crossed the eastern part of Frederick County passing through Emmitsburg, Libertytown, New Market, and Monrovia. After entering Montgomery County they would then turn west and return to Virginia at White's Ford (see map in Appendix C).

Following Lee's second invasion of the North in June 1863, the Army of the Potomac, commanded at first by General Hooker then by General Meade, came through Frederick County pursuing the invading Confederate army North. The armies would meet in deadly battle at Gettysburg on July 1-3. On June 28, 1863, the I and XI Corps camped west of Frederick, the II, III, and V Corps were around Frederick, and the VI Corps was south of the city. They all moved out in different directions the next day in accordance with Meade's "Pipe Creek Plan" (see Chapter 3).

In the summer of 1864, a Confederate army entered Maryland for the third time. On July 7, 1864, Confederate forces, having crossed the Potomac River near Sharpsburg the day before, entered Frederick County via Middletown. This army, commanded by Gen. Jubal Early, unlike the well-mannered and confident soldiers seen two years before, plundered and stole property and demanded ransoms in Middletown and Frederick. They were on their way to attack the capital city and capture it if they could, or at least draw Union troops away from central Virginia where they were making successful inroads. On July 9 the Confederates clashed with Federal forces at the Monocacy River two miles south of Frederick, delaying the planned action by the Confederates against Washington, D.C.

Monocacy Aqueduct

5A. MONOCACY AQUEDUCT AND LOCK #27

From Rt. 28 in Dickerson just north of the railroad underpass turn left on Mouth of Monocacy Road and go 1.2 miles to the fork and take the left fork to the parking area.

With its seven arches, the 516-feet-long Monocacy Aqueduct is the largest on the canal. Half of it is in Montgomery County and half in Frederick County. The pink quartz sandstone used to build the structure came from the base of Sugarloaf Mountain four miles away.

Confederates under Gen. D. H. Hill on September 2, 1862, tried to blow up the aqueduct, but did not have the equipment for such a large task. They contented themselves with damaging Lock #27 north of the aqueduct, burning some canal boats and breaking down the bank of the canal in several places. The lock-keeper, Thomas Walter, was charged with aiding the Confederates, but the charge was dropped after neighbors pleaded that he had convinced the rebels to destroy the lock instead of the aqueduct.

About a week later Confederate Gen. John Walker tried to destroy the aqueduct, but found the stone too hard for his drills to penetrate and had to abandon the project.

Sugarloaf Mountain

5B. SUGARLOAF MOUNTAIN

From Rt. 28 at Dickerson take Mt. Ephraim Road to the east for about 4 miles until it meets with Comus Road and the entrance to the Sugarloaf Mountain Park. The park is open dawn to dusk.

Sugarloaf Mountain was used as a lookout and signal station by both the Union and Confederates during the Civil War. When under control of the Union forces it connected, at various times, Washington, D.C. via Darnestown with stations on South Mountain, Fairview Mountain (north of Williamsport) and Catoctin Mountain (near Middletown).

Messages were transmitted by waving a pair of signal-flags in certain configurations. The soldier at the station receiving the message would view the flags through field glasses and report the letters or numbers transmitted to another soldier who would decipher the coded message using a cipher disk. At night torches were used instead of flags. The message was then either retransmitted to another signal station or run to the nearest army headquarters or telegraph office. The United States Signal Corps was established in July 1861 with Maj. Albert J. Myer in command.

A Signal Corps detachment stationed on Sugarloaf Mountain kept watch over the fords on the Potomac River. The report of Lee's army crossing into Maryland in September 1862, was seen and reported from here. From the lookout fort on the west side of the mountain or from the top of the mountain looking west you can see the Dickerson Power Plant smokestack in the distance. This was the approximate location of Spinks Ferry. About one mile to the left (south) of the smokestack is White's Ford, and about two miles further to the left is White's Ferry. Noland's Ferry near the Monocacy River was about two miles to the right (north) of the smokestack.

A short way down the road from the west overlook is a circle with a stone bench in the center. From this location, within shouting distance of the west overlook signal station, Darnestown can be viewed in the distance.

5C. URBANA

From the foot of Sugarloaf Mountain take Mt. Ephraim Road north about 4 miles to turn right on Park Mills Road. Follow Park Mills Road to a T intersection with Rt. 355. Turn right and travel 1.5 miles to Urbana.

This small town was the site of two Civil War events—one involving the advance of the Confederate army in the fall of 1862, and the other having to do with the aftermath of the Battle of Monocacy in July 1864. After Lee's army had crossed the Potomac River into Maryland at White's Ford on September 5, 1862, the bulk of the army went to Frederick but the cavalry units were scattered at different points to the south of the city to screen the main force from any Union advance from Washington, D.C. Jeb Stuart's cavalry was stationed at Urbana and after several days of enjoying the society of the local residents, most of whom were in support of the Confederacy, Stuart decided to give a ball. The large building of the Landon Female Academy was vacant and so was decorated with regimental flags, and the army band furnished the music for the dance held on the evening of September 11. When the dance was at its height it was interrupted by cannon and gunfire and the men grabbed their swords and rode off toward the fight. It turned out to be just a skirmish with McClellan's advance guard which withdrew, but when the men returned to resume the festivities, the wounded being brought in on stretchers quickly drew the attention of the ladies present, and the dance was over.

A few days later the empty Female Academy building hosted the Union soldiers of the 155th Pennsylvania Regiment and others of Humphrey's Division who had dropped out of rank because of exhaustion from the forced march from Rockville.

The 20-room Academy building had been constructed in 1754 on the Rappahannock River in Virginia. It was dismantled and moved to its present location in 1846, and has recently been restored. It is located just to the east of the southern intersection of Rt. 80 with Rt. 355. It is private, not open to the public, and difficult to see from the road, except in winter.

a. ZION EPISCOPAL CHURCH RUINS

Turn right on Urbana Church Road just north of the intersection with the road to I-270. The church ruins are on the right and the Confederate graves are on the east side.

      The church was built in 1802 but was destroyed by fire in 1861. The roofless stone walls served as a temporary hospital during the Battle of Monocacy, July 9, 1864. As Union troops retreated from the battle down the road to Monrovia (Rt. 80) they left behind a cavalry unit to guard their rear—Lt. David Clendenin's 8th Illinois Cavalry. Fresh from the battle, McCausland's Confederate cavalry stopped at the well at the church for water, being unaware of the Union cavalry nearby. The Union cavalry attacked and scattered the Confederates. Two of the soldiers in gray, Maj. Frederick Smith (Company G, 17th Virginia Cavalry) and Lt. Col. William C. Tavenner (Company C, 17th Virginia Cavalry), lost their lives in the encounter and are buried in this churchyard.

5D.   MONOCACY BATTLEFIELD

4801 Urbana Pike (Rt. 355). From Urbana travel north on Rt. 355 four miles and turn right into the National Park entrance. The battlefield is a National Battlefield Park and is open 8 a.m. to 4:30 p.m. Wednesday through Sunday year-round. Details of the battle and directions to the five monuments on the battlefield can be found at the Visitor Center which has interpretive programs, a small museum, and bookstore. 301-662-3515.

New Jersey Monument

      On July 6, 1864, under orders from General Lee to menace Washington in order to draw Grant's forces away from Virginia, Gen. Jubal Early led his 14,000-man Army of the Valley across the Potomac River at Shepherdstown to attack

Washington, D.C. from the north. On the morning of July 9, 1864, Early's army left Frederick traveling down the Georgetown Pike (Rt. 355) toward Washington. A force of about 5,800 Union troops under the command of Gen. Lew Wallace were waiting for them at the bridge crossing the Monocacy River. The day-long battle ended in a victory for the Confederates, who routed the numerically weaker Union forces. The Confederates lost about 900 killed and wounded, while the Union lost 1,968 killed and wounded. The importance of the battle, however, lies in the fact that Wallace's troops saved the Lincoln government from major disaster by delaying the Confederate army a day, giving General Grant time to bring in troops to reinforce the protection of the capital city.

The visitor center for the park is located in the 1830 Gambrill Mill, owned at the time of the battle by James H. Gambrill. During the battle Union forces were positioned in the yard of the mill and the mill was set up as a hospital.

On the battlefield are two important houses that are not open to the public: the Thomas Farm ("Araby" during the Civil War) where General Grant met with General Hunter on August 7, 1864, and removed him from command, replacing him with General Sheridan who arrived in Frederick on the train the next day; and the Worthington House where Glenn Worthington at age six watched the Battle of Monocacy rage around him and later wrote an account of his experience. Araby is a private residence and the Worthington House is owned by the National Park Service.

There is an "overlook" off I-270-northbound, between the Urbana and first Frederick exits which has an interpretive sign about the Battle of Monocacy. Unfortunately neither the battlefield nor Old Frederick can be seen well from this vantage point because a line of trees blocks the view to the northeast.

5E. BEST'S GROVE

From the Monocacy National Battlefield Visitor Center turn right onto Rt. 355, cross the Monocacy River and travel 1 mile to the two monuments on the left. From this spot the grove of three or four trees can be viewed about 200 yards to the south halfway along the farm driveway.

When Confederate forces occupied the area September 6 to the tenth in 1862 there was an army hospital located in this grove of trees (there were many more trees there at the time than today) as Gen. Stonewall Jackson's troops camped in the surrounding fields. General Jackson himself, having been thrown from a spirited horse given to him by local citizens, was a patient at the hospital for several days. Three days later, on September 13, Federal troops from McClellan's army camped in the same spot and two soldiers from the 27th Indiana Volunteers found General Lee's orders wrapped around three cigars—the famous "Lost Order 191." The order outlined Lee's strategy of dividing his army, sending General Jackson to attack Harpers Ferry, and General Longstreet toward Hagerstown. Knowledge of this maneuver would have allowed McClellan to move his Union forces between the two Confederate armies to "divide and conquer." But McClellan moved too slowly and was further delayed by heavy resistance of the enemy on South Mountain, so Lee was able to reunite his armies to fight the Battle of Antietam on September 17.

The monuments were erected in 1914 and 1965 on the site of the center of the Confederate line during the Battle of Monocacy.

5F. FREDERICK CITY

Thousands of soldiers tramped through the streets of the major crossroads city of Frederick as the residents played host to the Confederate army twice and the Union army also two times.

Frederick was invaded by Lee's Confederate army on September 6 to 12, 1862, an invasion many in the town welcomed with open arms. Company C of the 1st Potomac Home Brigade, USA, under the command of Capt. William T. Faithful, stationed in Frederick to protect the railroad, had retreated from the town the night before after burning all military supplies. A native of the town, Gen. Bradley T. Johnson, CSA, was made provost marshal for the Confederate stay. Appeals for volunteers for the Confederate army from General Lee and General Johnson went largely ignored, but gifts of food and clothing came in abundance. The fact that the area gave few volunteers to the Confederate army at the time was probably due to the fact that most of the young men who had ardently wanted to join the Southern cause had already done so. The Union army that pressed through the town a few days later in pursuit of the Confederates also found few local men ready to jump into their ranks.

After the Battles of South Mountain and Antietam all of the churches and many other public buildings in Frederick served as temporary hospitals and many of the ladies of the community offered their services as nurses.

President Lincoln, on his return from visiting the Antietam Battlefield on October 1-4, 1862, stopped briefly at Frederick and addressed the people at the Frederick train station which was located at 100 South Market Street.

In late June 1863, as the Federal forces followed Lee's second invasion of the North, Gen. Joseph Hooker came with his Union army through town and camped just to the west. When that army broke camp it was under the command of Gen. George Meade.

Frederick was again invaded by Confederates, this time under the command of Gen. Jubal Early, on July 8 and 9, 1864. Some fighting had occurred near the western edge of town on July 7 as advance cavalry from the enemy armies skirmished. This time the Southern army received a less than warm reception which cooled even more when the Confederates demanded a ransom of $200,000 to keep them from burning down the town. Many public buildings in town were again converted to temporary hospitals for the wounded after the Battle of Monocacy.

The central downtown area of Frederick retains many of the 18 and 19th-century buildings and streetscapes that existed at the time of the Civil War. Self-guided walking tours are available at the visitor center at 19 East Church Street (800-999-3613), or at the National Museum of Civil War Medicine (site #5Fi).

National Museum of Civil War Medicine

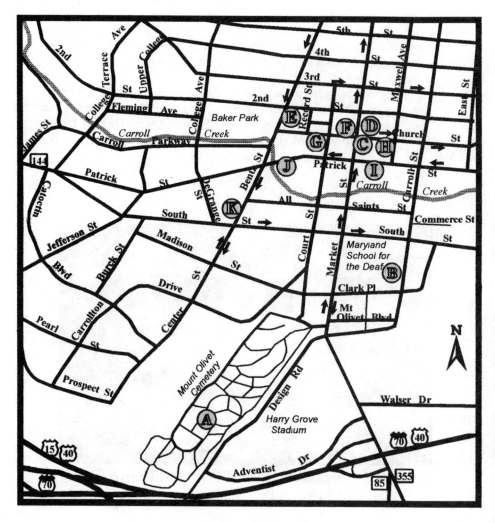

City of Frederick

a. MOUNT OLIVET CEMETERY

From the Monocacy Battlefield continue north on Rt. 355 two miles to the cemetery entrance on the left.(From I-70 take the Market Street/Rt. 355 exit and turn left on Market Street.) Once inside the cemetery take the right fork in the cemetery road and follow this lane to the line of Confederate gravestones on the right and the Confederate statue on the left. Turn right at the Confederate statue and continue straight for three cemetery blocks west to the Barbara Fritchie monument in the center of the roadway.

The graves of more than 400 Confederate soldiers who died in the Battles of Monocacy, South Mountain, and Antietam line the north boundary of this cemetery. They were placed here by the Frederick County Confederate Memorial Association, which also raised the money to place the statue to watch over the graves in 1881. The Association was granted $2,000 by the State of Maryland in 1869 to aid their efforts. Most of the remains of Union soldiers from those battles who had been buried in this cemetery were transferred to Antietam National Cemetery in 1867.

The Barbara Fritchie Monument was erected in 1914 by the Barbara Fritchie Memorial Association. The entire text of the poem by John Greenleaf Whittier that was inspired by the action of the elderly patriot is inscribed on the monument (see Barbara Fritchie House #5Fj).

b. HESSIAN BARRACKS

101 Clarke Place. From Market Street a few blocks north of Mount Olivet Cemetery turn right on Clarke Place and the barracks can be seen to the left. The barracks are on the grounds of the School for the Deaf. Open by appointment only. Call 301-663-8687.

This stone building was built in 1777 to house soldiers during the Revolutionary War. It was used as a prison for captured Hessian soldiers. In 1803 it was used by Capt. Merriweather Lewis as a staging area for his expedition into the Louisiana Territory.

Even before the Battles of South Mountain and Antietam the barracks had been made the Union Military Hospital. There were several frame buildings erected around the barracks at the time. The director of the hospital was Dr. R. F. Wier, assistant surgeon general. In June 1862 it held 690 patients. It continued to serve as a hospital throughout the war.

Kemp Hall

c. KEMP HALL
Southeast corner of Church and North Market Streets.

On April 26, 1861, the Maryland General Assembly met at the City Courthouse and then convened here at Kemp Hall the next day. The special session was convened in Frederick because Annapolis had been taken over by the Union army and was under martial law. Governor Hicks had delayed calling a special session of the legislature for fear that those assembled might vote for secession from the Union. When finally convened here in Frederick beginning in late April they did not, however, vote to secede, only appointing commissions to meet with President Lincoln and President Davis to plead for a peaceful solution. The legislature adjourned May 14, but met again on June 4 and passed more resolutions condemning military rule and the arbitrary arrest of citizens. When the General Assembly attempted to meet in Frederick again in September more than thirty delegates who had Southern sympathies were arrested (between September 12 and the 17) along with the mayor of Baltimore. When the legislature met on September 17 it did not have a quorum of members and so had to adjourn.

d. OLD CITY HALL
124 North Market Street.

Originally an opera house, this building was serving as the seat of the Frederick City government in 1864 when Mayor William C. Cole received the ransom demand of $200,000 from the Confederate forces under the command of Gen. Jubal Early on July 8, 1864. The city's five banks came up with the money and delivered it to General Early just before he left on June 9 on his way to threaten Washington, D.C. The city repaid half of the debt to the banks by 1868, but the rest was not repaid until the 1950s.

e. RAMSEY HOUSE
119 Record Street.
     Brig. Gen. George Lucas Hartsuff, USA, was seriously wounded at the Battle of Antietam and was being nursed at the home of Mrs. Mary Tyler Ramsey. President Abraham Lincoln visited General Hartsuff here when he was passing through Frederick on his way back from visiting the battlefield at Antietam on October 4, 1862, and gave a brief message to a small crowd of people gathered around the house.

f. EVANGELICAL REFORMED CHURCH
15 West Church Street.
     On Sunday, September 7, 1862, Gen. "Stonewall" Jackson came into Frederick from his camp outside the city to attend church. With him were Col. Henry Kyd Douglas and Major Morrison. There being no service at the Presbyterian Church that day, Jackson attended the Evangelical Reformed Church. It is reported that he slept through most of the service delivered by Dr. Zacharias.

g. ALL SAINTS EPISCOPAL CHURCH
108 West Church Street.
     From 1844 to 1853 the future Brig. Gen. William Nelson Pendleton, CSA, was the pastor of this church. He was the pastor at Grace Episcopal Church in Lexington, Virginia when the Civil War erupted and immediately joined the Confederate forces. Less than a year later he was a brigadier general. He officiated at the funeral of Gen. Robert E. Lee, being again the pastor at Grace Episcopal Church in Lexington, Virginia and also a long-time friend of the famous Confederate leader.

h. FREDERICK COUNTY HISTORICAL SOCIETY
24 East Church Street. Call 301-663-1188 for hours and information.
     This lovely Federal-style building was built as a residence by Dr. Baltzell in the 1820s. It is decorated in mid-19th-century style and has a room with displays from the Civil War period. There is a fine research library in the basement.

i. THE NATIONAL MUSEUM OF CIVIL WAR MEDICINE

48 East Patrick Street. Open Tuesday through Friday 10 a.m. to 4 p.m., Saturday and Sunday 12 noon to 4 p.m.. Call 301-695-1864 information.

Displays, videos, and interpretations at The Museum of Civil War Medicine describe the advances made in medical treatment during the war, as well as telling the stories of many of the thousands of wounded who passed through Frederick in the fall of 1862. More than 3,000 Civil War medical artifacts are on display. During the Civil War the building housing the museum was a shop for a carpenter who also served as an undertaker.

A map on the wall shows where the numerous temporary hospitals in Frederick were located, and a Civil War walking tour of the city is available. The museum also has an extensive and unique bookstore covering all aspects of medicine during the Civil War.

j. BARBARA FRITCHIE MUSEUM

154 West Patrick Street. Call 301-698-0630 for hours and information.

This reconstruction of the house of Dame Fritchie is operated as a museum. Barbara Fritchie, according to the legend that inspired John Greenleaf Whittier's poem of the same name, was an old woman who flew the United States flag from her attic window as the Confederate army marched by on September 10, 1862. The poem states that when Gen. "Stonewall" Jackson saw the flag he ordered his men to shoot it down, but the widow Fritchie held it up again and said, "Shoot if you must this old gray head, but spare your country's flag." Whence Jackson, touched by remorse said, "Who touches a hair of yon gray head dies like a dog! March on!" Actually General Jackson never rode by the Fritchie house, having taken a different route in order to deliver a message to the Presbyterian minister, but the legend and the poem certainly brought fame to the "clustered spires of Frederick."

k. ROGER B. TANEY HOUSE

121 South Bentz Street. Take Patrick Street West to turn left onto Bentz Street. The house is on the right. Call 301-663-8687 for hours and information.

Chief Justice Roger Brooke Taney lived in Frederick for 22 years, from the time of his graduation from Dickinson College and post-graduate work in Annapolis, until 1823. During that time he practiced law in Frederick, became one of the incorporators of the Frederick County National Bank, served as a member of the Maryland Senate, and was Attorney General of Maryland. In 1806 he married Anne Key, sister of his life-long friend, Francis Scott Key, and they had six daughters. The Taneys resided at 121 South Bentz Street from 1815 to 1823. The house is now a museum. Taney, who died October 24, 1864, is buried in St. John's Cemetery on East and 4th Streets.

Prospect Hall

1. PROSPECT HALL

Take Patrick Street west to Jefferson Street which becomes Rt. 340. Keep following the Rt. 340 west signs and keep to the right after you cross over Rt. 15/I-270, then bear right at the first exit onto Rt. 180/351. Turn left at the traffic light at the top of the ramp and Prospect Hall is on the right. There is parking in the rear of the building, off Butterfly Lane, but please contact the school office before walking the grounds. The monument to General Meade is located on the exit ramp back onto Rt. 340/west on the left side.

Built as a Catholic school, Prospect Hall was purchased in 1855 by Judge William Maulsby, a colonel with the local militia that went to Harpers Ferry to put down the disturbance instigated by John Brown in 1859. Both Colonel Maulsby and his son were defending Harpers Ferry with the Potomac Home Brigade when it was shelled and captured by Gen. "Stonewall" Jackson September 15, 1862. The sounds of the cannon fire could be heard by Maulsby's family here.

The grounds were used as a campground first for Confederate and then for Union troops before the Battle of South Mountain.

On June 27, 1863, part of the Union Army of the Potomac under Gen. Joseph Hooker camped on the grounds as they pursued the Confederate army that had crossed the Potomac River further north a few days before. Early the next morning Hooker received the message that President Lincoln had transferred the command of the Army of the Potomac to General Meade. General Meade immediately set to work on what would be known as the "Pipe Creek Plan" (see Chapter 3), sending various corps off in different directions. But that plan was never realized, the enemy armies clashing instead at Gettysburg. The transfer of command was formally made in the dining room of Prospect Hall on June 29, 1863. A monument was placed on the southeast side of the grounds in 1930 to commemorate the event.

Prospect Hall is still a school—St. Joseph Literary Institute.

5G. MIDDLETOWN

The town is located on Alternate Rt. 40, five miles west of Frederick.

Middletown—lying in the valley between Catoctin Mountain range and the South Mountain range, and on the National Road (Rt. 40)—saw the passing of the main body of the Confederate army on their way to Hagerstown on September 12, 1862; and then the passing of the Union IX Corps and I Corps on September 14 on the way to attack Confederate defenses at Turner's and Fox's Gaps in the Battle of South Mountain.

Although overshadowed by the Battle of Antietam three days later, the Battle of South Mountain on September 14, 1862, was strategically important because it delayed the Union forces trying to form a wedge between the divided Confederate army. The Confederates were then able to complete the capture of Harpers Ferry and regroup at Sharpsburg. Details of the battle can be found at the Antietam National Battlefield Visitor Center.

The Battle of South Mountain was fought on three fronts as the Union army (three corps plus Pleasanton's cavalry division—about 30,000 troops in all) advanced from Frederick, and the Confederate Third Division (about 5,000 men) under command of Gen. D. H. Hill defended the gaps on South Mountain through which the Union army had to pass. These were Turner's Gap on the National Road (Rt. 40), Fox's Gap about a mile further south on the road to Sharpsburg, and the southernmost Crampton's Gap on the road from Frederick to Harpers Ferry.

After fierce fighting all day the Union army finally forced its way through Crampton's and Fox's Gaps, some of the fighting continuing after nightfall. The third pass, Turner's Gap, was given up by the Confederates after the other two had fallen into Union control. The Union army remained on the top of the mountain for the better part of two days before moving toward

Sharpsburg. The Union lost about 1,800 killed, wounded or missing, and the Confederates about 2,700 in this battle. Many buildings in Middletown were used as hospitals after the Battle of South Mountain and the Battle of Antietam.

The town was visited by Confederates again on July 6 and 7, 1864, as Gen. Jubal Early's Confederate army moved through on the way to Frederick. The Confederates demanded a $5,000 ransom, threatening to burn the town if it was not given them. General Early accepted $1,500 from the town when that seemed to be all that they could raise. On the morning of July 6 the 8th Illinois Cavalry, USA, under the command of Col. D. R. Clendenin, skirmished with the 1st Maryland Cavalry, CSA, under the command of Brig. Gen. Bradley T. Johnson, about two miles east of Middletown on Catoctin Mountain.

a. CHRIST REFORMED CHURCH
12 South Church Street (Rt. 17).

The steeple of this church was used as a look-out by General McClellan during the Battle of South Mountain, September 14, 1862. The church was used as a hospital after the battle.

b. ZION LUTHERAN CHURCH
Corner of Main Street (Alt. Rt. 40) and Jefferson Street.

The entire church was taken over by the Union army and used as a hospital after the Battle of South Mountain and continued as a hospital for about a year after the battle.

c. CROUSE HOUSE
204 West Main Street (Alt. Rt. 40).

Seventeen-year-old Nancy Crouse was living in this house when Gen. "Stonewall" Jackson's troops came through Middletown on September 10, 1862. Being a staunch Unionist Nancy had a large United States flag hanging from her second-story window. About a dozen Confederate cavalrymen dashed into the house to tear down the flag only to find that Miss Crouse had wrapped the flag around her body and refused to give it up. When a gun was held to her head she declared, "You may shoot me, but never will I willingly give up my country's flag into the hands of traitors." The flag, however, was finally wrested from her, but was later returned to her when the Confederate cavalryman carrying the flag was captured by Union troops.

d. RUDY HOUSE
504 West Main Street (Alt. Rt. 40).

Future President Rutherford B. Hayes, major of the 23rd Ohio Infantry at the time, was wounded at Fox's Gap in the Battle of South Mountain on September 14, 1862. He was brought here to the home of Jacob

Rudy where Hayes' wife, Lucy Webb Hayes, came to nurse him back to health. He recovered from his wounds going on to fight in many more battles, being wounded five more times, and ending the war as a brigadier general (breveted to major general).

5H. TURNER'S GAP

Take Alternate Rt. 40 five miles north from Middletown to the South Mountain Inn at Monument Road.

Turner's Gap was the passageway through South Mountain for the National Pike (Alt. Rt. 40). The fighting took place mainly to the northeast of Alt. Rt. 40 below Monument Road and occurred late in the day on September 14 when Gen. Joseph Hooker's I Corps, USA, attacked Gen. D. H. Hill's left which had been reinforced by Gen. D. R. Jones' Brigade. The Confederates held out against great odds until nightfall when General Lee ordered them to fall back to Boonesboro.

a. MOUNTAIN HOUSE (SOUTH MOUNTAIN INN)

The stone house on Alt. Rt. 40 opposite Monument Road was built by Robert Turner between 1755 and 1765. It was used as an inn until 1876 when it was bought for use as a summer home by Madeline Dahlgren, the widow of Adm. John Dahlgren, USN, and mother of Union hero Ulric Dahlgren. The chapel on the other side of the road was built by her.

During the Battle of South Mountain the building, called Mountain House at the time, was used as a headquarters by Confederate Gen. D. H. Hill, and it is from here that he directed the Confederate defense of the three gaps of South Mountain. After the battle it served as a hospital and sheltered the body of Confederate General Garland, killed at Fox's Gap.

b. WASHINGTON MONUMENT

From I-70 three miles west of Frederick take the Alternate Rt. 40 exit. Go 6.5 miles to Washington Monument Road on the right at the top of South Mountain.

This first monument to the first President of the United States was completed in one day—July 4, 1827—rising fifteen feet. It had collapsed by the time of the Civil War, but was used as a signal station by the Union on July 8, 1863, as fighting erupted around Boonsboro between the Confederates retreating from Gettysburg and Union troops trying to block their way. There is a good view of Boonsboro from here. The monument was rebuilt in 1902 and again in 1936 and now is 30 feet tall.

Washington Monument

5I. FOX'S GAP

From Monument Road turn back toward Middletown on Alternate Rt. 40 and turn right (west) onto Bolivar Road, then right onto Reno Monument Road and go to the top of the mountain where the Reno monument is surrounded by a concrete wall on the left.

Gen. Samuel Garland's Confederate brigade was sent by Gen. D. H. Hill to defend Fox's Gap, which was attacked by the Kanawa Division of the Union IX Corps on the morning of September 14, 1862. The Confederates slowly pulled back toward Turner's Gap under heavy fire, but the Kanawa Division was too tired to press on against them until reinforced that afternoon by the rest of the IX Corps in the afternoon. The combined forces then attacked and drove the Confederates back. Confederate Gen. Samuel Garland of Lynchburg, Virginia was mortally wounded in the morning fighting, and

Union Gen. Jesse Reno was killed in the afternoon offensive. There are monuments to both generals at the Gap. The old Sharpsburg Road is now Reno Monument Road, but has been moved several yards from where it was during the battle.

On the same side of the road as the monuments, but across Ridge Road, was the cabin of Daniel Wise. The burial detail after the battle, tired of digging graves, dumped the bodies of 58 Confederate dead into his well next to the road. These bodies have since been reinterred at Washington Cemetery.

5J. CRAMPTON'S GAP

From Fox's Gap continue west on Reno Monument Road 2 miles and turn left onto Rt. 67. Continue about 5 miles and turn left onto Gathland Road and travel to the top of the mountain.

A handful of Confederate troops from McLaws' Division desperately defended this defensive position from attack by Gen. William B. Franklin's Union VI Corps on the afternoon of September 14, 1862. The fighting lasted into the night until the Confederates were finally pushed back. The exhausted Union troops slept in their battle lines. General Franklin kept his men at Crampton's Gap until called to Antietam on September 17, even though Harpers Ferry did not surrender to Confederate forces until September 15.

5K. WAR CORRESPONDENTS ARCH

A memorial to honor the correspondents and artists of the Civil War was the brainchild of writer George Alfred Townsend, who purchased property on the top of South Mountain in Maryland and built his home there after the war. During the war he had been a correspondent for the *New York Herald* and *New York World*. He began raising money for the monument in 1891 and the monument was dedicated October 16, 1896.

The finished monument is a 50-foot crenelated tower flanked by a horseshoe-shaped Moorish arch (standing for the horse that the correspondent depended on for speed), topped by three open Roman arches symbolizing "description, depiction, and photography." The monument is made of fieldstone, much of which came from nearby Civil War battlefields. The faces of the muses of "Electricity" and "Poetry" appear above the words "Speed" and "Heed." The statue in the niche of the tower is most probably a personification of the war correspondent idealized in the form of a Greek youth. He is shown sheathing the sword of Ares (Mars), the god of war; wearing the helmet of Hermes (Mercury), the swift messenger of the gods; and taking up the pipes of Pan, the satyr-god who was known as a beguiler with music and words. Texts from war correspondents of the past deck the walls, and even the weathervane (now in the Townsend Museum on the property) is symbolic, being a pen breaking a sword. On the rear, or west face, of the monument are listed the names of 151 war correspondents and artists of the Civil War, both Northern and Southern.

Although the park at Crampton Gap is part of the state park system, the Arch is under the care of the National Park Service. The park is cared for by a non-profit organization: The Friends of Gathland, P.O. Box 192, 900 Arnoldsville Road, Burkittsville, MD, 21718.

Phillipides

5L. BURKITTSVILLE

From Crampton's Gap go east 1 mile on Gapland Road to the foot of the mountain. The churches used for hospitals are on the left just past Potomac Street (Rt. 17).

This little village appears almost the same today as it did when it underwent the ravages of the Battle of South Mountain and its aftermath. Nineteenth-century homes line either side of the main street, many still retaining their outbuildings. Two churches were used as hospitals for both Union and Confederate wounded after the battle: the United Church of Christ (Reformed Church during the war), and St. Paul's Lutheran Church. President Lincoln visited the hospitals as he passed through to view the battlefield at Antietam.

5M. BRUNSWICK (BERLIN)

From the center of Burkittsville take Rt. 17 south 6 miles (past Rt. 340) to turn right on Petersville Road and take this road about 1 mile to the C & O Canal (Canal mile 55).

The town now known as Brunswick was laid out in 1780 with the name Berlin, a name it retained until 1890. A bridge over the Potomac River here was burned by Drake's Confederate cavalry June 9, 1861, but the Federal army under Major General McClellan built a pontoon bridge here in October 1862 in order to pursue Lee's Confederate army into Virginia after the Battle of Antietam. Maj. Gen. Joseph Hooker used this same bridge to bring part of the Union Army of the Potomac from Virginia into Maryland in June 1863, where he was replaced by Maj. Gen. George Meade before the Battle of Gettysburg. After the Battle of Gettysburg in July 1863, Gen. Alfred Pleasanton, USA, stationed his army here and used the Short family home as his headquarters (site now occupied by the American Legion Hall at the foot of Maple Street). Brunswick was a major Union supply depot during the war.

5N. POINT OF ROCKS

From Brunswick take Rt. 464 seven miles south to Point of Rocks.

The Baltimore and Ohio Railroad began its double tracks here for the 12-mile run to Harpers Ferry. There were no bridges across the Potomac River here during the war, but there was a ford. On May 23, 1861, Col. (later General "Stonewall") Thomas Jackson devised a plan to convince the B & O Railroad to concentrate its coal shipments to a specific time, then captured 56 locomotives and more than 300 cars by stopping all train traffic headed east at Point of Rocks.

On July 5, 1864, Lt. Col. John Mosby, CSA, in support of Gen. Jubal Early's invasion of Maryland, crossed the Potomac River from Virginia with 250 cavalry and attacked a Union garrison at Point of Rocks consisting of two companies of Loudon Rangers and two companies of Home Guards. The Union troops took cover on the other side of the C & O Canal at the pivot bridge. About 2 p.m. they were reinforced by Colonel Clendenin's 8th Illinois Cavalry and after a 30-minute exchange of gunfire, the Confederates went back across the Potomac River to Virginia. Two USCT infantrymen from the Home Guard were killed.

The railroad station and tracks to Washington, D.C. in the town were built after the war.

FREDERICK CITY AND COUNTY

SUGGESTED READING

Adams, Charles S. *The Civil War in Frederick County, Maryland.* Self-published, 1995.

Cooling, Benjamin Franklin. *Jubal Early's Raid on Washington: 1864.* Baltimore: The Nautical and Aviation Publishing Co. of America, 1989.

Gordon, Paul and Rita. *A Playground of the Civil War.* Frederick, Md.: Heritage Publications, 1994.

Priest, John Michael. *Before Antietam: The Battle for South Mountain.* Shippensburg, Pa.: White Mane Publishing Co., 1995.

Roe, Alfred S. *Monocacy.* Baltimore: Toomey Press, 1996.

Townsend, George Alfred. *Katy of Catoctin.* Tidewater Publications, 1959.

Schildt, John W. *Drums Along the Monocacy.* Chewsville, Md.: Antietam Publications, 1991.

Shields, Jerry. *Gath's Literary Work and Folk and Other Selected Writings of George Alfred Townsend.* Wilmington, Del.: Delaware Heritage Press, 1996.

Williams, Byron L. *The Old South Mountain Inn: An Informal History.* Shippensburg, Pa.: White Mane Publishing Co., 1995.

Worthington, Glenn H. *Fighting for Time: The Battle That Saved Washington.* Shippensburg, Pa.: White Mane Publishing Co.: 1988 (from original published in 1932).

FOR INFORMATION ON OTHER SITES, ACCOMMODATIONS, ETC.

Tourism Council of Frederick County, Inc.
19 East Church Street
Frederick, MD 21701
800-999-3613, 301-663-8687
www.co.frederick.md.us

Historical Society of Frederick County
24 East Church Street
Frederick, MD 21701
301-663-1188

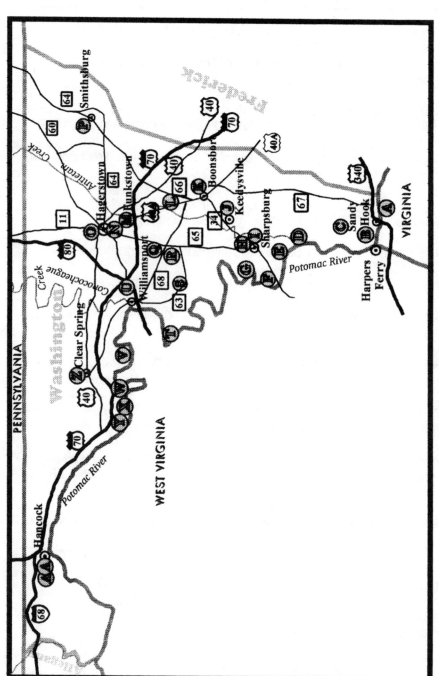

Washington County

CHAPTER 6

WASHINGTON COUNTY

Washington County had more engagements between Union and Confederate forces than any other county in Maryland. The Great Valley of the Appalachian Mountain Range, where Lee concentrated his efforts to invade the North with his Confederate army, runs through Washington County with the Allegheny and Cumberland Mountains on the west of the valley and the Blue Ridge Mountains (South Mountain and Catoctin Mountain in Maryland) on the east.

Washington County also has more than 75 miles of border along the Potomac River which divided Northern from Southern states during the war. This area of the Potomac River contains many easy fords across the river, used many times by both Union and Confederate forces for raids into enemy territory. The need to use the fords was increased after the only bridges across the Potomac River in the county at Shepherdstown and Harpers Ferry were destroyed in 1861.

The C & O Canal runs along the entire length of the Potomac River in Washington County. At the beginning of the war the Confederates were intent on the destruction of the canal, used as a supply line for the Union forces, but toward the end of the war they realized that it was just a small vein among many supply arteries. The most important of these arteries was the Baltimore & Ohio (B & O) Railroad, completed to Wheeling and the Ohio River in 1853. Although this railroad only crossed the southern edge of Washington County, the bridge that took the tracks across the Potomac River into Virginia at Sandy Hook/Harpers Ferry was extremely important. Even if the Union had control of the rest of the railroad tracks in Virginia (West Virginia after June 20, 1863), the railroad was unusable for many months when the Harpers Ferry bridge was destroyed. Another railroad, the Cumberland Valley Railroad, had just been completed to Hagerstown from Harrisburg, Pennsylvania before the war. This made Hagerstown, on the National Pike, a vital supply station.

The heaviest fighting in Washington County took place in September 1862 when McClellan thwarted Lee's first invasion of the North at the Battle of Antietam. The Battle of South Mountain on South Mountain to the southeast of Sharpsburg preceded the Battle of Antietam. The division between Washington and Frederick Counties lies along the crest of South Mountain. Since most of the action of the Battle of South Mountain took place on the Frederick County side of the mountain, it is described in the chapter on Frederick County.

Following General Lee's orders to capture Harpers Ferry, Gen. "Stonewall" Jackson's Confederate troops marched from Frederick west on the National Pike (Alt. Rt. 40) and took Rt. 68 just north of Boonsboro to Williamsport. Here they crossed the Potomac River to go on to Martinsburg, Virginia, and then Harpers Ferry, which they took through a three-pronged attack on September 15. The rest of Lee's army went on toward Hagerstown, leaving a protecting force defending the passes at South Mountain.

Lee was able to regroup most of his army at Sharpsburg by the morning of September 17, 1862, and there the Union and Confederate forces fought what has been called the "Bloodiest Battle of the Civil War" because there were more casualties in one day than in any other Civil War battle. At the end of the day the opposing armies were in practically the same positions that they had held at dawn, but the Confederates, feeling their heavy losses, retreated across the Potomac River that night.

More heavy fighting took place in Washington County in July 1863 when the Confederates, retreating after the Battle of Gettysburg, had to wait for nine days for the flooded waters of the Potomac River to subside so that they could cross back into Virginia. During these nine days they fought many small battles and skirmishes with Union forces around Williamsport and from Hagerstown to Boonsboro.

In early July 1864 Gen. Jubal Early led a Confederate army across the Potomac at various fords south of Williamsport and proceeded to Frederick to eventually threaten Washington, D.C. McCausland's cavalry brigade went first to Hagerstown, demanding a ransom from the town. After Early's retreat back into Virginia, General Lee commanded him to again invade the North in order to continue to draw Union forces away from the seige at Petersburg, Virginia. Early sent the cavalry brigades of McCausland and Bradley Johnson across the Potomac River on July 29 south of Clear Spring. They drove a Union cavalry unit from Williamsport, destroyed a trainload of supplies at Hagerstown, burned the city of Chambersburg, Pennsylvania, ransomed the city of Hancock, and fought a skirmish near Cumberland, Maryland before returning to Virginia August 2. A corps of General Early's Confederate forces was attacked at their camp at Keedysville on August 6, 1864. They drove the Union troops back and went on to a brief visit to the Hagerstown area.

Washington County had a large German immigrant population, many of whom had been in the area for generations. Strong support for the Union permeated the county. By August 1862 Washington County had exceeded its quota of volunteers for the Union army by more than 100 men (quota—943, volunteers—1,048). Maj. Henry Kyd Douglas, CSA; Col. Like Brien, CSA; Maj. James Breathed, CSA; Maj. George Freaner, CSA; and Father Abram Ryan were from Washington County.

6A. SANDY HOOK

Travel 28 miles west of Frederick on Rt. 340 and go past the Rt. 67 exit and turn right onto Sandy Hook Road just before the Rt. 340 bridge across the Potomac River (Canal mile 59.60). It is a good idea before visiting Sandy Hook and the Maryland Heights to go to the Harpers Ferry Visitor Center, just 3 miles further on Rt. 340, to get maps, guides, and information.

Sandy Hook got its name from a quicksand deposit that used to exist at the edge of the river. The little village was a busy railroad depot before the B & O Railroad was centered in Brunswick. During the Civil War the Frederick-Harpers Ferry toll road passed through here and Sandy Hook had a railroad repair shop, warehouses, and many stores as well as a depot.

In June 1859 John Brown, using the name Isaac Smith, entered Maryland from Chambersburg, Pennsylvania and stayed the night of June 30, 1859, at the Washington House in Hagerstown. He and his sons Owen and Oliver, along with Jeremiah Anderson, then lodged at Sandy Hook until they located a permanent base of operations at the Kennedy farm at Sample's Manor (see site #6C). On October 17, 1859, a detachment of 90 U.S. Marines coming by train from Washington, D.C. disembarked at Sandy Hook where they were joined by their commander, Col. Robert E. Lee, and marched to Harpers Ferry to take over the siege of John Brown's raiders at the armory.

a. WEVERTON COTTON MILLS

The ruins of the mills are about 1.5 miles downstream (east) from Sandy Hook on the C & O Canal. By car take Sandy Hook Road east, turn right on Keep Tryst Road and go about 1 mile.

The abandoned mill buildings were used as a Union barracks during the Civil War for soldiers guarding the railroad. Built by Casper W. Wever in 1832, the cotton mills operated using water power from the Potomac River. Today all that is left of the extensive manufacturing and dormitory buildings are the 15-feet-tall stone walls next to the river that were the entrance to the intake sluice for the water to power the mills.

b. B & O RAILROAD BRIDGE

Go about a mile west of Rt. 340 on the Sandy Hook Road. The stone piers of the old bridge are on the downstream side of the current bridge. Canal mile 60.67.

In 1859 this bridge was covered and carried both the railroad and pedestrian traffic across the river. This is where John Brown and his men entered on the night of October 16, 1859, captured the night watchman, William Williams, and shot and killed the free black man, Hayward Sheppard.

The bridge was burned by Confederates on June 14, 1861, before their evacuation of Harpers Ferry. The bridge was rebuilt from March 4 to 18, 1862, but the trestling on the Maryland side was destroyed by a storm in April 1862. Although Lee's army destroyed every B & O Railroad bridge between

Cumberland and Harpers Ferry before their march to invade Maryland in September 1862, the Harpers Ferry bridge was spared. It was, however, destroyed by the orders of a Union commander on July 5, 1863, but the railroad line was back in operation by August of that year.

6B. MARYLAND HEIGHTS

A path leads up to the Heights from the C & O Canal near a small parking area on the right side of Sandy Hook Road about 2 miles west of Rt. 340. The path is steep and the trail takes from three to four hours to hike. You can get a trail guide from the Harpers Ferry Visitor Center. There are gun emplacements at several points along the trail.

Maryland Heights, with an elevation of 1,460 feet, overlooks Harpers Ferry from the Maryland side of the Potomac River. On April 18, 1861, the Heights were occupied by Confederate troops under the command of Col. (later Gen.) Thomas J. Jackson, as was Harpers Ferry. In June, Brig. Gen. Joseph E. Johnston took over the command of troops at Harpers Ferry and Maryland Heights. Realizing that Harpers Ferry could not be held without the protection of the Heights, and the difficulty of holding the Heights when the main force was on the Virginia side of the river, Johnston decided to evacuate. The B & O Railroad Bridge was destroyed on June 14, 1861, and the Confederates left Harpers Ferry, taking the machinery from the armory, cannon, and other equipment with them. Union troops soon took their place.

During the Confederate attack on Harpers Ferry on September 12-14, 1862, before the Battle of Antietam, Confederates of Maj. Gen. Lafayette McLaws' brigade, along with Kershaw's and Barksdale's brigades, began the attack on Maryland Heights on September 12, coming down the ridge of the mountain from the north, having crossed South Mountain at Brownsville Gap and camped overnight in Pleasant Valley. Maryland Heights was defended by the 32nd Ohio; three companies of the 1st Maryland Home Brigade under Maj. John Steiner; Companies H and I of the 1st Maryland Cavalry; the 5th New York Artillery; and a squadron of the Rhode Island Cavalry under Maj. Augustus W. Corliss, with Col. Thomas H. Ford of the 32nd Ohio in overall command. The Union forces were reinforced at noon by seven companies of the 115th New York Regiment, but they were still unable to hold onto the Heights when the Confederates resumed the attack on the morning of September 13. After taking Maryland Heights the Confederates then had to haul heavy artillery up the cliffs as the Federals had destroyed the cannons.

Confederate General Walker's division occupied Loudon Heights overlooking Harpers Ferry from the south on September 13, and Gen. "Stonewall" Jackson's troops took Bolivar Heights overlooking Harpers Ferry from the west. All three Confederate forces opened fire on Harpers Ferry on the morning of September 15. The Union army in Harpers Ferry soon surrendered. Approximately 11,500 prisoners were taken, and large amounts of ammunition and supplies were captured. Led by Col. Benjamin "Grimes" Davis and Col. Arno Voss, 1,200 U.S. Cavalry escaped from Harpers Ferry on the night of September 14, and captured a Confederate supply train near Williamsport on the morning of September 15.

6C. KENNEDY FARM

From Sandy Hook take Harpers Ferry Road north about 5 miles. Turn right on Chestnut Grove Road, and proceed about 1 mile to the log farmhouse on the left. The farmhouse is private and only open to the public on weekends May through October from 9 a.m. to 1 p.m. jefferson.village.virginia.edu/jbrown/kfarm.html

Kennedy Farm

This farm near Harpers Ferry was rented by John Brown, using the name Isaac Smith, in July 1859. Here he made his headquarters for a planned revolution to free the slaves that would begin with the capture of the Federal armory at Harpers Ferry. On October 16, 1859, Brown and 19 of his 22 men (three were left to guard the farm) left for Harpers Ferry with a wagon load of arms and pikes. Along the way they cut the telegraph wires leading into the town and took over the B & O Railroad bridge at about 10:30 p.m., then seized the armory building. The next day, after a siege, Brown and six of his followers were captured by U. S. Marines under the command of Col. Robert E. Lee. Brown was given a trial and hanged in Charlestown, Virginia (now West Virginia) December 2, 1859. The other captured men were tried and hanged later. Ten of Brown's men had been killed in the fighting. A plaque listing the names of Brown's men has been placed in front of the house by the Sons of Confederate Veterans.

6D. ANTIETAM VILLAGE

From the Kennedy Farm return to Harpers Ferry Road and travel north about 5 miles to the junction with Canal Road. This was the location of Antietam Village (Canal mile 69.30). CAUTION! Harpers Ferry Road is narrow and winding and extreme care and obedience to the speed limit must be observed.

A large iron furnace and associated factories and shops occupied the area for a half mile along Antietam Creek during the Civil War, the first iron furnace having been opened here in 1765. During General Early's raid in July, 1864, Gordon's Division, CSA, camped here while participating in a movement to flank the Union soldiers holding Maryland Heights. General Early later decided not to take the Heights. Nearby is the Antietam Aqueduct (mile 69.36) of the C & O Canal, damaged by Gordon's men.

6E. BOTELER'S FORD (also known as Shepherdstown, Packhorse, or Blackford's Ford)

From Antietam Village turn left on Canal Road and continue about 4 miles. CAUTION! Do not take this road in inclement weather. The ford can also be reached by taking Harpers Ferry Road to Rt. 34, turning left and proceeding to the parking at the Canal parking area next to the Rt. 34 bridge to Shepherdstown on Canal Road and walking downstream on the Canal towpath 1 mile (Canal mile 71.39).

This ford was used frequently by both sides during the war for small raids. Gen. Stonewall Jackson's army crossed here from Virginia to Maryland on September 16, 1862, en route to the Battle of Antietam after taking Harpers Ferry. Here the battle-worn Confederates retreated back to Virginia on September 18-19, 1862, after the Battle of Antietam, protected by 33 guns of the artillery of Brig. Gen. William Pendleton on the other side of the river. On September 19 there was an artillery battle between these guns and those of the Union V Corps under Maj. Gen. Fitz-John Porter.

In July 1864 Maj. Gen. Franz Sigel's Union forces crossed here retreating from Martinsburg on their way to Maryland Heights, and were closely followed by the Confederates under Maj. Gen. John B. Gordon, part of General Early's army (see Site #6D).

On August 4, 1864, Gen. Jubal Early's Confederate Division again entered Maryland by way of this ford and others nearby, driving off Union troops guarding the area consisting of Cole's cavalry and elements of the 14th Pennsylvania. The Confederates made camp in Keedysville.

6F. FERRY HILL PLACE

From Rt. 34, just before the bridge to Shepherdstown over the Potomac River, the house is on the north side of Rt. 34 (Canal mile 72.80). 301-739-4200.

This 1812 house was the home of Col. Henry Kyd Douglas, aide to

Gen. "Stonewall" Jackson, and author of *I Rode With Stonewall*. Douglas visited his home in secret several times during the war, sometimes with narrow escapes from Union soldiers nearby. On November 3, 1862, Rev. Robert Douglas, Henry's father, was arrested here and charged with giving signals to the Confederates across the Potomac River. He was held at Fort McHenry for six weeks. Henry Kyd Douglas also made a brief visit here in June 1863 on his way to the Battle of Gettysburg where he was wounded. After the war Henry Kyd Douglas was active in veterans affairs and was on the Washington Cemetery Commission (see site #6N).

The house is now a National Park headquarters for the C & O Canal.

6G. KILLIANSBURG CAVES

From Ferry Hill Place travel east on Rt. 34 four miles to Sharpsburg. Turn left (north) on West Chapline Street, which becomes Snyders Landing Road. Go for 1.6 miles to the boat ramp where there is limited parking. Walk almost 1 mile downstream on the C & O Canal to mile 75.73. One cave is 50 feet above the towpath on a steep cliff face, the other nearer ground level.

According to local lore these caves were used by some of the residents of Sharpsburg to hide during the Battle of Antietam, September 17, 1862.

6H. ANTIETAM NATIONAL BATTLEFIELD

In Sharpsburg, turn north onto Rt. 65 from Rt. 34 and the Battlefield Visitor Center is 2 miles on the right. This is a National Battlefield Park and is open daily. Recorded auto tours, a film, museum displays, and many brochures and books on the battle are available at the center. 301-432-5124.

The bloodiest day in the Civil War occurred here on September 17, 1862, when about 41,000 Confederates were pitted against 87,000 Union troops. More than 23,000 from both sides were killed, wounded, and missing in one day in the Battle of Antietam (Battle of Sharpsburg).

Led by Gen. George B. McClellan, the Union offensive began with an attack by Maj. Gen. Joseph Hooker's I Corps against the Confederate left under the command of Maj. Gen. "Stonewall" Jackson. The fighting continued with Union troops under Generals Manfield, Sumner, Franklin, and Porter attacking the Confederate center held by Generals Early, McClaws, Walker, Anderson, and D.H. Hill. Some of the heaviest fighting occurred on the Confederate right flank as General Longstreet's troops repulsed attack after attack of General Burnside's Union troops at the Rohrbach Bridge over Antietam Creek (later called Burnside's Bridge) until the Union finally pushed the Confederates back in the afternoon. Burnside's men were gaining on the town of Sharpsburg when a counterattack by the division of Maj. Gen. A. P. Hill—just arrived from Harpers Ferry—forced them back to the bridge.

Neither side gained a decisive victory, but the Confederates retreated across the Potomac River the following evening, giving up, for the moment, their invasion of the North.

Although a few monuments were erected earlier, part of the battlefield was purchased by the Federal government in 1890. It was made into a national park in 1933. The following sites on the battlefield have associations with Maryland units. There are also two sites of interest which are not on the battlefield tour.

a.   MARYLAND MONUMENT

North of the Visitor Center.

This is the first monument erected to soldiers who fought on both sides. It honors six Union and two Confederate units from the state of Maryland that participated in the Battle of Antietam. It is in the form of an

Maryland Monument

Italian tempietto with a dome supported by eight pillars—one for each unit. The monument is called the "Temple of Liberty" and on the top of the dome is a statue of "Peace." Four bronze bas-reliefs on the outside of the monument depict the action of: the 2nd Maryland Infantry, USA, at Burnside Bridge (see Site #6Hf); the 5th Maryland Infantry, USA, closing in on Roulette's barns (see Site #6He); Wolcott's Battery A of the 1st Maryland Artillery, USA (see Site #6Hd); and Brockenbrough's Battery of the Baltimore Light Artillery, CSA (see Site #6Hc). The other units honored on the monument are: the 3rd Maryland Infantry, USA (see Site #6Hb); Purnell's Legion, USA (see Site #6Hc); Dement's Battery of the 1st Maryland Artillery, CSA (see Site #6Hf); and Snow's Battery B of the 1st Maryland Light Artillery, USA (see Site #6Hd). The monument was dedicated May 31, 1900, with the Governor of Maryland and President McKinley speaking. Over 10,000 people attended.

b. DUNKER CHURCH
Across from the Visitor Center. Battlefield Tour Stop #1.

The original church was built in 1852 by the German Baptist brethren, referred to as Dunkers because of their practice of complete submersion in baptism. This is where some of the fiercest fighting took place as the Confederates were forced back into the woods behind and to the north of the church. The Union troops attacking them in a battle line got disoriented in the thick smoke, the battle line curved in at the ends, and they started shooting at each other. Taking advantage of the confusion the Confederates, being reinforced, drove the Union troops back. The 3rd Maryland Infantry, USA, took part in this action. There is a Maryland marker honoring them across the road from the church.

The building was used as a mortuary after the battle. It was destroyed by a storm in 1921, but was rebuilt from the original pieces which had been preserved, in 1962.

c. PHILADELPHIA BRIGADE PARK
Battlefield Tour Stop #5.

Early on the morning of September 17, 1862, the Baltimore Battery of Light Artillery, CSA, under the command of Capt. J. B. Brockenbrough, formed the left line of defense of Gen. "Stonewall" Jackson's Division as it was attacked by General Hooker's Division of Federal forces. There is a Maryland marker honoring this unit to the rear of the Park.

The Purnell Legion Infantry (from Maryland), USA, in the 3rd Brigade of General Greene's Division, General Mansfield's XII Corps, USA, overran this position later in the day, and defended it against the onslaughts of the Confederates. The Maryland marker to them is on the south side of the park.

d. MILLER'S CORNFIELD
Cornfield Avenue, Stop #3 on the Battlefield Tour.

Snow's Battery B, under the command of Lt. Theodore J. Vanneman, of the 1st Maryland Light Artillery in the 2nd Division of General Franklin's VI Corps, USA, was situated here at mid-morning of the battle.

Wolcott's Battery A of the 1st Maryland Light Artillery, 1st Division of General Franklin's VI Corps, USA, defended the East Woods from a position near the intersection of Smoketown Road and Mumma Lane. A Maryland marker is at the spot.

e. OBSERVATION TOWER

From the Visitor Center turn right and then take the first right on Smoketown Road. Follow the tour road to the Sunken Road. The tower is at the end of the road, Stop #8 of the Battlefield Tour.

On August 30, 1890, Congress passed an act authorizing the preservation and marking of the battlefield at Antietam. The battlefield was put under the authority of the Department of War. Although several veterans groups had already purchased small plots of ground from farmers and erected monuments where their units had fought, the War Department was interested in marking lines of battle with cast-iron explanatory signs, and erecting inverted cannons at the spots where the six generals (three USA and three CSA) were slain in the battle. The battlefield was used as a training ground for officer candidates in the U.S. Army War College, and the observation tower was put up so that the strategies and progression of the battle in relation to the lay of the land could be viewed.

Unique to this battlefield, the inverted cannons placed wherever a general was mortally wounded were placed there when the battlefield was under the War Department.

In 1933 the Antietam Battlefield was transferred to the Department of the Interior, which built a visitor center, allowed more monuments to be erected, and expanded the original 35 acres to more than 2,000 acres by 1990.

The 5th Maryland Infantry fought from a position at the top of the hill to the east of the Sunken Road. A monument erected by veterans occupies the top of the hill, and a Maryland marker is on the north side of Richardson Avenue to the north of the Sunken Road.

f. BURNSIDE BRIDGE

Continue on the park tour road across Rt. 34 to Rodman Avenue and follow the signs to Burnside Bridge, Stop #9 on the Battlefield Tour.

The Rohrbach Bridge, as it was called at the time of the battle, was the site where about 500 riflemen from the 20th and 2nd Georgia Regiments, on a bluff overlooking the bridge, held off many attacks by the Union IX Corps commanded by Maj. Gen. Ambrose Burnside. Burnside's objective was to force the Confederates back to Sharpsburg and have his army stand between the Confederates and their path of retreat at Boteler's Ford. The Union forces began their attack at about 10 a.m. and made several unsuccessful attempts to take the bluff before finally succeeding at about 1:30 p.m. when the 51st Pennsylvania and the 51st New York Regiments finally reached the top. There they stopped to rest for two hours. Before they were ready to push on, the Confederates were reinforced by 2,500 men under Maj. Gen. A. P. Hill who had just marched 17 miles from Harpers Ferry. The enlarged Confederate force drove the Federals back to the bridge. Brig. Gen. Isaac Rodman, USA, who had brought a Union unit across the Snavely Ford a mile to the south of the bridge, was killed in the afternoon fighting.

The 2nd Maryland Infantry, USA, participated in the Federal push across the bridge. There is a marker at the bridge.

In the afternoon Capt. William Dement's Battery of the 1st Maryland Artillery in Ewell's Division, CSA, helped to push the Federals back to the bridge from their position at Old Harpers Ferry Road just north of Branch Avenue. There is a marker on the road.

g. LEE'S HEADQUARTERS SITE

Travel west on Rt. 34 from Rt. 65. The headquarters site is on the right .5 mile past Mechanic Street.

Gen. Robert E. Lee commanded the movements of his Confederate forces during the battle from his headquarters tent in a grove of trees here. Lee was much closer to the actual fighting than was McClellan who was at the Pry farm about one mile east of the battlefield. Although McClellan was on higher ground, not much of the battle could have been viewed because of the heavy smoke which accumulated and stayed close to the ground throughout the battle. There is a small monument to mark the spot, erected by the United Daughters of the Confederacy in 1942.

h. STEPHEN GROVE FARM

From Sharpsburg travel west on Rt. 34 for about 1 mile and the large brick house is on the left, set far back from the road. This is private property and not open to the public.

This large house of Stephen Grove on his farm called Mount Airy, was used as a hospital for both Union and Confederate soldiers after the Battle of Antietam. President Abraham Lincoln visited the wounded at the hospital on October 3, 1862, and also met with Major General McClellan and several other generals to discuss future strategy for the Army of the Potomac.

Across the road from the farm, where the old railroad station is, there was a monument made of cannons and cannon balls placed there to greet the veterans who came by train to visit the battlefield after the train line was completed in 1880. A path led from the monument to the battlefield. Nothing is left of this monument but the base.

6I. ANTIETAM NATIONAL CEMETERY

From the Antietam National Battlefield Visitor Center return to Rt. 65 and turn left going 2 miles to Rt. 34. Turn left and go up the hill to the cemetery on the right.

Antietam National Cemetery

This cemetery was established in March 1864 by the Maryland General Assembly in a bill which stipulated that both the Union and Confederate dead from the Battles of Antietam and South Mountain be buried there. The Board of Trustees for the cemetery, however, was made up of representatives only from the Northern states and it refused to bury the Confederate dead in the same cemetery as the Union dead. The cemetery was formally dedicated September 17, 1867, containing the remains of 4,776 Union soldiers of which 1,836 are unknown. The dedication ceremony was attended by the governor of Maryland and President Andrew Johnson. In 1868 a new commission was formed to establish a cemetery for the Confederate dead still lying in the battlefield (see Washington Cemetery, site #6N). The huge statue of a Union soldier at parade rest (nicknamed Old Simon) was erected in 1880. The cemetery now contains the remains of other soldiers from the Civil War and other U.S. wars.

6J. KEEDYSVILLE

From Sharpsburg travel 3 miles east on Rt. 34 and turn right at South Main Street, Keedysville.

Being so near the bloody battlefield at Antietam many homes and buildings in the town were used for hospitals after the battle, although no actual fighting took place here at that time. A number of Federal units were encamped at Keedysville for some time after the battle, and again after the Battle of Gettysburg in July 1863.

On August 5, 1864, a Confederate division under Maj. Gen. Jubal Early was encamped near Keedysville when they were attacked by Cole's Union cavalry regiment being led by Lt. Col. W. F. Vernon. Colonel Vaughn's Tennessee cavalry held them off, incurring severe casualties, until pushed back to the rest of the command which had been roused by the sound of fighting. The Union cavalry then retreated across South Mountain.

6K. BOONSBORO

From Keedysville travel 3 miles east on Rt. 34.

The little town on the National Road did not expect to be visited by the spectre of war, but it just happened to be in the path of major army movements of both sides and was caught in the crossfire between these armies on several occasions.

Boonsboro was first visited by Confederate troops on September 10, 1862, as Gen. "Stonewall" Jackson's corps camped to the south of town on their way to cross the Potomac River at Williamsport, invade Martinsburg, and attack Harpers Ferry. While they were in Boonsboro one of Jackson's aides, the 21-year-old Capt. Henry Kyd Douglas, rode with some companions through town on the way to visit Douglas' home near Sharpsburg

Boonsboro I.O.O.F. Hall

and met with a detachment of 21 Union cavalry led by Captain Schaumberg in front of the U.S. Hotel at the crossroads in the center of town. The sharp report of gunfire was heard in the streets of Boonsboro as the Confederates first retreated toward their camp, then were joined by others and drove the Federals back through town, wounding a few and capturing some others. General Jackson was on South Mountain at the time.

As Lee's army moved west toward Sharpsburg after the Battle of South Mountain, Union advance troops skirmished with the Confederate rear guard in and to the west of Boonsboro on September 15, 1862.

After the Battle of Antietam the little town was inundated with the wounded of both sides from the battle. Practically all the public buildings and many private homes were used as hospitals.

Boonsboro felt the sting of war again during the Confederate retreat from Gettysburg. At dawn on the morning of July 8, 1863, Gen. Jeb Stuart's brigade, coming from Funkstown, attacked the divisions of Buford and Kilpatrick on the north side of Boonsboro. The Union forces were deployed in a large semi-circle from the Williamsport Road on the west to east of the National Pike leading to Hagerstown (Rt. 40A). The enemy batteries fired at each other all morning. Cavalry and infantry slogged back and forth through deep mud until the Confederates finally pushed the Union back into Boonsboro. Maj. O. Howard's XI Corps, sent by Meade from Frederick as reinforcements, arrived at South Mountain about 5 p.m. and General Stuart withdrew his men because he had achieved his objective of keeping the Union army from attacking the wagon train and main body of the Confederate army holed up at Williamsport waiting for the Potomac River to subside—and he was out of ammunition.

a. DISCIPLES OF CHRIST CHURCH
From the intersection of Rt. 34 and Alt. Rt. 40 follow St. Paul Street (opposite Rt. 34) one block to the church on the right.

The church had not even been completed when it was taken over as one of the main hospitals after the Battle of Antietam. It continued to be used as a hospital well after the battle. Soldiers camped on the grounds around the church.

b. I.O.O.F. HALL
105 South Main Street (Alt. Rt. 40).

The International Order of Odd Fellows was a very popular men's benevolent association in the second half of the 19th century. The large open hall of this building was perfect for a hospital and it was used for this purpose after the Battles of South Mountain and Antietam.

c. MURDOCK HOUSE

6524 Main Street (Alt. Rt. 40). Go about 1 mile east from Boonsboro and the house is on the right. This is a private residence and not open to the public.

On his way from the Frederick area to Martinsburg and eventually Harpers Ferry, Gen. "Stonewall" Jackson used John Murdock's house as his headquarters for the night on September 10, 1862. His cavalry camped in the fields across the road. Murdock was a farmer and businessman who later became justice of the peace in Boonsboro. He was known by Jackson's aide, Henry Kyd Douglas, who was from the area, to have Southern sympathies in this area of strong Union support.

d. BOONSBOROUGH MUSEUM OF HISTORY

113 North Main Street (Alt. Rt. 40). Turn around from the Murdock House and travel back through Boonsboro. The museum is on the right after passing the Rt. 34 intersection. Open Sunday 1 to 5 p.m. May through September, or by appointment. 301-432-6969.

This private museum contains many Civil War relics and weapons, memorabilia, including journals and letters, of Henry Kyd Douglas and John Murdock, as well as eclectic collections of various other artifacts from around the world. Much of the collection pertains to the Battle of Antietam and other disturbances near the town of Boonsboro such as John Brown pikes and relics from the local military hospitals.

6L. BENEVOLA (Beaver Creek)

Travel 3 miles north of Boonsboro on Alternate Rt. 40.

The day after Gen. Jeb Stuart's attack on Boonsboro on July 8, 1863, General Buford's Union 1st Cavalry Division—Colonel Gamble's 1st brigade and Colonel Devin's 2nd brigade—moved north along the National Pike (Alt. Rt. 40) and across the Beaver Creek bridge at Benevola. Just beyond the creek they came across a Confederate cavalry camp and routed them, chasing them back toward Funkstown. About three miles south of Funkstown the Federal assault was stopped by Chew's battery.

6M. FUNKSTOWN

Continue north from Benevola on Alt. Rt. 40 for about 7 miles north of Benevola, just past the I-70 underpass.

After their attack on the Union forces at Boonsboro on July 8, 1863, Gen. Jeb Stuart's troops rested in camps around Funkstown while the Federals regrouped. At dawn on July 10 the Union division of General Buford attacked from the Boonsboro Road (Alt. Rt. 40) and fanned out to the east to Beaver Creek Road with Merrit's brigade on the right, Devin's on the left, and Gamble's in the center, supported by two sections of Tidball's artillery. Stuart's Confederates had been reinforced by the addition of Gen. Fitzhugh Lee's regiment which supported Jones' brigade on the Confederate left at Beaver Creek Road, while Chambliss', Robertson's, and Baker's regiments were strung out to the right as far as Antietam Creek to the south of town. Manly's artillery provided support to the center, while Chew's battery of artillery protected the right flank to the west of Alternate Rt. 40 above the creek. The Confederates were further reinforced later in the day by the addition of two Georgia brigades sent by Longstreet.

The Battle of Funkstown began south of town and seesawed several times during the day. By mid-afternoon the Union artillery was running out of ammunition. They were finally reinforced by Brig. Gen. Albion Howe's 2nd division. At the end of the day the Confederate line broke and they retreated to the north and west and through the town to camp on the north side of Antietam Creek northwest of Funkstown. Sporadic fighting continued the next day with both sides holding their ground. On July 12 Brig. Gen. Horatio Wright advanced the Union 1st Division and Eustis' brigade through the town and attacked the Confederate position to the west of town. The Confederates retreated through the day down the Sharpsburg Pike (Rt. 65) toward St. James College.

The casualties from the Battle of Funkstown are difficult to compute since some reported figures include the fight at Boonsboro as well, but they are most probably: **196 Union killed, wounded, and missing; and 283 Confederate killed, wounded, and missing.** Several houses and barns in and around the town were damaged by cannon. The Stonebreaker Barn that marked the extent of the fighting to the east (Stuart's left flank) is no longer there.

a. JACOB HAUK BARN

The barn is just to the right (east) of Alt. Rt. 40 before entering Funkstown from the south. This is private property.

This barn anchored the right of the Confederate defenses during the Battle of Funkstown. Across the road to the west is Antietam Creek which marked the extent of Stuart's right flank. Chew's Confederate artillery was positioned on the hill above the creek. The large stone-foundation barn looks much as it did in 1863 and is still in the Hauk family. Just beyond the barn is an historical marker and a National Pike milepost.

b. DAVIS GENERAL STORE
The store is located on Alt. Rt. 40 where it turns sharply to the west and becomes Baltimore Street.

This little general store was quite in the middle of the Battle of Funkstown, and probably lost much of its merchandise to the Confederate and Union soldiers who passed through. It was visited by Confederates again two months later. On September 12, 1863, Confederate General Longstreet's division passed through Funkstown on the way to Hagerstown. Some of the officers demanded that Davis' Store be opened, and the key was finally obtained from Mrs. Davis and the store looted. Some members of the 2nd Louisiana Tigers Infantry got in a fight among themselves and one of the group was killed and is buried near the town.

Chaney House

c. DR. JOSEPH CHANEY HOUSE (now Ruth's Antiques)
The building is on the southwest corner of the intersection of High Street and Baltimore Street (Alt. Rt. 40).

This house served as the main hospital after the Battle of Funkstown. The sugeons had a tent set up in the yard and the wounded were laid on the floor inside the house in rows. Many women of the town helped out as nurses.

The amputated limbs were piled up to the west of the house. Except for the addition of a front porch, the house looks much as it did at the time of the battle.

d. KELLER HOUSE

The house is on the northwest corner of the intersection of High Street and Baltimore Street (Alt. Rt. 40).

Several wounded soldiers were cared for at this house after the battle, among them Confederate Maj. Henry D. McDaniel of the 11th Georgia Infantry. He suffered from a serious wound in his abdomen, but recovered and became governor of Georgia after the war. The house has been meticulously restored.

6N. WASHINGTON CEMETERY
Continue on Alt. Rt. 40 and turn left on Memorial Boulevard. The main entrance to Rose Hill Cemetery is on the left at the intersection of Memorial Boulevard with South Potomac Street. Take the right lane once inside the cemetery to the Washington Cemetery section on the right marked by a statue of "Hope."

After the Board of Trustees of the Antietam National Cemetery refused to bury the Confederate dead from the Battle of Antietam in that cemetery (see Site #6I), Governor Oden Bowie had a survey taken of the number of Confederate dead left in the battlefield and found that many of the remains were in such shallow graves that they were being turned up by farmers' plows. In 1870 the Maryland

Washington Cemetery Statue

General Assembly appropriated money, later added to by Virginia and West Virginia, to establish a new cemetery. A Board of Trustees made up of Confederate veterans and one non-veteran was appointed. A section of Rose Hill Cemetery in Hagerstown was chosen by the Board in 1872 and named Washington Cemetery. The locating and exhuming of the bodies took five years and on June 12, 1877, the cemetery and memorial statue representing "Hope" were dedicated with a crowd of 6,000 attending. In 1963 the Maryland Civil War Centennial Commission put up a bronze map of the cemetery with the names and locations of the known dead. There are 2,447 individuals buried in the cemetery and it is the only cemetery still under the direct control of the state of Maryland.

60. HAGERSTOWN

From Rose Hill Cemetery turn right on Potomac Street and follow Potomac Street until it intersects with Washington Street at the main square of the town. There is street-metered parking along with several parking lots.

Founded in the 18th century, Hagerstown was a prosperous city by the mid-19th century. Located at the intersection of the National Pike (Rt. 40) and several other major roads, the city had several newspapers and many factories. The only railroad in Hagerstown at the time of the Civil War was the Cumberland Valley Railroad which came from Harrisburg and Chambersburg, Pennsylvania and terminated in Hagerstown. Battle scars can still be seen on many of the old buildings from the fighting that occurred in the streets during the summer of 1863.

As the advance of Lee's main army on the retreat from the Battle of Gettysburg moved southwest to ford the Potomac River at Williamsport, Lee's troops began to receive serious Federal resistance on July 6, 1863, at Hagerstown.

When Confederate Col. John R. Chambliss led the 9th, 10th, and 13th Virginia regiments along with the 2nd North Carolina into the city from the northeast at about 11 a.m., there were no enemies to be found. But at the same time Union Gen. Judson Kilpatrick was leading his 3rd Cavalry division (two brigades) up the National Pike (Alt. Rt. 40) from Funkstown and east from the Williamsport Road (Rt. 11) toward Hagerstown. The Confederates were soon joined by General Robertson's 4th and 5th North Carolina regiments and part of the 1st Maryland Cavalry led by Capt. Frank Bond of Company A.

The two forces met in the middle of Hagerstown at the intersection of Baltimore and Potomac Streets. Joined by the 1st West Virginia Cavalry coming from the east, the Federals pushed the Confederates back to the city square (Washington and Potomac Streets). The conflict raged from city square to Baltimore Street, as well as on many side streets. The Union artillery of Lieutenant Elder opened fire from Seminary Hill (Mulberry Street and Antietam Street). Capt. Chew's Confederate artillery came from the east and, after a fierce artillery battle with Elder's guns, drove the Federals away and set up their own guns on the hill.

More Confederates came pouring in from the northeast by way of Leitersburg Pike (Rt. 60) and Old Forge Road. Brig. Gen. Alfred Iverson's brigade of Ewell's corps and Gen. Jeb Stuart's cavalry came rushing in to the aid of the beleaguered troops toward the end of the day and pushed the Union forces out of the city. The Federals set up defenses around a toll house about two miles southwest on the Williamsport Road (Rt. 11), but they were eventually pushed back by the 11th Virginia.

All of this action prevented Kilpatrick's forces from joining General Buford's division, which was attacking the Confederate wagon train of wounded and supplies at Williamsport.

The following summer Hagerstown again saw the Confederates, as described below.

a. CITY SQUARE

Potomac and Washington Streets. The Washington County Convention and Visitors Bureau is located in the Elizabeth Hager building in the Square (800-228-7829).

There are just a few buildings left from the Civil War period around the town square, among them 1-4 West Washington Street, St. John's Lutheran Church (141 South Potomac Street). The building at 148-152 West Washington Street (J. Dixon Roman House) and the Zion Evangelical Church (201 North Prospect Street) are nearby, as well as many of the houses along South Prospect Street. Some of these buildings still show the scars from the fighting of July 6, 1863.

On July 6, 1864, after fighting off a force of 150 Federal Cavalry (Company A, 1st Maryland) under the command of Lt. George Shearer south of town, Brig. Gen. John McCausland, CSA, rode into town with 1,500 Confederate cavalry, set up headquarters at the square and demanded that the town pay him $20,000 and 1,500 suits of clothing or he would burn down the town. The town paid, although not quite the amount of clothing required was produced, and the Confederates rode out of town at dark.

The 1818 City Hall, where negotiations for the ransom took place, was located at the site of the present City Hall, one block north of the Square on North Potomac Street. The ransoming of Hagerstown is celebrated with an annual fall festival.

b. SEMINARY SITE

Southeast corner of King and E Streets, now occupied by the Washington County Hospital.

Key-Mar College, a female seminary at Mulberry and Antietam Streets, was used as the main hospital in the area for treating the wounded from all the fighting in and around Hagerstown during July 6-13, 1863.

The college had also been used as headquarters by Union Gen. Robert Patterson commanding defense forces in the first year of the war.

The pharmacy building of the present hospital is all that is left of the buildings of the old seminary.

The Episcopal Church Cemetery near the hospital on Mulberry Street contains the graves of several Civil War soldiers.

c. MILLER HOUSE

135 West Washington Street. Operated by the Washington County Historical Society Wednesday through Friday from 1 p.m. to 4 p.m., and Saturday, 2 p.m. to 5 p.m. from April through December. 301-797-8782. There is an admission fee.

The 1824 house is a museum furnished in mid-19th-century style, except the kitchen, which is from an earlier period. The courtyard garden in the rear of the house is a wonderful example of a Victorian townhouse garden. In an upstairs room is an exhibit of Civil War memorabilia including an 1869 photographic copy of General McCausland's ransom note. The basement of the building houses a reference library.

6P. SMITHSBURG

From Hagerstown take Jefferson Boulevard (Rt. 64) east 6 miles to Rt. 66. Turn left (north) on Rt. 66 and go 1 mile.

The mostly German immigrant inhabitants of this little town were staunchly Union in their sentiments. In the summer of 1863 they were faced with a merry-go-round of Union and Confederate armies marching to and from Gettysburg.

On June 21, 1863, 5,700 Confederates commanded by Maj. Gen. Jubal Early marched through town. Then on June 29, 1863, the 8th Illinois Union Cavalry rode through.

On July 4, 1863, George Custer, just promoted to general, led his Union cavalry to overwhelm a Confederate cavalry unit led by Gen. Bradley T. Johnson just to the east of town at Monterey Pass. Custer led his captured men and wagons into Smithsburg that evening and the conquerers were given a grand feast by the townspeople.

On July 5 Jeb Stuart's Confederate cavalry division—consisting of Gen. Milton J. Fergusen's brigade, Gen. John R. Chambliss' brigade, and a portion of Gen. "Grumble" Jones' brigade—retreating from Gettysburg met two entrenched Union brigades at about 5 p.m. at Smithsburg. The Federals, under the command of Brig. Gen. Judson Kilpatrick, consisted of the 3rd Cavalry Division and Col. Pennock Huey's brigade of Brig. Gen. David McMurtrie Gregg's 2nd Cavalry Division. Lt. William Fuller's Battery C of the 3rd U.S. Artillery guarded the Raven Rock Road to the east; Lt. Alexander Pennington's Battery M of the 2nd U.S. Horse Artillery was guarding the road from Leitersburg along with Brig. Gen. Custer's Michigan Brigade; and Elder's Battery E of the 4th U.S. Artillery, a battery from the 5th U.S. Artillery and Col. Nathaniel Richmond's brigade guarded the south.

Fergusen approached the enemy first along the Raven Rock Road, but was not able to get through and so joined Stuart and the rest of the Confederates to the northeast. The combined forces were able to push the Federals back after an artillery battle that lasted two hours. Kilpatrick's Union forces retreated to Boonsboro and Stuart's men went on to Leitersburg, and then to Hagerstown.

6Q. ST. JAMES SCHOOL

From Smithsburg return to Hagerstown and take Rt. 65 south. One mile south of I-70 turn right on College Road and travel about 2 miles to the school on the left. The school is private.

Founded in 1842 as a diocesan school of the Episcopal Church, St. James was fashioned after the British "public schools" for young men in preparation for attending a university. It was very successful and had 195 students in 1861, but only 16 in 1862. Eighty-seven former students served in the Confederate army and 78 in the Union. The faculty, led by the head of the school, Rev. John B. Kerfoot, was pro-Union.

In the summer of 1861 Federal troops started pouring into the area south of Hagerstown and as many as 4,000 Pennsylvania Volunteers under Brig. Gen. Alpheus Williams made temporary camp on the grounds of St. James College.

On September 20, 1862, thousands of Union soldiers chasing Gen. Jeb Stuart back into Virginia at Williamsport stopped a while at the college to take food from the pantries and gardens and converted the spring house into a bath house. The stone spring house is currently the only building left on the campus from the Civil War period.

From July 6-13, 1863, the Confederates retreating from Gettysburg set up defenses near the college, and skirmishes were fought several times back and forth before the Confederates were well dug-in by the eleventh. After the Confederates had left, the faculty discovered a good deal of wanton destruction at the College.

Invading Maryland again after threatening Washington, D.C. in July, Gen. Jubal Early arrested Reverend Kerfoot and Reverend Coit at St. James College on August 7, 1864, and charged them to work for the release of Dr. Hunter Boyd who had been arrested by Federals at Winchester, Virginia in 1863. This they set about doing after the Confederates had left, realizing that they had a school to run after the war that counted on the enrollment of Southern as well as Northern students. Dr. Boyd was released August 19, 1864.

6R. JONES CROSSROADS

From St. James School continue south on Rt. 65 about 4 miles to the intersection with Rt. 68.

During the Confederate retreat from Gettysburg the Confederate defenses protecting the troops waiting at the Falling Waters Ford were situated to the north and east of this crossroads. On July 7, 1863 the 6th New York Cavalry, led by Colonel Devin, attacked the Confederate defenses here. After being driven back to about two miles east where the road crosses Antietam Creek, they were joined by the 17th Pennsylvania Infantry, and then the 9th New York Infantry and set up a defense line, but the Confederates failed to attack. On July 10, 1863, elements of Maj. Gen. George Sykes' V Corps, including the 83rd Pennsylvania Regiment, clashed with Confederate pickets at this crossroads.

6S. DOWNSVILLE

From Jones Crossroads (Rt. 65 and Rt. 68) turn right (west) on Rt. 68 and travel 2.9 miles to turn left on Rt. 632. Travel 2.3 miles to the intersection with Rt. 63.

Camp Williams of the 1st Maryland Infantry, USA, was established here in July 1861.

On July 7, 1863, General Woolford's infantry brigade, part of the Confederate defenses set up by General Imboden to protect the wagon train waylaid at Williamsport, skirmished with Union troops here at the easternmost point of the Confederate defenses.

6T. FALLING WATERS FORD

From Downsville turn right (north) on Rt. 63 and travel about 2 miles to turn left on Falling Waters Road. Take this road about 6 miles to the end. The ford was about 1/2 mile upstream at Canal mile 94.44. The ford and road are named for the town across the Potomac River in West Virginia.

123

On June 17, 1863, some of Lee's Confederate army, on the way to Gettysburg, used a pontoon bridge here that was later destroyed by Federal troops. After the Battle of Gettysburg General Lee wanted to use this ford for his retreating army. When the first wagons of the 17-mile-long wagon train of wounded and supplies, guarded by General Imboden's cavalry, reached Williamsport on July 5, 1863, they found the Potomac River at ten feet above flood stage. The Confederates completed a pontoon bridge at Falling Waters during the next week using wood from warehouses in Williamsport and parts of the old pontoon bridge. As the waters subsided, the wagons and army crossed on the night of July 13 and 14 in a driving rain and ankle-deep mud. The I and III Corps, CSA, crossed the river at Falling Waters, and the II Corps, CSA, crossed the river further north at Williamsport. While waiting for the river to subside, Confederate troops, wagons, and horses filled the entire five miles between the ford and Williamsport. Confederate skirmishers protecting the rear of the retreating army fought a desperate battle with General Custer's Michigan brigade all along Falling Waters Road and in the brush adjacent to the road. Brig. Gen. J. J. Pettigrew, CSA, was mortally wounded in the fight. The final troops marched over the makeshift bridge about 9 a.m. July 14. The Union regiments of Kilpatrick and Buford arrived too late to engage the enemy.

6U. WILLIAMSPORT

From Falling Waters Ford return to Rt. 63 and turn left. Go about 1 mile to Williamsport.

A thriving town in the 1860s, Williamsport was situated both on the C & O Canal and on the major road southwest from Hagerstown. Although there was no bridge, good fords across the Potomac River lay both to the north and south of town. General Braddock had crossed here in 1755 during the French and Indian War.

The town's first contact with the Civil War came in May 1861 when an advance guard of 1,500 Confederates camped nearby. The following month, as Union soldiers massed in the area, Capt. Abner Doubleday set up an artillery battery on a hill overlooking the Potomac. This battery was later dismantled because it had no clear view of the fords. Throughout the war Union regiments camped around the town, and when the Union troops were gone Confederate raiders came.

On September 10, 1862, Gen. "Stonewall" Jackson's army passed through on the way from Frederick to West Virginia to capture Martinsburg and Harpers Ferry before the Battle of Antietam. After that battle, on September 19, 1862, Maj. Gen. Jeb. Stuart's Confederate cavalry crossed the river here to make a demonstration to attract the attention of McClellan's army around Boonsboro. About a mile east of Williamsport Stuart's cavalry fought off 7,000 green Pennsylvania troops commanded by Gen. John F. Reynolds and the more seasoned cavalry brigades of Brig. General Pleasanton and Gen. Charles Lovell as well as accompanying artillery. The Confederates returned to the Virginia (West Virginia) side of the river the next day.

Doubleday Hill

The advance of Lee's army into the North which would end at the Battle of Gettysburg began as the bulk of his forces crossed the Potomac at Williamsport June 14-25, 1863, some units crossing north of the town at other fords, and some crossing south of town on a pontoon bridge. After the great battle, as the Confederates waited for the river to subside so that they could go back to Virginia, the wounded were treated at makeshift hospitals in homes and buildings all around town. Most of the wounded had been left at Gettysburg, but there were still quite a number being transported in the wagon train. From July 5 to the thirteenth Confederate defenses were built in an arch around Williamsport that reached from the Conococheague Creek on the north to St. James College on the east to Downsville and Dam #4 on the south. Fighting at these defensive lines was intense at times. General Meade finally put the full weight of his Union troops against these defenses on the morning of July 14, but the Confederates had all left during the night, most having crossed the Potomac by that time. They had left campfires burning and fake log cannons placed to make it look like they were still there. After viewing the Confederate rifle pits, breastworks, and cannon parables, General Meade remarked that he was happy he had not blindly attacked these defenses while they were still manned, or it may have ended as a Gettysburg in reverse.

6V. DAM #5

Take Rt. 68 northwest out of Williamsport for 4.6 miles. Bear left onto Big Pool Road (Rt. 56). Go .5 mile to turn left on Dam #5 Road. Travel about 3 miles to the parking lot for the dam (Canal mile 106.80).

   On December 7, 1861, Confederates from the Virginia side of the Potomac River fired cannon at the Maryland side, apparently trying to damage the dam, but all they hit was a nearby home which burned to the ground. From December 17 to 20, 1861, men under Gen. "Stonewall" Jackson's command worked at night in the frigid water to loosen stones to breach the

Dam #5

dam. Col. S. H. Leonard with the 13th Massachusetts, 5th Connecticut, reinforced by the 29th New York and the 1st Maryland, kept the Confederates at bay during the day and blocked any attempt to cross the river into Maryland. The Confederates finally breached the dam, but the damage was repaired a few days after the Confederates left.

6W. FOUR LOCKS

From Dam #5 go back up Dam #5 Road to turn left on Big Pool Road (Rt. 56). Travel about 4 miles, then turn left on Four Locks Road to the Four Locks Recreation Area (Canal mile 108.64).

This was the winter camp for the 1st Maryland Regiment, USA, in 1861/62, and the headquarters for the 7th Maryland Regiment, USA, guarding the Potomac crossings in the fall of 1862 after Stuart's cavalry had used the nearby McCoy's Ford to cross the Potomac.

Confederate troops camped near here after crossing the Potomac on the way to Pennsylvania in June 1863.

6X. McCOY'S FERRY FORD

From Four Locks go back to Big Pool Road (Rt. 56), turn left and travel about 2 miles to McCoy's Ferry Road. Take this road about 1 mile to the recreation area just beyond the culvert under the railroad. The railroad did not exist during the Civil War (Canal mile 110.42).

The ferry had long ceased operation but the ford was still frequently used when, on the night of May 23, 1861, several Confederates tried to steal some boats from the Maryland side. The local Clear Spring Guards, hearing the noise of the oars, rushed out and started firing into the darkness. At least one Confederate was hit and they all left the boats and swam back to the other side.

Maj. Gen. Jeb Stuart with 1,800 of his best cavalry and Pelham's light artillery crossed the Potomac here in a heavy fog on the morning of October 10, 1862, entering Maryland on his second "Ride Around McClellan's Army." They crossed the National Pike (Rt. 40) three miles to the north and went on to Pennsylvania. Two days and more than 100 miles later they would cross back into Virginia at White's Ford (site #4Q).

McCoy's Ferry Ford was also the ford used by the Confederate cavalry under Gen. John McCausland June 29, 1864, entering Maryland and Pennsylvania to attract the attention of the Union army away from Virginia. This Confederate force would burn Chambersburg, Pennsylvania, ransom Hagerstown and Hancock, Maryland, and fight a Union force at Folcke's Mill and Old Town near Cumberland before returning to West Virginia August 2.

6Y. FORT FREDERICK

From McCoy's Ferry go back to Big Pool Road (Rt. 56) and turn left and go about 2 miles to the park entrance (Canal mile 112.40).

This massive stone fort was constructed in 1756 as part of a chain of forts along the eastern side of the Allegheny Mountains during the French and Indian War. It was garrisoned by the 1st Maryland, USA, under Col. (later Gen.) John Kenley during the Civil War, but the only action that it saw was the shooting at Confederates tearing up railroad tracks across the Potomac River, for which purpose a hole was made in one of the walls to allow a cannon to have a good bearing on the target. Confederates made attempts to drive the Union troops out of the fort several times during 1861 and 1862, but were unsuccessful.

6Z. CLEAR SPRING

From Fort Frederick return to Big Pool Road (Rt. 56) and turn left. Travel 2 miles to I-70 and take I-70 east to the next exit (Rt. 68, Clear Spring).

Being on a main route and at the foot of an observation mountain, this little town could not avoid seeing some action during the Civil War. During the retreat of the Confederates after the Battle of Gettysburg, the 74th New York Regulars and the 29th Pennsylvania Cavalry were camped near town. On the morning of July 10, 1863, they sent out reconnaissance parties and one of these ran into about 500 Confederates on the road to Williamsport (Rt. 68) about one half mile from Clear Spring. A fight began immediately, but when the rest of the Union troops arrived the Confederates retreated.

On July 29, 1863, the 1st Maryland Cavalry, CSA, under Gen. Bradley T. Johnson—as a part of General McCausland's raid and the burning of Chambersburg, Pennsylvania—drove a small a Union picket force out of Clear Spring and proceeded to raid the town and surrounding farms. The Confederates had also paid the town a brief visit on July 8, 1862.

a. FAIRVIEW MOUNTAIN

The mountain is to the west of Clear Spring off Rt. 40. The top of the mountain is fenced off for the protection of radio and television towers, but the mountain can be viewed from several vantage points on the road.

This high knoll overlooking the Potomac gave a good view of activities in Williamsport, and a signal station was established at the top of the mountain early in the war. On October 10, 1862, a Confederate company in Wade Hampton's command cut the telegraph lines here and captured two signalmen. This was part of Gen. Jeb Stuart's Confederate cavalry's second "Ride Around McClellan" (see Appendix C for map of route).

6AA. HANCOCK
Take Rt. 40 or I-70 west from Clear Spring about 15 miles. The C & O Canal Visitors Center, 326 East Main Street, is open daily from 8:30 a.m. to 4:30 p.m.

About 800 Federal troops entered Hancock on July 9, 1861, and established military rule as Confederates across the Potomac River took over control of the ferry. A telegraph wire was established between Hancock and Hagerstown by December 1861, while the 5th Connecticut Regiment wintered here.

Following their occupation of Bath, Virginia (now Berkeley Springs, West Virginia) in the winter of 1861/62, Confederate cavalry under Gen. "Stonewall" Jackson pursued Union troops in the area until they crossed the Potomac River to Hancock. On January 5, 1862, Jackson's batteries shelled Hancock in retaliation for the Union shelling of Shepherdstown and to keep the Federals on their side of the river as the Confederates continued to control the B & O Railroad line on the Virginia side. The Union cannon did not have the range of the Confederate guns and their return fire fell short, although they did catch a barn on fire on the Virginia shore. The next day Jackson sent Col. Turner Ashby under a flag of truce into Hancock to demand surrender. Brig. Gen. F. W. Lander refused to give in, so Jackson continued the shelling. At the end of the day, however, the Confederates left for Romney, knowing that Union reinforcements were on the way and that it would take several days to build a bridge across the Potomac River in order to invade the town.

As the Confederate invasion of the North began in the summer of 1863, McNeill's Rangers ran into a small force of Union cavalry at Cherry Run, six miles downriver from Hancock on June 17. The swift and forceful attack of the Confederates threw the Federals off guard and they retreated leaving 15 prisoners.

On June 28, 1864 Imboden's Confederate cavalry came through on a raid to try and capture some Union dignitaries in Pennsylvania.

The final incident of the war in Hancock came very close to destroying the town. On August 1, 1864 General McCausland and his Confederate cavalry entered Hancock and demanded that the citizens pay a ransom of $30,000 and 5,000 cooked rations or he would burn down the town. The Confederates had just burned Chambersburg, Pennsylvania (July 30) for refusing to pay a ransom, so the townspeople knew that the threat was real. But one of McCausland's brigade commanders, Gen. Bradley T. Johnson, who was from Frederick, Maryland, argued that a town with a population of just 700 couldn't possibly come up with that amount of money. The argument was settled when the Union cavalry brigade of Brig. Gen. W. W. Avery came galloping up the road from Hagerstown. Johnson fought a rear guard action as the Union cavalry chased the Confederates west.

SUGGESTED READING

Adams, Charles S. *The Civil War in Washington County: A Guide to 66 Points of Interest.* Self-published, Shepherdstown, W.V., 1996.

Douglas, Henry Kyd. *I Rode With Stonewall.* Mocking Bird Books. University of North Carolina Press, 1940.

Frassanito, William A. *Antietam: The Photographic Legacy of America's Bloodiest Day.* New York: Charles Scribner's Sons, 1978.

Keller, S. Roger. *Events of the Civil War in Washington County, Maryland.* Shippensburg, Pa.: Burd Street Press, 1995.

Murfin, James V. *Gleam of Bayonettes.* Baltimore: The Maryland Historical Trust Press, 1965.

Priest, John Michael. *Antietam: The Soldiers' Battle.* Shippensburg, Pa.: White Mane Publishing Co., 1989.

Priest, John Michael. *Antietam: The Soldiers' Battlefield: A Self-Guided Tour.* Shippensburg, Pa.: White Mane Publishing Co., 1989.

Scharf, J. Thomas. *History of Western Maryland.* Baltimore, Md.: Regional Publishing Company, 1968 (reprint of 1882 edition).

Sears, Stephen. *The Landscape Turned Red: The Battle of Antietam.* New York: Ticknor and Fields, 1983.

Stotelmyer, Steven R. *The Bivouacs of the Dead.* Baltimore, Md.: Toomey Press, 1992.

Williams, Thomas J. C. *History of Western Maryland.* Vols. 1 & 2, Baltimore, Md.: Regional Publishing Co., 1906.

INFORMATION ON OTHER SITES, ACCOMMODATIONS, ETC.

Washington County Conference & Visitors Bureau
Elizabeth Hager Center
16 Public Square
Hagerstown, MD 21740
800-228-7829, 301-791-3246

C & O Canal Museum and Visitor Center
326 East Main Street
Hancock, MD 21750
301-739-4200
    www.nps.gov/choca/co_life.htm

Washington County Historical Society
135 West Washington Street
Hagerstown, MD 21740
301-797-8782

Western Maryland

CHAPTER 7

WESTERN MARYLAND
ALLEGANY AND GARRETT COUNTIES
(Garrett County was not formed until 1872)

The mountainous area of western Maryland would have probably never been involved in the Civil War had it not been for the Baltimore and Ohio Railroad which was completed from Baltimore to Wheeling in 1853. This railroad entered Virginia at Harpers Ferry and then ran mainly along the Potomac River touching Maryland briefly again in tunnels near Paw Paw. Running along the North Branch of the Potomac River above Old Town, it crossed back into Maryland again for a short distance at Cumberland where it met with the Chesapeake and Ohio (C & O) Canal and National Pike (Rt. 40), and finally crossed Maryland for the last time from Bloomington to Oakland. The C & O Canal to Washington, D.C. had reached Cumberland, Maryland by 1850. It carried coal, stone, lumber and produce from the west to the capital city, but was too slow to be of strategic importance to the military for transporting troops and artillery—that was the job of the trains. So the main objective of the Confederates entering the area was to destroy railroad bridges and the telegraph lines that ran along the railroad tracks—and the main objective of the Union army was to protect the same.

West Virginia was a part of Virginia until it officially became a state on June 20, 1863. The area of what is now West Virginia that lies across the Potomac River (and North Branch of the Potomac River) from Maryland was frequently in contention between the two armies. Martinsburg and Romney were held by the Confederates for the better part of the war, but New Town, near Cumberland, was a bastion of the Union.

All through the summer of 1861 the Confederates had been ripping up railroad tracks and destroying bridges of the B & O Railroad on their side of the Potomac River. The only way that the Union would be able to use the B & O Railroad would be to capture the land through which it lay and retain control of that area. To that end the Federal War Department created a new military area in October 1861—the Department of Harpers Ferry and Cumberland. The department was first under the command of Brig. Gen. Frederick Lander, but when he was wounded at the Battle of Ball's Bluff on October 21 (see site #4N), then Brig. Gen. Benjamin Franklin Kelley took over command of the department. The Federal troops drove the Confederates out of Romney, Virginia (West Virginia) on October 26, 1861, and repairs were made on the B & O Railroad so that trains began running again between Cumberland and Hancock by December 16, 1861. But the Confederates still controlled Martinsburg and had taken up all of the railroad track between there and Harpers Ferry. Gen. "Stonewall" Jackson was using his troops with skill in order to retain the railroad in Virginia and prevent the Federal troops under General Kelley in Cumberland and those under General Banks in Frederick from uniting to take control of that area of Virginia. Jackson retook Romney at the beginning of January 1862, but was ordered by the Confederate Secretary of War to withdraw. The Federals came back to Romney and the railroad was again opened from Cumberland to Hancock on February 4, 1862. A strong push by the Union army took Winchester, Virginia on March 12, 1862, the Harpers Ferry bridge was rebuilt, and by March 29, 1862, the entire line of the B & O Railroad was open again.

In order adequately to protect the railroad the Department of Harpers Ferry and Cumberland was reorganized in June 1862 into the Mountain Department, west of the western boundary of Maryland, under the command of Gen. B. F. Kelley; and the Cis-Allegheny Department, covering the area from the Mountain Department to Cumberland, under the command of Col. Dixon F. Miles. Both were under the jurisdiction of Gen. John E. Wool (Gen. Robert E. Schenck in December 1862) in Baltimore. Troops assigned to the guarding of the railroad were constantly being commandeered by generals needing more soldiers to fight various battles, but permanent guards at most of the bridges were able to construct block houses and mount heavy artillery on bluffs overlooking the bridges.

The railroad line was sporadically interrupted several more times during the war, especially during the Confederate invasions of the North in September of 1862, June of 1863, and July of 1864, but most of the damage was below Martinsburg.

The worst incursions by Confederates into Allegany County (and present Garrett County) came in the spring of 1863 when a coordinated double-pronged raid by Confederate Generals William E. Jones and John D. Imboden made an effort to open the Allegheny arena to Confederate control and draw Union troops away from the Shenandoah Valley by destroying railroads and telegraph lines in western Maryland and northwestern Virginia (West Virginia). On April 25, 1863, both units left the Shenandoah Valley in Virginia, Imboden's cavalry would head west and remain in Virginia, Jones' cavalry would go north to Oakland, Maryland, then west to destroy the Cheat River bridge, and the forces would then meet and combine to attack Clarksburg, Virginia. Things did not go as planned because swollen rivers impeded the progress of the cavalries. They did not destroy the Cheat River bridge or attack Clarksburg, but they were able to destroy some railroad bridges and interrupt Union communications to confuse the enemy into thinking that there was a much larger force attacking. So a large number of

Federal troops was indeed drawn away from the valley. The B & O Railroad was able to reopen on May 17, 1863. General Imboden struck Cumberland on June 15, 1863, when the Federal troops were elsewhere and captured the town for the day without bloodshed.

The Department of West Virginia, named after the new state, was created on June 24, 1863. It included western Maryland and eastern Ohio as well as eastern and central West Virginia and Gen. B. F. Kelley was put in command. The last commander of the Department of West Virginia was Brig. Gen. George Crook. Sporadic raids by the Confederates in the spring of 1864 forced the Federals to assign 15 additional regiments to the Department of West Virginia, but the raiders continued destroying bridges, and even capturing two generals. This continued enemy activity forced the Federal War Department to use a large number of Union troops that could well have been used elsewhere to protect the long railroad line.

7A. FOLCK'S MILL AND TURKEY FLIGHT MANOR

(Now the Ali Gahn Country Club) 13100 Ali Gahn Road. Take exit #46 from I-68 northeast of Cumberland and turn right at the bottom of the exit. The creek is a short distance from the exit, and the inn is above the creek on the south. The inn is named for the tract of land on which it stands. L'Osteria Restaurant is open for dinner, but the interior of the second floor where the wounded were tended to is not open to the public. 301-777-3553.

Turkey Flight Manor

After burning Chambersburg, Pennsylvania on July 30, 1864, the Confederate cavalry of Brig. Gen. John McCausland, heading west toward Cumberland, met a large Union force blocking the way at Folck's Mill on Evett's Creek two miles east of Cumberland on the afternoon of August 1, 1864. Brig. Gen. B. F. Kelley had ordered the 156th Ohio National Guards under Col. Caleb Marker, and four companies of West Virginia Infantry under Maj. J. L. Simpson to defend the bridge carrying the National Pike (Rt. 40) over Evett's Creek. Marker set up a battery of cannon, Lt. John McAfee commanding, on a hill overlooking the bridge. On meeting enemy fire the Confederates took cover behind the bridge and mill and set up their own artillery on their side of the creek. The fighting lasted until after dark when McCausland withdrew to Old Town leaving 8 dead and 30 wounded.

Above the creek on the west side sat a tavern which today has been handsomely restored and is operating as a restaurant at the Turkey Flight Manor Motel. The tavern was used as a temporary hospital for the wounded of both sides after the battle.

7B. OLD TOWN
From Folck's Mill return to I-68 and take Rt. 51 (exit #43). Go about 12 miles to Old Town at the junction of Rt. 51 with Rt. 28, just above the confluence of the South Branch of the Potomac River (Lock #70, Canal mile 166.70). About four miles south of Cumberland is a marked turn-off to a canal boat replica at lock #74.

At Old Town there was a ford across the Potomac River and a covered wooden bridge over the canal near the lockhouse. Thomas Cresap's Mill was nearby. On August 2, 1864, Confederate cavalry under the command of Gen. Bradley T. Johnson, part of McCausland's cavalry, were returning from the burning of Chambersburg to cross the Potomac River at Old Town when their path was blocked by Federal troops firing at them from a ridge of Alim Hill above the canal. These Ohio troops under the command of Col. Israel Stough were soon routed by the Baltimore Light Artillery, under Johnson's command, firing at them from one side and McCausland's cavalry, returning from a skirmish at Folck's Mill, coming down on them from another. The Federals took refuge in a blockhouse and armored train across the Potomac River on the Virginia (West Virginia) side, but the Confederate artillery landed a shot to the smokestack of the train, exploding the boiler and routing the Federals.

7C. CUMBERLAND
From I-68 take Exit #43C (#43A if coming from the west). Turn left on West Harrison Street and follow the signs to the Western Maryland Station Center and "Tourist Information." Plans are under way at this time to restore the C & O Canal terminus and turning basin. Information is available at the Tourist Office.

Cumberland lies in a steep valley surrounded by mountains. It is bordered by the Potomac River on the south and is divided into two halves by Wills Creek, which empties into the Potomac River. The C & O Canal ends here where it meets with the National Pike (Rt. 40). The B & O Railroad completed its train line through here from Baltimore to Wheeling in 1853. Marking a crucial juncture of canal, rail, and road transportation, Cumberland was well-protected by Union troops throughout the war. During most of the war the Confederates were only 24 miles away in Romney, West Virginia, a constant threat to the city. First occupied by the 11th Regiment Indiana Zouaves under Col. Lew Wallace on June 11, 1861, Cumberland subsequently hosted up to 20,000 Union troops in the Department of Harpers Ferry and

Cumberland—later the Cis-Allegheny Department, and finally the Department of West Virginia in June 1863. The area was commanded by Brig. Gen. Benjamin Franklin Kelley, then by Brig. Gen. George Crook. The main military camps in Cumberland were Fort Hill, where Fort Hill High School is today at 500 Greenway Avenue, and Campobello Fort where Allegany High School is today at 616 Sedgewick Street.

From June 14, 1861, when Confederates destroyed the bridge at Harpers Ferry, to March 29, 1862, there were no through trains on the B & O line between Baltimore and Wheeling, and there were interruptions of service at other times during the war. The wooden railroad bridge at North Branch, a few miles east of Cumberland, was destroyed May 28, 1861, again on June 18, 1863, and still again in February 1864. The bridge at New Creek, Virginia (West Virginia), just west of town, was burned June 19, 1861.

On June 16, 1863, the two regiments of infantry garrisoned in Cumberland were transferred to New Town, Virginia (West Virginia) to guard against Confederates coming north after the defeat of General Milroy at Winchester, Virginia. The following evening 350 Confederate cavalrymen under Maj. John Imboden demanded the surrender of Cumberland and entered the town for a few hours to purchase clothing, steal horses, and cut telegraph lines.

Most of the Civil War-era buildings in the town have been destroyed, including the original train station and Civil War-era hotels. The architecture today is mainly late 19th and early 20th century. The earlier residences, some pre-dating the Civil War, are located mainly along Washington Street on the west side of Wills Creek.

Two churches and three public buildings were used as hospitals during the war. The Belvidere Hall at 143 Baltimore Street, and the Old Mill on South Mechanic Street below Harrison Street (near the entrance to the Railroad Station parking lot) are now gone, but still standing are The Academy (now the Allegany County Library) at 31 Washington Street, The First Baptist Church at 212 Bedford Street, and the First Presbyterian Church at 16 Liberty Street.

Col. William Wallace McKaig, Jr., CSA, was from Cumberland.

a. C & O CANAL VISITOR CENTER

The visitor center is housed in the Western Maryland Station Center which also houses the Allegany County Visitors Bureau and a transportation museum. Open Wednesday through Saturday 10 a.m. to 5 p.m., Tuesday and Sunday from 1 p.m. to 4 p.m. 301-722-8226.

Located on the second floor of the 1913 train station, the center has displays about the history of the C & O Canal and an extensive bookstore. Although not many artifacts that pertain particularly to the Civil War are displayed in the museum, the canal itself, which terminates in Cumberland, did play a part in the war (see site #7B). The Western Maryland Station Center is a good place to begin a tour of Cumberland. Maps are available at the tourist office on the first floor. You can also get a ticket for a ride on an authentic steam train from April 6 to December 15 at the center.

C & O Canalboat

b. MONUMENT TO THE CAPTURE OF UNION GENERALS CROOK AND KELLEY

Baltimore Street and Queen City Drive.

The plaque locates the site of the Revere House Hotel where Brig. Gen. George Crook stayed when he was in town. The Barnum House Hotel where Brigadier General Kelley stayed was located at the northeast corner of Baltimore and George Streets.

In the early morning hours of February 21, 1865, a group of about thirty Confederates—volunteers from McNeill's Partisan Rangers, formed from the 18th Virginia Cavalry, and volunteers from Company F of the 7th Virginia Cavalry and Company E of the 11th Virginia Cavalry—were led by 1st Lt. Jesse McNeill into Cumberland to capture Brig. Gen. Benjamin Franklin Kelley and Brig. Gen. George Crook, from their beds in their hotel rooms in the midst of about 8,000 Union troops stationed around Cumberland.

Jesse McNeill had taken over command of the Rangers after the death of his father, the former commander, John Hanson McNeill, in the fall of 1864. Both father and son had a grudge against General Kelley for arresting members of their family. The scheme to capture General Kelley was apparently formulated by Jesse, and his men convinced him also to capture General Crook who was then staying at a nearby hotel.

The Confederates came across the mountain from Moorefield, leading their horses through snow drifts; they crossed the North Branch of the Potomac River between New Creek and Cumberland, and proceeded to the city on the New Creek Road. They charged the first pickets they encountered and overwhelmed them before they could give the alarm. Tying the sentries up, they went on and captured the next sentries through trickery. The cavalry rode down the main street of Cumberland after crossing the Chain Bridge over Wills Creek. It was still dark and the Confederates wore heavy overcoats, so Union soldiers in the street mistook them for Union cavalry. They divided into three groups, one to capture General Crook, one to capture General Kelley, and one to destroy the telegraph lines. The plan went almost without a flaw, except the adjutant general, Captain Melvin, had to be captured along with the two generals because he was inadvertently awakened by the invaders trying to locate General Kelley in the Barnum House. The groups met again at the stables near Chain Bridge, placed their captives on mounts and rode off down the C & O Canal. They were several miles away before the generals were missed. The captured generals were taken to Richmond and later exchanged. McNeill and his party were given commendations by Gen. Robert E. Lee, and Jesse McNeill was promoted to captain.

c. SPRIGG HOUSE
201 Washington Street. Not open to the public.

This house was at one time used as headquarters for Union officers. Although the inside of the building has been converted to offices, the outside looks almost the same as it did then.

d. HISTORY HOUSE
218 Washington Street. Open May through October Tuesday through Saturday from 11 a.m. to 3 p.m. and Sunday from 1:30 p.m. to 3:30 p.m. 301-777-8678.

This 1867 house of Judge Josiah Hance Gordon is headquarters of the Allegany County Historical Society. Judge Gordon was a member of the Maryland Legislature and was one of those arrested in Frederick in September 1861. He was president of the C & O Canal Company from 1869-70. The house is decorated in high Victorian style, and there are displays on the upper floor of Civil War memorabilia including arms and equipment, photos and letters.

e. ROSE HILL CEMETERY
535 Fayette Street.

There is a wonderful view of the city from this cemetery. Here is a monument to Union soldiers from the area and another to Confederate soldiers who died in nearby skirmishes or hospitals. The Union monument is

Union Monument at Rose Hill Cemetery

in the form of a bronze private soldier. It was erected in 1895 by the Women's Relief Corps of Cumberland (Women's Auxiliary of the Grand Army of the Republic).

The Confederate monument is in the form of a 25-foot obelisk and was erected in 1912 by the "Ladies of Cumberland." Six of the soldiers buried under the monument were reinterred here from the Clarysville Hospital in 1900 by the James Breathed Camp, United Confederate Veterans.

Col. William Wallace McKaig, Jr., CSA, is one of the Civil war soldiers buried in the cemetery.

f. SUMNER CEMETERY

Yale Street, upper (north) part of Hillcrest Cemetery.

A monument marks the spot where six local soldiers who were enlisted in the U.S. Colored Troops (USCT) are buried. This is the oldest known black cemetery in Allegany County. Long before the Civil War this was the site of many slave burials, so it seemed the natural final resting place for six veterans of that war who had fought valiantly as members of the United States Colored Troops. Their names were Frank Tyler, Abraham Craig, Thomas Lindsey, Thomas Simpson, David Kinner, and Sam Parry.

In January 1991 the Cumberland Historic Cemetery Organization made this cemetery its project. It was joined by The Ebenezer Baptist Church, the Metropolitan AME Church, the McKendree United Methodist Church, and the Sons of Union Veterans Harpers Ferry Camp 6, in cleaning up the cemetery and erecting the monument and flag pole to the USCT.

Clarysville Inn

Michael Zimmerman

7D. CLARYSVILLE INN
Take Rt. 40 west from Cumberland 5 miles to the intersection with Rt. 55. The inn is on the south side of Rt. 40 at Rt. 55. It is open for lunch and dinner. Call 301-722-3900.

Now operating as a restaurant, the inn was the center of the largest hospital complex in the area during the Civil War. The inn was built as a stagecoach stop on the National Pike in 1807 by Gerard Clary. It was officially established as the site for a Federal hospital on March 5, 1862, because the hospitals in the churches and public buildings in Cumberland were inadequate and it was feared by the local inhabitants that they were spreading disease. By the end of that spring six long ward buildings had been built around the inn on both sides of the National Pike, as well as 15 support buildings (stables, kitchens, laundry, etc.). The inn served as officers' quarters and a house was built next to it for the director of the hospital, Dr. J. B. Lewis. Thousands of sick and wounded soldiers from both sides were treated there in the three years it was in operation. Those who died here have since been removed to Antietam National Cemetery (Union), and Rose Hill Cemetery, Cumberland (Confederates).

7E. BLOOMINGTON BRIDGE

From the Clarysville Inn take Rt. 55, then Rt. 36 south 18 miles to Westernport. Go west on Rt. 135 from Westernport about 1 mile and after crossing a small bridge over the Savage River the Bloomington railroad bridge over the Potomac River can be seen on the left. It cannot be approached from this point. To view the bridge from the other side follow Rt. 135 over the tracks and make the first left on Hamill Street then left on Owens Avenue, following the gravel road to the end where there is an unloading area for canoes. You can then walk a short path through the woods to the river and see the bridge to the left.

At daybreak on May 6, 1864, a company of about 60 Confederate raiders under the command of Capt. John Hanson McNeill descended on Bloomington from West Virginia. Their objective was to destroy railroad bridges and telegraph lines in the vicinity. Part of the company took a captured train into Piedmont to wreak havoc there, and while they were gone the eleven men left behind under Capt. John T. Peerce captured a train carrying more than 100 armed Union soldiers by using trickery to make them believe that there were many more Confederates surrounding the cars. They were soon rejoined by McNeill and the rest of the company and proceeded to burn the captured trains and destroy the stone bridge. Before they could finish setting the charges to blow up the bridge, a second train carrying many more Union soldiers and armed civilians descended on them from the east and a battle ensued. Several citizens were killed or injured, but no Confederate soldiers were killed.

Bloomington Bridge

7F. OAKLAND

Continue on Rt. 135 twenty-two miles west.

In the spring of 1863 Confederate Gen. Robert E. Lee commanded Gen. John Imboden and Gen. William Jones to lead an expedition into western Virginia and western Maryland to destroy strategic railroad bridges in order to disrupt supply lines of the Union army.

As a part of this "Great Raid" Confederate forces under Gen. William E. Jones, Col. Asher V. Hartman, Maj. Ridgely Brown, and Capt. John Hanson McNeill left Harrisonburg, Virginia on April 20 and crossed the North Branch of the Potomac River at Gorman, Maryland (Rt. 50 & Rt. 560) on the morning of April 26, burning the bridge behind them. The main force under General Jones went west on Rt. 50 toward Aurora and thence to Cranberry Summit (Terra Alta, West Virginia). Colonel Harman's 12th Virginia Cavalry, Brown's Maryland Cavalry, and McNeill's Partisan Rangers divided into several groups and traveled north toward Oakland. One group led by captains McDonald and Dangerfield crossed the North Branch of the Potomac River at Kitzmiller and reached the railroad line at Altamont, where Rt. 40 crossed the railroad at the top of the mountain. While the crew was taking a break they commandeered a train with about four empty cars. Thinking that the train was in reverse one of the Confederates opened the throttle and mistakenly sent the unmanned train down the mountain into Oakland where it careened recklessly through the town and eventually stopped, with two wheels hanging over the edge of what was left of the trestle over the Youghiogheny River west of town that their compatriots had just finished burning. The train was later dumped into the river. Meanwhile, the rest of the Confederates had been burning bridges, cutting telegraph lines, stealing horses and food all around Oakland, pushing as far north as Deep Creek. Before the day was over, the whole contingent had moved west to join General Jones' forces at Cranberry Summit.

a. GARRETT COUNTY HISTORICAL SOCIETY

123 Center Street. Entering Oakland on Rt. 135 turn right on Third Street and go three blocks to turn left on Center Street. The museum is one and one-half blocks on the left. For hours call 301-334-3226 or 301-334-3403.

Housed in a late 19th-century building, the Historical Society has an exhibit of Civil War memorabilia, including Gen. B. F. Kelley's saddle, and items that once belonged to Gen. George Crook.

b. CROOK'S CREST

From the Historical Society turn left on Center Street, right at the next street, North Wilson, left at the next street, Pennington, and the second right on North Scott Street. Go to the top of the hill, around a curve and "Crook's Crest" is the yellow house on the right. This is a private residence.

Crook's Crest is the home built by Brig. Gen. George Crook and occupied by his wife after he died in Chicago, never having lived in the house himself. His wife was Mary Daily, the daughter of the owner of the Revere House in Cumberland, and the sister of one of General Crook's captors in the McNeill raid (see site #7Cb). General Crook continued in the army in the west after the Civil War and rose to major general. His funeral in Oakland in 1890 was attended by William McKinley and "Buffalo Bill" Cody.

SUGGESTED READING

Scharf, J. Thomas. *History of Western Maryland*. Baltimore: Regional Publishing Company, 1968 (reprint of 1882 edition).

Schlosnagle, Stephen, and the Garrett County Bicentennial Commission. Garrett County: A History of Maryland's Tableland. Parsons, W. V.: McLain Printing Co, 1978.

Scott, Harold L., Sr. *The Civil War Hospitals at Cumberland and Clarysville, Maryland*. Cumberland, Md., self-published (no date).

Stegmaier, Harry I., et al. *Allegany County: A History*. Parsons, W.V.: McLain Printing Company, 1976.

Thomas, James W. and T. C. Williams. *History of Allegany County*. Cumberland, Md.: L. R. Titsworth & Co., 1923.

INFORMATION ON OTHER SITES, ACCOMMODATIONS, ETC.

Allegany County Visitors Center
13 Canal Street
Cumberland, MD 21502
800-50-VISIT, 301-777-5905

Western Maryland Scenic Railroad
13 Canal Street
Cumberland, MD 21502
800-TRAIN-50
www.wmsr.com

Allegany County Historical Society
218 Washington Street
Cumberland, MD 21502
301-777-8678

Garrett County Chamber of Commerce
200 South Third Street
Oakland, MD 21550-1581
301-334-1948
www.gcnet.net/gctourism/gct.html

Garrett County Historical Society
123 Center Street
Oakland, MD 21550
301-334-3226

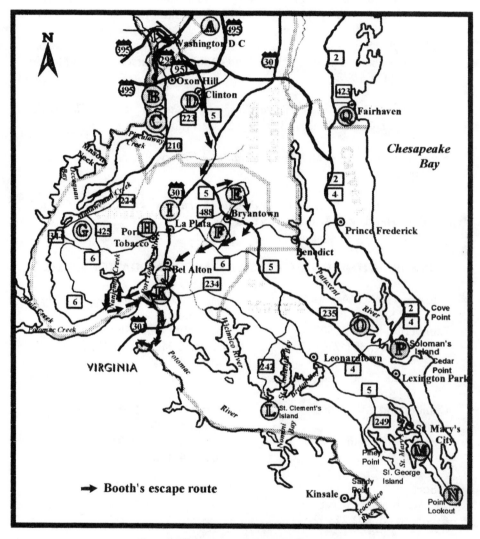

Southern Maryland

CHAPTER 8

SOUTHERN MARYLAND
CALVERT COUNTY, CHARLES COUNTY, ST. MARY'S COUNTY, AND SOUTHERN PRINCE GEORGE'S COUNTY

Except for the area near Washington, D.C. southern Maryland was remote and isolated before and during the Civil War. Surrounded on three sides by water, with few roads and many rivers and inlets, the culture of the land was based on plantation life and fishing villages. The large plantations produced mainly tobacco, using slave labor. Beginning in the 1830s steamships made regular stops at several landings on the shores of the Patuxent and Potomac Rivers picking up hogsheads of tobacco and other local produce. But passengers for these "Queens of the Bay" were scarce in southern Maryland until the area's first resort on the Chesapeake Bay appeared with the opening of Fair Haven in 1839. Others at Point Lookout and Solomons Island soon followed.

Being Southern in culture, most of the people in this part of Maryland favored the Confederate cause. Before the draft of 1862 there were only seven volunteers for the Union army from the entire aggregate of Prince George's, Calvert, Charles and St. Mary's Counties. It is not known exactly how many men from the area joined the Confederate army, but Gen. Joseph Lancaster Brent, CSA ("Brentland" in Welcome), Adm. Raphael Semmes, CSN ("Efton Hills" in Nanjemoy), and Maj. William Dement, CSA ("Eutaw" in Pomfret), were all from Charles County. The homes are today all private residences and not open to the public.

The Civil War sites in southern Maryland are focused on three activities: Confederate smuggling and mail routes, the escape of John Wilkes Booth after the assassination of President Lincoln, and the Union army camps. Since southern Maryland, except for the northern border, is surrounded by water, a fourth type of Civil War activity in the area—raids and smuggling by boat—actually took place in the Potomac River or near the western shore of the Chesapeake Bay.

The landowners of Charles and St. Mary's Counties formed a close-knit group, some tied by family and some by friendship, but all steadfastly loyal to each other—like an exclusive club. So it is not surprising that they would band together in clandesdine activities to aid a common cause. During the summer of 1861 numerous boats made secret crossings of the Potomac River from southern Maryland carrying people and contraband. Mail from the

South was often delivered through the regular post offices in the area. But all this open activity came to a halt in November 1861 when Col. L. C. Baker with three companies of the 3rd Indiana Infantry, detached from General Hooker's division at Budd's Ferry, began patrolling the area and set up detachments at Ledlow's Ferry, Pope's Creek, and Port Tobacco, putting an end to blatant smuggling.

A few brave and wily souls continued the smuggling, sometimes under the very noses of the soldiers. The smugglers usually worked at night using rowboats with muffled oars (with rags wrapped around the oarlocks), or Indian-rubber boats, although sometimes they would use small sailing vessels. In the spring of 1862 Thomas A. Jones was hired as an official agent of the Confederate Secret Service. Operating from his home near Pope's Creek, Jones set up a Confederate mail line, "the Secret Line," that used a number of operatives and ran mail up to Bryantown or Surratt's Tavern or Leonardtown where it was usually "re-packaged" and sent through the regular mail. One operative ran mail directly to Canada. Because of the secretive nature of this activity the number and names of all the people involved in the mail line, and the many tricks that they used to fool the Union soldiers, will probably never be known.

Separate from the "Secret Line," but with some of the same contacts, was the communications network established by the Confederate spy Capt. Thomas Nelson Conrad. Conrad had a base of operations in King Georges County, Virginia, across the Potomac River from Charles County. His parents had moved from Alexandria, Virginia to Leonardtown, Maryland, though whether they were a part of his activities is unknown. His network connected Virginia to Washington, D.C. through Charles County, Maryland, and he would frequently travel to the capital city himself, dressed as a chaplain.

In the winter of 1864-65 John Wilkes Booth made contact with some of the Confederate operatives in southern Maryland in order to set up a route to secretly carry President Lincoln off to Virginia after kidnapping him in Washington—a plan that had to be abandoned.

After shooting President Lincoln at Ford's Theatre on the evening of April 14, 1865, the carefully laid plans that Booth had made in the previous months in anticipation of kidnapping the President benefited him in his escape. Booth left Washington, D.C. by way of the Navy Yard bridge and met up with his cohort, David Herold, at Soper's Hill on Good Hope Road just outside the current Capital beltway. The two then traveled to Lloyd's (Surratt's) Tavern in what is now Clinton, then south to the town of T.B. where Rt. 5 and Rt. 301 intersect today. From there the pair went south to Beantown and turned east to Dr. Mudd's house where Booth's broken leg was cared for and where they rested. From there Booth and Herold sought out

Samuel Cox near Bel Alton, who then put them in touch with Confederate agent Thomas A. Jones. The fugitives lay in hiding near Bel Alton for several days since the whole area was crawling with soldiers searching for them. Jones was finally able to put Booth and Herold on a boat near Pope's Creek to cross the Potomac River to Virginia on the night of April 20.

Losing their bearings on the dark river, the two fugitives ended up back on the Maryland shore at dawn. They remained at Nanjemoy Creek for two days, then set off again on the evening of April 22. They made contact with Thomas Hardin on the Virginia shore and eventually ended up at the Garrett Farm where Booth was killed and Herold was captured by Federal troops on April 26.

Federal troop occupation had come early to southern Maryland. In June 1861 the first detachment of Federal troops under the command of Col. Charles Graham were sent into the area, making temporary headquarters first at Port Tobacco, then near Budd's Ferry, opposite where Confederates across the Potomac River had set up batteries. They were joined in October by a whole division under General Hooker who established the winter quarters at Chicamuxen Creek. Most of these troops left in the spring of 1862, posting detachments at various "hot spots." Camp Stanton, camp of the 7th U.S. Colored Infantry, Col. James Shaw, Jr. in command, existed for a short time just west of Benedict in the spring of 1863, but the large number of deaths due to disease forced the closing of the camp. There is no trace left today of this camp.

The most permanent encampment was at Point Lookout, at the southernmost tip of Maryland. Here a military hospital was established in the summer of 1862, and a prisoner of war camp was built the following year.

Late in 1862 a permanent fuel distribution point for the Potomac Flotilla was established at Cross Manor on St. Inigoes Creek in St. Mary's County, and remained there until the end of the war. Although the Confederate batteries on the Virginia side of the Potomac River were mostly abandoned in the second year of the war, Confederate raiders continued to destroy and disable lighthouses and capture ships in the river and bay. The Potomac Flotilla increased in size as the war went on, and was continually active.

8A. FORT LINCOLN

From the Capital Beltway take Rt. 50 west (exit #19) toward Washington. Follow Rt. 50 past the Baltimore-Washington Parkway to exit onto South Dakota Avenue. From South Dakota Avenue turn right onto Bladensburg Road, and the entrance to Fort Lincoln Cemetery is four blocks ahead on the right. Once inside the cemetery continue to the right until you see the cannon on the hill to the right just past the mausoleum.

Battery Jamieson is all that is left of Fort Lincoln, one of the first forts built to form a ring of defenses around Washington, D.C. The fort was constructed in the summer of 1861 and named in honor of President Lincoln. The cannon were placed to commemorate the brigade of General Hooker, the first to occupy the fort.

The old Capitol Cemetery was expanded in 1931 to include parts of Fort Lincoln, and the battery was preserved in the park-like landscape design created by landscape architect Horace Peasley.

A statue of President Lincoln created by sculptor Andrew O'Connor was placed in the cemetery in 1947 and sits across from the battery.

Statue of Lincoln at Fort Lincoln Cemetery

8B. FORT FOOTE

Take the Indian Head Highway (Rt. 210) exit #3 from the Capital Beltway. Take the first right onto Oxon Hill Road (Rt. 414) and follow south. Turn right on Fort Foote Road and follow the signs to the fort. It is located in a park open from dawn to dusk.

Fort Foote was built in 1863 on Rozier's bluff eight miles from Washington, D.C. as a part of the defenses of Washington and named for Rear Adm. Andrew Hull Foote. It was manned by the 2nd Battalion of the 9th New York Heavy Artillery, Col. Henry Seward (son of Secretary William Seward) commanding.

Not a whole lot is left of Fort Foote, but the remains of the fort demonstrate how these forts were constructed and the guns placed. There are two 15-inch Rodman naval guns mounted overlooking the Potomac River.

Rodman Gun at Fort Foote

Fort Washington

8C. FORT WASHINGTON

From Fort Foote turn right on Fort Foote Road and travel 1.6 mile to Oxon Hill Road. Turn right and go .5 mile to Livingston Road. Turn right and go 1 mile to Fort Washington Road. Turn right and travel 2.7 miles to the park entrance. The fort is a National Historic Park and there is a parking fee. Open daily 8:30 a.m. to 4 p.m. 301-763-4600.

Fort Washington overlooking the Potomac River just south of the capital was constructed in 1809 to defend Washington from attack by sea. Unfortunately, the British attacked first by land and the fort had to be disabled by the U.S. forces in 1814 to keep it from falling into British hands since it was practically defenseless from the land side.

In January 1861, when a crisis seemed imminent, a Marine force of forty men was sent to man the fort. With them, charged with putting the fort in operating order, was Army Engineer Lt. George Washington Custis Lee, son of Col. Robert E. Lee. In just three months both Custis and his father would resign their commissions to join the Confederate forces.

On April 15, 1861, the day after Fort Sumter surrendered to Confederate forces, the 1st U.S. Artillery commanded by Capt. Joseph A. Haskin manned Fort Washington. It was garrisoned throughout the war.

The fort has been restored and has examples of cannon used in both the Civil War and the War of 1812, as well as the restored barracks, kitchen, and sutler's stores which present a picture of garrison life.

8D. SURRATT'S TAVERN

From Fort Washington take Fort Washington Road to turn left on Piscataway Road (Rt. 223) and travel 5 miles to turn right on Brandywine Road. Surratt's Tavern is immediately to the left.

From the Capital Beltway take the Branch Avenue (Rt. 5) exit and go 3 miles. Turn right onto Woodyard Road, then turn left at the second traffic light onto Brandywine Road and the house is immediately to the left.

Surratt's Tavern is currently run by the Surratt Society and has an excellent research library as well as a museum. The house is open March 1 through mid-December on Thursdays and Fridays 11 a.m. to 3 p.m., and Saturdays and Sundays noon to 4 p.m. 301-686-1121.

Surratt's Tavern

www.somd.lib.us/museums/surratt.htm

About midnight on April 14, 1865, John Wilkes Booth and David Herold stopped at Surratt's Tavern to pick up some field glasses, a rifle and some ammunition which were given to them by the proprietor of the tavern, John Lloyd. Booth had shot President Lincoln about two hours before.

The combination home, inn, tavern, and post office had been built by John Surratt in 1852. A town called Surrattsville (now Clinton) grew up around the tavern. Strong Southern sympathizers, the Surratts ran a secret Confederate mail depot at the tavern during the Civil War. When John died in August 1862, his wife, Mary, tried to keep the place operating, but finally decided to move with her children in December 1864, to Washington, D.C. where she ran a boarding house at 541 H Street. She leased the old tavern to John Lloyd.

Mary Surratt knew Booth well since he had been a boarder at both the tavern and the boarding house. On Friday afternoon, April 14, Mary, accompanied by one of her boarders, traveled to Surrattsville to collect a debt from a man living there. On the way she stopped at the tavern to deliver a package to Mr. Lloyd as requested earlier that day by John Wilkes Booth. The package contained field glasses. When she met with Lloyd she reminded him to have the "shooting irons ready." That visit and statement would later seal Mary Surratt's fate.

With one son in the Confederate army, and another (John) a known Confederate courier, Mary Surratt faced a hostile military commission at her trial for conspiring in the Lincoln assassination plot. She was convicted and hung on July 7, 1865. Whether or not she was truly guilty is still a matter of conjecture. Her son John, who had first brought Booth to the tavern, was acquitted by a civilian jury several years later.

8E. DR. SAMUEL MUDD HOUSE

From the Surratt House continue south on Rt. 5 for 18 miles and turn left onto Rt. 205 and then left on Poplar Hill Road. Take this road about 4 miles to turn right onto Dr. Samuel Mudd Road. The house is about 1/2 mile on the right. Open April through November, Wednesday 11 a.m to 3 p.m., and Saturday and Sunday noon to 4 p.m. 301-645-6870.

John Wilkes Booth had broken the smaller bone of his left leg when jumping down to the stage from the President's box after shooting President Lincoln. About 4 a.m. on April 15 Booth and his companion, David Herold, stopped at the home of Dr. Samuel Mudd to have his leg attended to. Dr. Mudd set the injured leg and put Booth to bed in his home. Booth slept there until that afternoon when he and Herold left. During the trial Dr. Mudd

Dr. Samuel Mudd House

claimed that he did not recognize Booth, even though he was witnessed meeting with Booth on two separate occasions. He was tried and convicted of helping the assassin, and sentenced to life imprisonment at Jefferson Prison on Dry Tortugas Island in Florida. Dr. Mudd was granted a full and unconditional pardon by President Johnson in 1869 for his medical attention to his fellow prisoners during a yellow fever epidemic.

Recent historic evidence has shown that Dr. Mudd actually met with Booth three times before the assassination and was most probably involved in the conspiracy to kidnap President Lincoln. Although he probably had no knowledge of the murder of the president when Booth and Herold came to his house in the early morning of April 15, evidence proves that he was aware of that fact before they left his home and he sent them on their way with directions and names of contacts.

The house, with most of its original furnishings, is operated by the Dr. Samuel A. Mudd Society.

8F. BRYANTOWN TAVERN

Turn right from the Dr. Mudd House and go about 1.5 miles to turn right on Bryantown Road. Travel 3 miles and cross Rt. 5, then turn right immediately onto Trotter Road. The second house on the right is the old Bryantown Tavern. This is a private residence.

On December 18, 1864, John Wilkes Booth was introduced to the Confederate Signal Service agent Thomas Harbin by Dr. Samuel Mudd at Bryantown Tavern. Booth enlisted Harbin to aid in the proposed kidnapping of President Lincoln (the plan before the assassination plan). The tavern was later used by Federal soldiers as a place for interrogating residents of the area about the Booth escape.

The Confederate agent Thomas Nelson Conrad often stayed at the tavern, usually disguised as a Union army chaplain. He had many clandestine meetings at the tavern with informers and other spies.

8G. CHICAMUXEN METHODIST CHURCH

From Bryantown return to go north on Rt. 5 one mile. Turn left onto La Plata Road (Rt. 488), go 6 miles to turn right onto Doncaster Road (Rt. 6) and go about 12 miles. Turn right on Rt. 344 and then right on Rt. 224. Chicamuxen is about 2 miles north. The church is on the left.

From October 1861 to April 7, 1862, General Hooker made his headquarters in this church while his division camped between here and Budd's Ferry which was located about five miles to the south—but about a mile off the current road. The Confederate batteries across the Potomac River at Quantico were a constant worry to the Union troops stationed in the area in the winter of 1861-62: they wanted to know what those Rebs were up to. So when General Hooker heard of a recent balloon demonstration in Washington, D.C. he asked the aeronaut Thaddeus Sobieski Constantine Lowe to bring the balloon to his camp. The tethered balloon went up on November 10, 1861, with General Sickles, serving under Hooker, in the basket with Lowe. From the balloon General Sickles could see all the way to Occoquan and Dumfries, Virginia and viewed a large number of enemy troops camped in the area. In the next few months observations were made regularly from the balloon. The Confederates fired at the flying monstrosity with their cannon, but the range was too far.

8H. PORT TOBACCO

From Chicamuxen return to Rt. 6. Travel east on Rt. 6 for about 8 miles.

Port Tobacco, the county seat of Charles County during the war, was also a center of smuggling activities during the Civil War. Brawner's or St. Charles Hotel (now gone) was one notorious hangout for the smugglers, but the many taverns in town also served as rendezvous points at times. George Adzerodt, who was later hanged for his part in the Lincoln assassination plot, had a carriage-painting business in the town with his brother. His brother left at the beginning of the war to join the office of the provost marshal of Baltimore, so George changed his occupation to smuggling. In the plot he was supposed to assassinate Vice-President Johnson, then join Booth and Herold to lead them through southern Maryland. But he opted instead to escape Washington and head north to his old home town of Germantown, Maryland, where he was captured a few days later. He was tried, convicted, and hanged.

Olivia Floyd lived northwest of Port Tobacco at "Rose Hill" and was one of Jones' operatives in the Confederate mail service. In the winter of 1864 she hid an important missive for the Confederate government in the andirons of her fireplace. Union soldiers searching her house rested their feet on the andirons, but never discovered the message. Rose Hill is just west of town off Rt. 6 and overlooks the town. It is a private residence.

8I. ST. IGNATIUS CHURCH/CHAPEL POINT

From Port Tobacco travel south 3 miles on Chapel Point Road to the chapel on the right.

The high bluff on which St. Ignatius Church sits has a perfect view across the Potomac River and was used as a site for both Union and Confederate signal stations at different times during the war. Confederate agent Annie Olivia Floyd is buried in the cemetery.

The traveler looking out from this bluff can get a good idea of the vastness of the wide Potomac River in this area and how difficult it must have been to patrol the area by both land and water.

8J. RICH HILL (COX HOUSE)

From St. Ignatius Chapel travel east on Chapel Point Road 2 miles to cross over Rt. 301 onto Bel Alton-Newtown Road. Take the first right onto Wills Road and follow to the end. This is where the pine thicket was. Proceed about .5 mile east on Bel Alton-Newtown Road to the plaque on the left. The house, Rich Hill, can be viewed across the field just west of the plaque. It is a private home.

After leaving Dr. Mudd's house on April 16 John Wilkes Booth and David Herold lost their way several times before finding a guide, Oswald Swann, a free black. Swann led them, at their request, to the home of Samuel

Cox called "Rich Hill." Cox was a wealthy planter and had been prominent in Charles County politics before the war. He was also a known Confederate sympathizer. Cox hid Booth and Herold in a nearby pine thicket where they stayed until the evening of April 20.

Huckleberry

8K. HUCKLEBERRY

From Rt. 301 about 1.5 miles south of Bel Alton turn right onto Pope's Creek Road. Huckleberry cottage (reconstructed) is about 1 mile ahead on the right at the entrance to the Loyola Retreat House. The creek from which the fugitives left the Maryland shore in a skiff is just to the south of the bluff on which the Retreat House sits, but it is private property and permission from the Retreat House is required to approach the site from land.

Thomas Jones and Maj. Roderick Watson owned the land on which Huckleberry sits near Pope's Creek that included an 80-foot bluff overlooking the Potomac River. From this bluff the river could be viewed for miles in either direction. This came in mighty handy when Jones, after serving a term of six months in a Federal prison for smuggling, was enlisted into the Confederate Secret Service in the spring of 1862 and became the director of the Confederate Mail Line through Southern Maryland. He had many tricks for eluding the Federal guards. Sometimes he would take a boat across the river near the bluff at sunset when the glare from the sun obscured the view of the Union soldiers keeping watch. Signals were made across the river from Major Watson's House next door by putting different-colored curtains in a window. The Confederate mail was hidden in various containers and carried by many different people to a number of drop-off points. The operation was very well coordinated and many of the "mail carriers" did not know the identity of the others, or of their boss. The Confederate Mail Line operated for three years with no one involved being caught.

Major Watson died in November 1861, but at least two of his children were known to have helped in the "Secret Line." One of Jones' most trusted mail carriers was Dr. Stowton W. Dent of "Dent's Palace" in Dentsville. The doctor would hide mail in the heavy folds of his overcoat and deliver it as he made his rounds visiting the sick.

On the morning of April 16, 1865, after he had deposited Booth and Herold into hiding in a pine thicket, Samuel Cox contacted Confederate agent Thomas A. Jones, his foster brother, who lived at "Huckleberry" cottage. Jones brought the two fugitives food and drink for five days as they hid until the coast was clear to send them across the Potomac River. He also disposed of their horses which were described on the "Wanted" posters along with the fugitives.

On the evening of April 20 Jones took Booth and Herold to his house, then to Pope's Creek nearby where he had hidden a small skiff. He put Booth and Herold in the boat and directed them toward the Virginia shore. The two missed their way on the dark river and ended up in Nanjemoy Creek, still on the Maryland side of the Potomac, but made it across to Virginia the night of April 22. They traveled through Virginia until finally being caught at the Garrett farm in the early morning hours of April 26 where Booth was shot and Herold was captured.

8L. ST. CLEMENT'S ISLAND AND THE POTOMAC RIVER MUSEUM

From Pope's Creek Road return to Rt. 301 and follow south to turn left (east) onto Rt. 234. Go 16 miles to Clements. Turn right on Colton Point Road (Rt. 242) and follow 8 miles.The Potomac River Museum demonstrates the history of the river and there are boat tours to St. Clement's Island, the first landing place of the Maryland colonists. Call 301-373-2280 for hours.

St. Clement's Island was known as Blackistone Island during the Civil War and there was a lighthouse on the island tended by Jerome Williams. On May 19, 1864, the 30-foot sloop *Swan* landed on the island with a dozen Confederates led by Capt. John Goldsmith, a former resident of the area. The raiders were about to burn down the lighthouse, which also served as a home, but the keeper, who knew Goldsmith well, pleaded for the safety of his pregnant wife. The invaders only destroyed the lens and lamps of the lighthouse, and then returned to the Virginia shore.

Although many hidden coves and inlets on the Potomac River were used by smugglers in southern Maryland, the usual destination point of the smugglers was either the Coan River or the Yeocomico River in Virginia. A Tennessee regiment occupied the town of Kinsale on the Yeocomico early in the war and were the contact for many of the smugglers. Confederate batteries existed at one time or another at Quantico, Boyd's Hole, Potomac Creek, Matthias Point, Freestone Point, Shipping Point, and Cockpit Point on the Virginia shore, threatening all shipping on the Potomac River.

In May 1861 the Potomac Flotilla, created and commanded by Comdr. James H. Ward, USA, began patrolling the Potomac River and the Chesapeake Bay, but the flotilla did not have enough ships in the beginning to do much damage to the smuggling activities or the Confederate batteries. On June 26, 1861, Commander Ward, directing an attack on batteries at Mathias Point from the *Thomas Freeborn*, was shot and killed—the first U.S. Navy officer to die in the Civil War.

On June 28, 1861, Capt. George N. Hollins, CSA, boarded the steamer *St. Nicholas* at Point Lookout. His cohort, Richard Thomas Zarvona, had boarded the steamer in Baltimore disguised as a French woman, along with sixteen henchmen. Once out of sight of the port the Confederates took over the ship and headed for the Coan River Landing on the Virginia shore. There they put ashore about fifty prisoners who had been passengers on the ship and picked up reinforcements from the 1st Tennessee Infantry and the CSS *Patrick Henry*. Their plan of capturing the Union gunboat *Pawnee*, which had a regular rendezvous with the *St. Nicholas*, was thwarted because the *Pawnee* had made an emergency trip to Washington, D.C. So the Confederates took their prize and used it to capture three supply ships in the Chesapeake Bay: the *Monticello*, the *Mary Pierce*, and the *Margaret*.

The most notorious smugglers in this area were the Irishman, Mr. Maddox, and Dr. Coombs who worked out of Herring Creek. They had many helpers and would hide people and goods bound for Virginia during the day, and cross the Potomac River at night. In August 1861, a Union raiding party captured three of the smugglers' sailing vessels moored in the creek.

On October 7, 1862, Confederate raiders under the command of John Taylor Wood captured and burned the schooner *Frances Elmor* off Pope's Creek using small boats they had brought overland to the Virginia shore by attaching wheels to them.

8M. ST. INIGOES CREEK

Return to Rt. 234 and travel south to the intersection with Rt. 5. Go south on Rt. 5 fifteen miles south of Leonardtown to St. Mary's City, then continue 4 more miles to turn right on Villa Road. Go 1 mile and turn right on Grayson Road. After .6 mile turn left on Cross Manor road and proceed to the gate of the manor. Park on the side of the road outside the gate and walk 100 yards to the right along the outside of the fence to the monument at the edge of the Creek.

Cross Manor was owned by Dr. Caleb Jones, a strong Union supporter, during the Civil War. In late 1862 the U.S. Marines stationed at the distribution point for the Potomac Flotilla at Piney Point (see site #8K) realized that the Point was much too exposed to the elements for the ships to be able to dock in rough weather. The whole operation was moved to Cross Manor on St. Inigoes Creek in a nice quiet inlet. More than 100 marines were stationed at the center which provided wood and coal for the steamships and food for the sailors. The flotilla couldn't have operated without this depot and operational headquarters. New wharves were built with trolly tracks leading to them for transporting heavy goods. Carpenter and blacksmith shops were built for repairing ships, and sutlers set up semi-permanent stores, all interspersed with coal bins and warehouses. A telegraph line ran from the depot to Washington, D.C. The center became a dumping ground for captured ammunition, torpedoes, prisoners, and contraband.

During the Civil War many aging commercial steamships were rigged with guns to serve in the flotilla. The USS *Tulip* was one of the smaller steamships. In November 1864 one of her two steam boilers was condemned and she was ordered to Washington for repairs. The master of the ship was William H. Smith from Pennsylvania. In order to avoid being a sitting duck for Confederate cannon across the river, Smith ordered that the condemned boiler be fired up. The explosion that came a few minutes later tore the ship to fragments, only part of the bow being recovered later. There were 57 enlisted men and two officers on the ship. Ten survived the blast, but two of these later died of their wounds. About eight of the bodies recovered were so mangled that they could not be identified. These were buried near the site of the explosion on the south shore of St. Inigoes Creek, along with parts of bodies found in the river. In 1940 the U.S. Navy erected a monument over this burial site, making it officially the smallest U.S. national cemetery.

8N. POINT LOOKOUT HOSPITAL AND PRISON CAMP

The cemetery is located on the west side of Rt. 5 about 8 miles south of St. Inigoes. The park visitor center is about 1 mile further and the site of the hospital is at the end of the road. The park is open year-round and the visitor center is open daily 10 a.m. to 6 p.m. in the summer, but only on weekends in April, May, September, and October. 301-872-5688.

Point Lookout is the southernmost point of Maryland—a triangle of marsh and sand at the confluence of the Potomac River with the Chesapeake Bay. Before the Civil War there was a popular seaside resort located there, with more than 100 summer cottages and a large hotel. In 1862 the U.S. government leased the property and began construction of a hospital.

Monument to Confederate P.O.W.s, Point Lookout

Fifteen rectangular ward buildings were arranged like the spokes of a wheel around a hub containing a chapel, library, and kitchen. The hospital began receiving patients August 17, 1862, and continued throughout the war. It was named Hammond General Hospital after Surgeon General W. A. Hammond.

In July 1863 a prisoner of war camp, Camp Hoffman, was established by the Union at Point Lookout to hold up to 10,000 prisoners at a time, although from April 1864 until the end of the war it held more than 20,000. A board fence enclosed 23 acres in which there were six wood buildings which served as dining halls and kitchens. The prisoners lived in tents. When smallpox broke out in the camp an isolated hospital was set up outside the fence, and the sick were attended by the nearby Sisters of Charity. In the summer of 1864 the prisoners were set the task of building fortifications around the camp and hospital. These earthworks were called Fort Lincoln.

Over 50,000 prisoners passed through the camp during the two years it was in operation, and, by the end of the war, 3,384 Confederate prisoners had died and were buried in a cemetery outside the camp. The bodies had to be moved about twenty years later because of river erosion. Two monuments can be seen marking the current location of the cemetery next to Rt. 5—the Maryland Monument erected by the state in 1876, and the U.S. Monument erected by the Federal government in 1911 which lists the names of all of the people buried there.

80. SOTTERLEY PLANTATION

From Point Lookout travel north on Rt. 5 seven miles to Rt. 235. Take Rt. 235 north 20 miles and turn right on Rt. 245 at Hollywood. Travel east 6 miles and follow the signs to the plantation which is open to the public and is run by the Sotterley Foundation. There is a fee. Call 301-373-2280 for hours.

During the Civil War there were many plantations along the rivers and streams in southern Maryland, but most are now gone or changed beyond recognition. Sotterley has fortunately been preserved and is a good example of what these rural plantations looked like and how they operated. Sotterley Plantation still retains its vista to the Patuxent River, its gatehouses, formal gardens, and even one of Maryland's very few original slave quarters. The original part of the house dates back to 1717 and was added to in 1727 and in the second half of the 19th century.

Since the 18th century there had been a deep-water wharf on the Patuxent River at the plantation. When steamships began plying the Chesapeake Bay in the 1830s the Weems Line had a run up the Patuxent River and would regularly stop at the Sotterley landing. Steamships continued to stop there intermittently until well into the 20th century.

The owners of the plantation during the Civil War were Dr. Walter Hanson Stone Briscoe and his wife, Emeline Dallum Briscoe. Three of their sons, Henry, Chapman, and David Stone Briscoe, were soldiers in the Confederate army. Although there is no recorded evidence, Sotterley could possibly have been a stop on the secret Confederate mail line, because of the Briscoe's obvious Southern sympathy and the proximity of a deep-water wharf where steamboats stopped. Family stories relate how Dr. Briscoe was hidden in the attic by the family during visits by Union soldiers so that he would not be arrested. In the dining room of the house a secret space carved out of the bottom of a pilaster provided a hiding place for important papers.

8P. CALVERT MARINE MUSEUM

From Sotterley return to Rt. 235 and travel south 4 miles. Turn left on Rt. 4, cross the bridge across the Patuxent River and follow the signs to the museum to the right. Open daily 10 a.m. to 5 p.m. There is a fee. 410-326-4702.

Although the Calvert Maritime Museum has no exhibits relating specifically to the Civil War, it does display the maritime histories of the Patuxent River and the Chesapeake Bay, and has examples of many of the types of boats that were used during the time of the war by Confederates for smuggling and raiding—such as log boats and brogans (see site #9F for descriptions of boats). The Drum Point Lighthouse, typical of lighthouse design in the 19th century, has been moved to the museum and there are pictures of past lighthouses of southern Maryland, including some that were raided by the Confederates. Cruises are available to the mouth of the Patuxent River aboard an authentic "bugeye" sailing craft.

There was a military camp during the war at the mouth of Battle Creek, and a prisoner of war camp at "Prison Point." Brooke Manor, across Battle Creek from the camp, is reported to have been a Confederate smuggling base.

On March 31, 1865, Confederate raiders aboard a yawl they claimed was sinking came alongside the 115-ton schooner *St. Mary's*. The raiders boarded the trading ship and took her over along with her cargo of $20,000 worth of merchandise. The Confederate leader was Master John C. Braine, CSN, who had been privateering along the Atlantic coast since 1863. Abandoning their yawl the raiders sailed the schooner down the bay and into the Atlantic Ocean where they captured another schooner and placed the crew of the *St. Mary's* aboard her after having robbed both crews of their valuables. The *St. Mary's* ended up in the Bahama Islands at the end of the war.

8Q. FAIRHAVEN

From Solomons take Rt. 4 north 26 miles. Turn right on Rt. 2 and travel north 5 miles. Turn right on Rt. 423 and travel 2 miles to Fairhaven.

In 1839 the steamboat magnate George Weems founded a summer resort at Fair Haven (original name of Fairhaven) on the Maryland shore of the Chesapeake Bay halfway between Baltimore and the Patuxent River.

The capture of the *St. Nicholas* by the Confederate raiders Capt. George Hollins and Richard Thomas Zarvona on June 28, 1861 (see site #8M) had Union officials on guard. They knew that Zarvona and his men were still on the loose in the Chesapeake Bay area and out for more prey. So when reports came to Baltimore police that Zarvona had been seen in Fair Haven, Lt. John Carmichael and John Horner set out for the resort with a detachment of police on July 4. Since they were out of their jurisdiction their avowed objective was the arrest of a barber by the name of Neale Green, vacationing at Fair Haven, for his part in the Baltimore riot of April 19. The party arrested Green and took him aboard the steamer *Mary Washington* bound for Baltimore. The suspicions of the police were confirmed when several passengers on the boat, former members of the crew of the *St. Nicholas*, informed them that Zarvona was aboard in disguise. When Carmichael ordered the steamer to dock at Fort McHenry instead of the Baltimore dock, Zarvona confronted him with a drawn pistol. The other police officers drew their weapons, as did Zarvona's men, and there was a stand-off as women ran screaming to their cabins. Finally other passengers and crew overwhelmed Zarvona and his men and they were held at bay until the ship docked. But Zarvona had disappeared. After an hour and a half search he was finally located hiding in a bureau in the ladies' cabin.

Another incident occurred at Fair Haven before the war was over. On the night of April 4, 1865, Capt. Thaddeus Fitzhugh, CSA, with Lieutenant Dutton and 28 Confederates, mainly from Company F of the 5th Regiment Virginia cavalry, stormed aboard the brand-new steamship *Harriet Deford*, docked overnight at Fair Haven, and captured her, putting ashore the captain and mate and all the white passengers. Retaining the engineer, fireman, and about 60 free black men and their families, the Confederates steamed down the bay with the ship. The Potomac Flotilla, commanded by Foxhall Parker, gave chase with 10 patrol boats, finally locating the steamer on April 7 in Dimer's Creek (now Indian Creek), Virginia, wrecked and burned.

SUGGESTED READING

Cooling, Benjamin Franklin III. *Mr. Lincoln's Forts: A Guide to the Civil War Defenses of Washington.* Shippensburg, Pa.: White Mane Publishing Co., 1988.

Holly, David C. *Tidewater by Steamboat: A Saga of the Chesapeake Bay,* Baltimore: Johns Hopkins University Press, 1991.

Klapthor, Margaret Brown, and Paul Dennis Brown. *The History of Charles County, Maryland.* La Plata, Md.: Charles County Tercentenary, Inc., 1958.

Mills, Eric. *Chesapeake Bay in the Civil War.* Centreville, Md.: Tidewater Publishers, 1996.

Posey, Calvert, and Judith L. *A History of the Role Charles County Played in the Civil War,* Self-published (no date).

Steers, Edward, Jr., and Joan L. Chaconas. *The Escape & Capture of John Wilkes Booth.* Marker Tours, revised May 1989.

Steers, Edward, Jr. *His Name is Still Mudd: The Case Against Dr. Samuel Alexander Mudd.* Gettysburg, Pa.: Thomas Publications, 1997.

Tidwell, William A. *April '65: Confederate Covert Action in the American Civil War.* Kent, Ohio: Kent State University Press, 1995.

Tidwell, William A., James O. Hall, and David Winfred Gaddy. *Come Retribution: Confederate Secret Service and the Assassination of Lincoln.* Oxford: University Press of Mississippi, 1988.

FOR INFORMATION ON OTHER SITES, ACCOMMODATIONS, ETC.

Calvert County Tourism
175 Main Street
Prince Frederick, MD 20678
800-331-9771,   410-535-4583
www.co.cal.md.us

Calvert County Historical Soc.
P.O. Box 358
Prince Frederick, MD 20678
410-535-2542

Charles County Tourism
P.O. Box B
LaPlata, MD 20646
800-766-3386,   301-645-0558
www.govt.co.charles.md.us

Prince George's County Conference
   and Visitors Bureau
9200 Basil Court, Suite 101
Largo, MD 20774
301-925-8300

Prince George's County Historical
   Society
5626 Bell Station Road
Glendale, MD 20769
301-464-0590

St. Mary's County Historical Soc.
P.O. Box 212
Leonardtown, MD 20650
301-474-2467

St. Mary's County Tourism
P.O. Box 653
Leonardtown, MD 20650
800-327-9023, 301-475-4411

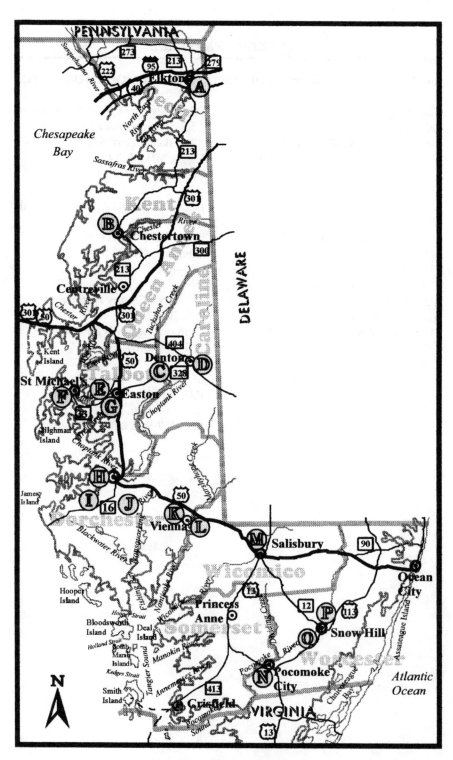

Eastern Shore

CHAPTER 9

EASTERN SHORE
Counties of
CAROLINE, CECIL, DORCHESTER, KENT,
QUEEN ANNE, SOMERSET, TALBOT,
WICOMICO, and WORCESTER

The Eastern Shore of Maryland had for centuries prior to the Civil War been a farming and fishing area, providing seafood, tobacco, and wheat to the mainland. Small isolated fishing villages sat at the mouths of rivers and along inlets, their only contact with the mainland being by water. Many shipbuilders in these towns enjoyed a wide reputation as builders of unique swift sailing vessels. Large plantations dotted the many rivers and creeks, their vast farmlands sweeping inland from the banks of the waterways. It had also been for centuries the home of pirates, slave kidnappers, and smugglers who knew the intricate waterways of "the Shore" (the Eastern Shore) intimately and could elude capture with ease.

At the outbreak of the Civil War most of the Eastern Shore was still isolated from the mainland, but steamships now visited many of the towns frequently, stimulating a new industry in packing and canning. Early in 1861 the Delaware Railroad had reached Salisbury, bringing commerce to the immediate area along the tracks, and providing a vehicle for Union troops to be transported to the center of what could have been a dangerous stronghold of the Confederacy.

In regard to sympathies for the North or South during the war, the Eastern Shore was a patchwork of allegiances. Several Quaker settlements had spread the concept of the evil of slavery, and the recent economic boost to farming and fishing industries in the area had strengthened people's confidence in the Union. On the other hand, it was an area dominated by slavery. The most powerful men were those who owned large plantations and many slaves. Also, being so isolated, the people of the Shore were fiercely independent. Many men from the Shore "went South" to join the Confederate army, but many also stayed home and made up the core of the 1st and 2nd Eastern Shore Home Guard. There were no large areas that could specifically be called pro-Union or pro-Confederacy—divisions occurred within families, towns, and counties throughout the Eastern Shore. Many volunteers for the U.S. Colored Troops also came from the shore, and some regiments were trained at Camp Upton in Salisbury, Camp Kirby in Easton, or other camps on the Shore.

During the summer of 1861 attempts were made by the U.S. military to assure that the Maryland Eastern Shore would remain in the Union. Several times troops were sent by steamer to the Eastern Shore to gather up the arms of local militia and disperse those units. In August 1861 Brig. Gen. Henry H. Lockwood, a Delaware man, was stationed at Cambridge where he established a training camp for volunteers for the U.S. Army. The 1st Regiment, Eastern Shore Infantry was commissioned in September, with Lockwood in command. It served mainly on the Shore until it was called to Gettysburg in July 1863. Lockwood was succeeded by Col. James Wallace. The 2nd Regiment Eastern Shore Infantry was commissioned in December 1861, with Col. Edward Wilkins in command; it also served mainly on the Shore until called to duty in the Shenandoah Valley campaign in the spring of 1863.

The myriad rivers, creeks, swamps, and inlets of the Eastern Shore made it ripe territory for smuggling from the very beginning of the war. The smuggling was fairly flagrant until General Dix sent 4,500 Union troops under the command of Brig. Gen. Henry Lockwood to the Eastern Shore in November 1861, to restore Federal authority in the Maryland section of the Shore and take control of the Virginia section of the Shore. The Federal troops were headquartered at Camp Upton in Salisbury and consisted of regiments from Wisconson, Michigan, Indiana, Massachusetts, New York, Delaware, and the Maryland Eastern Shore. They began their sweep south on November 13 expecting to encounter an estimated 1,500 to 3,000 rebel troops reported to be training south of the border between the two states, as well as smugglers and Southern sympathizers. But most of the enemy had gotten wind of the impending invasion and had moved out, felling trees across roads and burning bridges in their wake—all except about 175 local militia in Virginia who were captured. By November 22 the bloodless expedition had reached the southern tip of the Shore and manned the Cape Charles Lighthouse, making commerce on the Chesapeake Bay safe once again.

Some smuggling continued even after military occupation, as it had in the region for centuries. Because of the difficulty of policing the hundreds of hiding places in the waterways of the Shore some clandestine activities were never curtailed, but some captures were still made periodically throughout the war by troops stationed in Cambridge and Salisbury and by the Potomac Flotilla on the Chesapeake Bay (see sites #8L and #8M).

Caroline County

Mainly because of the influence of its many resident Quakers Caroline County was strictly for the Union during the war. Its location inland, away from navigable rivers, also protected it from smuggling activities and armed invasions. The only monument dedicated exclusively to Union soldiers on the Eastern Shore graces the top of a hill in the Hillcrest Cemetery in the center of Federalsburg. The marble statue is of a Union private soldier standing at parade rest, erected in about 1910 by the Federal Post of the Grand Army of the Republic (Union veterans). Federalsburg had adopted its name in 1780 during the Constitution debates.

Cecil County

At the northern end of the Chesapeake Bay and bordered by both Pennsylvania and Delaware, Cecil County was overwhelmingly pro-Union during the Civil War. More than 1,500 men from the county fought for the Union, mainly in the 5th and 6th Maryland Infantry, and Snow's Battery of the 1st Maryland Artillery. Cecil County had given more than its quota of volunteers by the 1862 draft.

Cecil County boasted four ranking officers in the Union army: Brig. Gen. Andrew Wallace Evans of the 1st Maryland Cavalry, and Brig. Gen. (brevet) James Watt Horn, Col. Joseph C. Hill, and Col. George R. Howard, all of the 6th Maryland Infantry. Also from the county was the Confederate Gen. William Whann McKall. One of the most distinguished Civil War personages from the county was a civilian, John A. J. Creswell, state delegate, Congressman, Senator, and adjutant general in charge of raising local troops during the war.

Dorchester County

Cambridge is the commercial center of Dorchester County. A port city for hundreds of years, it was where tobacco was weighed, oysters were shipped out, and slaves were bought and sold. The citizens of the county were of differing opinions during the Civil War. Although many favored the South, volunteers from the county for the Union army accounted for at least five companies: Companies A, B, C of the 1st Eastern Shore Infantry, and Companies G and H of the 2nd Eastern Shore Infantry. Camp Wallace was established in Cambridge in 1861 and curtailed smuggling activities on the Choptank River, but the Nanticoke River to the south continued to harbor smugglers throughout the war.

Gov. Thomas Holliday Hicks, Col. James Wallace, USA, of the 1st Eastern Shore Infantry, and Col. Clement Sullivane, CSA, of the 21st Virginia Regiment, were from Dorchester County. The county is also the birthplace of

Harriet Tubman, famous for leading more than 300 slaves to freedom. Anna Ella Carroll's family had a summer home (burned) in the county and she is buried at Trinity Church.

Kent County

It is recorded that Kent County filled the muster rolls of five companies in the 2nd Eastern Shore Infantry, USA (Companies A, B, C, D, E). Although the exact number is not known, probably less than 100 men from the county fought for the Confederacy. The county had given more Union army volunteers than its quota by the 1862 draft. Gen. George Vickers, USA, and Col. Edward Wilkens, USA, were both from Kent County and their graves can be found in the Chestertown Cemetery west of town. General Vickers helped to form and became the leader of the 2nd Eastern Shore Infantry Regiment, USA, of which Wilkens was second in command. The regiment fought in the Shenandoah Valley campaign as well as serving at home protecting the Eastern Shore.

After the war, Vickers was elected by the Maryland legislature to fill the vacant seat in the U.S. Senate after the Senate had refused to seat Philip Francis Thomas in 1867. Arriving by ice boat and special train, Vickers was just on time to cast his vote of "not guilty" in the Andrew Johnson impeachment proceedings.

Queen Anne's County

Queen Anne's County was of mixed allegiance during the war, though not as heavily Union as the two counties above it, Cecil and Kent. Before the 1862 draft, 76 men from the county had volunteered for the Union army (the county's quota was 405).

There were two instances that demonstrated the Confederate leaning of some of the local citizens. On the eve of the war a local militia, the Smallwood Rifles, had been formed and they had amassed 50 kegs of powder, as well as a number of weapons, to prepare for the protection of the residents of the county. This was stored at the county courthouse in Centreville. When a company of Federal soldiers came to collect the weaponry and ammunition on June 11, 1861, it was discovered that 30 kegs of powder had disappeared. On the morning of election day in November 1861 Southern sympathizers Madison Brown and John Palmer were arrested by soldiers for the theft of the powder, but the powder was never found. These were two of the arrests objected to by Judge Carmichael which later led to the judge himself being taken into custody (see site #9Ga).

On July 2, 1861, three companies of the 8th Massachusetts steamed across the bay from Baltimore on the *Hugh Jenkins*, docked about a mile up the Wye River and arrested Ogle S. Tilghman, captain of the local militia, after searching his house and finding two guns. Tilghman was taken to Fort McHenry.

Maj. Gen. William Hemsley Emory, USA, was from Queen Anne's County.

Somerset County

Being so close to Virginia the residents of Somerset generally favored the South. And of course much smuggling went on, as it had for generations, from the Manokin, Nanticoke, and other Rivers. Chrisfield was a special hotbed of such intrigue, and Deal Island was often a meeting place for dealers in smuggled goods. Bradford Barracks was a Union soldier camp near Princess Anne.

Anna Ella Carroll and Maj. Gen. Arnold Elzy, CSA, were both born in Somerset County. Kingston Hall, the childhood home of Anna Ella Carroll, is in Kingston. Elmwood, the Jones estate (Arnold Elzy was born Arnold Elzy Jones) is on Locust Point on the Manokin River near Champ. Their homes are now private residences.

Talbot County

Much of the Civil War activity in Talbot County centered around Easton, where there was a camp of Union soldiers. The steamship landing on the Miles River, just above Easton, was used to transport troops and prisoners.

Admiral Franklin Buchanan, CSN; Gen. Charles Sidney Winder, CSA; Brig. Gen. Lloyd Tilghman, CSA; Col. A. B. Hardcastle, CSA; Col. Charles Sears, CSA; Maj. A. C. C. Thompson, CSA; Capt. John W. Bennett, CSN; and Dr. Edward Napoleon Covey, surgeon general of the Confederate cavalry, were all from Talbot County. On the Union side, veteran of the Mexican War Captain James T. Slover, pilot of the USS *Monitor* after that ship's battle with the *Merrimac*, was from St. Michaels.

"The Rest," home of Adm. Franklin Buchanan is on the Miles River on the west side of Unionville Road (Rt. 370) three miles west of Easton. It is a private residence but there is a historical marker on the road next to the property.

Adm. Franklin Buchanan and Gen. Charles Sidney Winder are buried in the Wye House Cemetery on Rt. 370, about six miles northwest of Easton.

175

Wicomico County

Wicomico County was formed from part of Somerset and Worcester Counties in 1867. Gen. John Henry Winder, CSA, was born and raised at his family's home, "Rewston" (now a private residence), in the part of Somerset County that is now Wicomico County.

Worcester County

Since Worcester County forms the border between Maryland and Virginia, there were many family ties across the line and many men from the area actually went over that line to join the Confederate forces. Many who stayed, such as Dr. Costen, helped in the Confederate cause as best they could. Union troops were quartered at various times at Camp Halleck at New Town (Pocomoke City), Snow Hill, and at the Coventry Church in Rehobeth.

9A. SHERIFF JOHN DEWITT MUSEUM

135 Main Street, Elkton. Elkton is at the northern end of the Chesapeake Bay and can be reached from exit #109 of I-95. Rt. 40 runs through the south side of the town. The museum is open Monday and Thursday afternoons, Tuesday evenings, and the fourth Saturday. 410-398-1790. www.cchistory.org

This small museum, opened in 1992, contains displays of military gear and weapons—from the Civil War to Desert Storm. It is a unique collection and has displays of a number of Civil War artifacts. The museum adjoins the Cecil County Historical Society and is dedicated to Cecil County veterans of all wars.

John A. J. Creswell was a lawyer and a Unionist delegate to the Maryland legislature in 1861. In 1862 he was appointed assistant adjutant-general, charged with raising troops in the area, and was elected to Congress in 1863 and the Senate in 1865. Creswell is buried in the Presbyterian Cemetery on Main Street in Elkton, and his home, "Creswell Hall," is on Delaware Avenue between Main Street and Rt. 40 south of Elkton. Gen. William Whall McKall, CSA, was born and raised at "Wilna," near Childs on Blue Ball Road (Rt. 545) three miles north of Elkton. Both Wilna and Creswell Hall are private residences.

9B. CHESTERTOWN MONUMENT

From Elkton travel south 28 miles on Rt. 213 and turn right on High Street. From the Bay Bridge travel east on Rt. 301 and turn north on Rt. 213. Travel for 16 miles, then turn right on High Street in Chestertown. The monument in High Street Memorial Park is in front of the courthouse.

This monument to the men of Kent County who fought in the Civil War—both Union and Confederate—was donated to the city in 1917 by Judge James Alfred Pearce. Judge Pearce had not himself fought in the war, but his father, U.S. Senator from 1843 until his death in 1862, had been an ardent critic of martial law in Maryland and especially on the Eastern Shore. The monument was a peace offering according to its sponsor who said he hoped to "draw together the minds and hearts of our reunited people" with this tribute. The names of 37 Confederate soldiers are listed on one side of the monument, and the names of 22 Union soldiers are listed on the other side, with the common epitaph, "Under the sod the Blue and Gray, waiting alike the Judgement Day." Obviously, not all of the soldiers from the county are listed on the monument, as actually many more men from Kent County fought for the Union than for the Confederacy.

9C. SITE OF TUCKAHOE—BIRTHPLACE OF FREDERICK DOUGLASS

From Chestertown go south on Rt. 213 until it intersects with Rt. 50. Take Rt. 50 south 2 miles and turn left (east) on Rt. 404. Take Rt. 404 five miles east, following the Queen Anne business route, and turn right on Old Cordova Road (Rt. 303). Tapper's Corner is about 2 miles south where Old Cordova Road meets Lewistown Road. Tuckahoe was in this area, probably reaching east to the Tuckahoe River.

Frederick Augustus Washington Bailey was born as a slave at the plantation "Tuckahoe" in 1817, the son of Harriet Bailey and probably a white father. At the age of seven he was sent to his master's brother's house in Baltimore. When he was grown he was sent back to the Eastern Shore and escaped from there in 1838, ultimately finding a home in Bedford, Massachusetts where he changed his name to Frederick Douglass and wrote an autobiography describing his life in bondage (*Narrative of the Life of Frederick Douglass, an American Slave*). After a brief sojourn in England he returned to the United States and purchased his freedom. Douglass was an ardent spokesman for the cause of freedom from slavery. Through his writing and speeches he probably did more for freedom and civil rights than any other person of his time. Later in life he was Minister to Haiti and Recorder of Deeds in Washington, D.C.

In his autobiography, Douglass gives detailed descriptions of slave life on the Eastern Shore and of Wye House, the plantation of Col. Edward Lloyd, V, which Douglass often visited since his master worked for and leased his own farm from Colonel Lloyd.

9D. NECK MEETING HOUSE

Return to Rt. 404 and continue east 6 miles to Denton, taking the business route to Meeting House Road. Open Monday through Friday from 8 a.m. to 5 p.m. 410-820-8899.

This one-room Quaker Meeting House and its grounds were used as a camp by Union soldiers in 1861, and a site of abolitionist meetings before the war. It was built in 1802, one of the earliest places of worship built by the Society of Friends in America. It is in Caroline County. The Quakers definitely had an influence on the allegiances of the people of Caroline County. The county had very few of its men go over to the South and had very little trouble during the war.

9E. UNIONVILLE

From Denton travel south on Rt. 328 to Rt. 50. Turn right, then left onto the Easton Parkway (Rt. 322). Following the signs for St. Michaels turn right onto Rt. 33. After 2 miles turn right onto Unionville Road (Rt. 370). Cross the bridge across the Miles River and the Unionville A.M.E. Church is on the right about 1 mile beyond.

You won't find it on a map but the little town of Unionville has a very special history. After the Civil War many black veterans were not treated with the same respect as white veterans, and were not given employment after the war like their white counterparts. One white Union veteran by the name of John Cowgill tried to rectify the wrongs inflicted on his comrades-at-arms by giving seventeen black veterans parcels of land from his own property in Talbot County. These seventeen brought their families to the land, built houses, a school and a church, and called their village Unionville after the Union they had fought to protect. Today the graves of these black veterans can be found in the cemetery surrounding the little St. Stephens African Methodist Episcopal Church next to the road.

9F. CHESAPEAKE MARITIME MUSEUM

Return to Rt. 33 and turn right. Continue 7 miles to St. Michaels. Turn right on Mill Street in the center of town. The museum is open from 9 a.m to 4, 5, or 6 p.m. depending on the season. For more information call 410-745-2916. www.cbmm.org

"Fly"

This large outdoor and indoor museum has both originals and replicas of vessels that were probably used by locals to smuggle goods and people across the bay to the Confederacy. The collection includes log sailing canoes, sloops, pungies, and doryboats.

The log sailing canoes were from 30 to 40 feet long (the "brogan" type was 50 feet long with a cabin forward), made of from three to seven logs, and one or two masts with triangular sails. No inside framing or decks gave them more room for cargo and the double-ended hull made them extremely maneuverable. The log canoe, when not sailing, was propelled by a single sculling paddle worked by a man standing aft.

The sloop went back to the 18th century. It was a small sailing vessel with a deck and a cabin, but with only one mast. Pungies were developed in the 1840s and were deep-draft sailing vessels with two masts. These sleek boats were very fast, but could not go into shallow water because of their large keels. The favorite boat of the smugglers was the doryboat—flat-bottomed, two-masted, and about 20-25 feet long. They were fast, maneuverable, and could be hidden in shallow inlets and creeks. Sometimes the sails would be made of black cloth, and the hull painted black so that the boat could travel at night without being seen. A doryboat like this would be called a "Black Nancy."

There is a display in the "History Building" about blockade running, as well as a small tribute to Adm. Franklin Buchanan, CSN, with models of the *Monitor* and *Merrimac* (*Virginia*) and a cannonball from the battle between the two ships. Exploring the entire museum usually takes a full day and a fine restaurant is located on the site.

9G. EASTON

From St. Michaels return on Rt. 33 to the Easton parkway, but go straight across the intersection into Easton. Turn right on Washington Street and the courthouse is on the right.

Easton, the county seat of Talbot County, was a town occupied by soldiers and divided in sentiments during the Civil War. Union soldiers were stationed at Camp Kirby near Easton and would periodically visit the town on their off hours. According to a local history many of the ladies in town favored the South, it being the fashionable thing to do in the local high society, while their husbands supported the Union. At one point the provost marshal hung a large United States flag over the sidewalk in front of the hotel and many women took to the street rather than walk under it. Union supporting women, mainly from outside the town, formed the "Ladies Union Relief" society which brought food to the soldiers in the neighboring camps.

Easton Courthouse

An indication of the division between residents was the rivalry between the Unionist newspaper, *The Easton Gazette,* and the Democratic newspaper, *The Easton Star,* which is quite evident from their articles and news coverage. The editor of the *Easton Star,* Thomas K. Robson, was arrested in May 1863, and taken under armed guard to Easton Point where he was put on the steamer *Balloon* and taken to Fort McHenry. He was later released to the South where he spent the remainder of the war. The office of the *Easton Star* was ransacked. The arrest was supposedly directed by an order from President Lincoln himself, and was due to Robson's continual criticism of the Union and praise of the South in his editorials. In July 1862 Robson had printed on the front page of the paper a poem by 16-year-old John Martin of Trappe honoring the late Col. Turner Ashby, CSA.

Before it was clear that Maryland would not secede from the Union in the spring of 1861, General Tilghman suggested that the arms of the local militia at the Easton armory be seized by the self-appointed "Safety Committee" and made ready for use by the state of Maryland. Tilghman had already "gone South" and was not at hand when, on June 9, 1861, part of the 13th New York Regiment, under the command of Col. Abel Smith, arrived at the Miles River Landing, marched to Easton and seized all of the arms which had been so recently spruced up. The arms consisted of a number of old muskets and five or six cannon from the War of 1812. There was no active protest by the citizens, nor any injuries.

a. THE EASTON COURTHOUSE

The Easton Courthouse is famous in Maryland Civil War lore for being the site of the vicious arrest of Judge Carmichael. Judge Richard Bennett Carmichael was a very respected barrister with a distinguished Eastern Shore family lineage. During the state elections in November 1861, soldiers guarding the polls arrested many local people for being "disloyal." Carmichael—judge of the 7th district which included Talbot, Caroline, Queen Anne's, and Kent Counties—charged the grand juries of his courts not only to release those arrested, but to regard such arrests without warrants as crimes in themselves. The arresting soldiers who were served with bills of presentment were quickly reassigned elsewhere, but the bills had been published in the local papers for all to see.

Six months later, on Monday, May 26, 1862, the deputy provost marshal of Baltimore, James McPhail, and three of his officers burst into Judge Carmichael's courtroom at the Easton Courthouse and demanded that he surrender into their custody. When the judge asked what the charges were one of McPhail's men, James Bishop, jumped up to the bench and grabbed the judge by the beard. Carmichael resisted this insult to his person by kicking the assailant, who then beat the judge with his revolver until he lay unconscious on the floor. Prosecuting attorney Isaac C. W. Powell, who tried to help the judge, was also beaten. Both men were arrested and taken to Baltimore on the steamer *Balloon*. Judge Carmichael was held at Fort McHenry for six weeks, then taken to Fort Lafayette and Fort Delaware where he was released six months later, never having been tried.

The center section of the present courthouse is the part that existed during the Civil War, the wings having been added in 1958. The courthouse was built in 1794 as a two-story, five-bay brick structure topped by an open octagonal cupola. At the time of the war the clock was located in the pediment over the door instead of on the cupola, and the door and flanking windows were not arched; otherwise it looks today almost the same as it did in 1862. Judge Carmichael's courtroom is in the center section on the second floor. It is open to the public during business hours when court is not in session.

b. EASTON CONFEDERATE MONUMENT

The monument in front of the courthouse was erected in 1913 by a committee headed by Confederate veteran Oswald Tilghman. The bronze standard bearer, "a representation of youthful exuberance as portrayed in Longfellow's 'Excelsior'," was chosen by the committee to represent the Confederate soldiers of Talbot County because of an incident that occurred at the Battle of Gettysburg. On July 3, 1863, Talbot County men in the 2nd Maryland Infantry, CSA, fought on Culp's Hill against Talbot County men in the 1st Eastern Shore Infantry, USA. The color bearer for Trappe's Company H of the Union regiment was Robert W. Ross, and the color bearer for the Confederates was his cousin Percolus M. Moore, both from the Trappe area. "For long minutes as the struggle raged they stood almost face to face, while all around them boyhood friends from Trappe tried desperately to kill each other." Sergeant Moore was fatally wounded in the fight. Moore is listed on the monument along with 84 others. Talbot County had more than 300 sons who enlisted in the Union army, but not enough money could be raised to erect a monument to them.

9H. CAMBRIDGE
From Easton take Rt. 50 twenty miles south to Cambridge.
  Camp Wallace was established at Cambridge in the fall of 1861, after James Wallace organized the 1st Eastern Shore Infantry.
  Cambridge was founded in 1684 and served as a customs collection point before the Revolutionary War. It is a seafaring town centered around the Long Wharf on the Choptank River. Harriet Tubman arrived by boat at Long Wharf on one of her missions to help slaves escape to freedom, and came just in time to rescue her sister who was being auctioned at the courthouse stairs (206 High Street). Two blocks of lovely 18th- and 19th-century Georgian and Federal-style homes line the brick-paved High Street leading up to the Wharf.
  A self-guided walking tour is available from the Dorchester County Tourism Office, 501 Court Street (800-522-TOUR). Neither the courthouse nor Christ Church are the same buildings that were there during the Civil War, but most of the houses are original.
  There are two Cambridge natives famous for their Civil War activities who are buried in the city—Col. James Wallace, USA, and Col. Clement Sullivane, CSA, as well as Governor Hicks (#c). Wallace and Hicks are buried in Cambridge Cemetery, Cemetery Avenue and Academy Street. Sullivane is buried in Christ Church Cemetery, 213 High Street.

a. MEREDITH HOUSE—Dorchester County Historical Society
The house is in Cambridge, 16 miles south of Easton on Rt. 50. After crossing the Choptank River turn left (east) onto Maryland Avenue and follow several blocks to LaGrange Avenue where you make a left, then a quick right to the parking area. The house is operated by the Dorchester County Historical Society and is open 10 a.m. to 4 p.m. Thursday through Saturday year-round. 410-228-7953.

There is a room on the second floor of this 1850s house that is dedicated to the Maryland governors who came from Dorchester County. In the room can be found Governor Hick's writing desk, settee, and his wife's inaugural gown, as well as other memorabilia from this and other governors from Dorchester County. The house is decorated in mid-19th century style and is a good example of aristocratic sea-town life of the time.

The Dorchester County Historical Society sponsors periodic displays at the house that often feature the Civil War in this area.

b. BRANNOCK MUSEUM

210 Talbot Avenue, Cambridge. From the Meredith House take Maryland Avenue west into Cambridge, turn right onto High Street and turn left at the Long Wharf onto Water Street. Continue ten blocks west and turn left on Talbot Avenue. The museum is two blocks on the left. Open by appointment by calling 410-228-6938.

This little private museum is dedicated to Dorchester County's contributions to the US and CS navies and the "Oyster Navy" that policed the Chesapeake Bay, after the war. It features displays on Lt. Hunter Davidson, CSN, commander of the CSS *Teaser*, inventer of torpedoes, and the first leader of the post-war Oyster Navy; and Captain James Waddell, CSN, commander of the CSS *Shenandoah*. The museum also has an excellent research library.

c. APPLEBY

317 East Appleby Avenue, Cambridge. From Rt. 50 in Cambridge turn right (west) onto Rt. 343. Go for .25 mile and turn left onto Rt. 341 (Race Street). Go six short blocks to turn left onto Appleby Avenue. The house is on the left. This is a private residence.

Appleby was the home of Thomas Holliday Hicks, governor of Maryland from 1858 to 1862. Hicks moved there from Vienna, Maryland (site #9K) in the 1850s after being elected registrar of wills for Dorchester County. He was born near East New Market. He retained the house until his death.

When civil war seemed pending and the secession of Maryland from the Union a possibility in the early spring of 1861, Governor Hicks refused to call the Maryland General Assembly into special session for fear that the legislators might vote for secession. The legislature of Maryland was thus not able to meet until late April, and by that time it had to meet in Frederick because Annapolis, the state capital, had been taken over by Federal military forces.

The legislators did not vote for secession, but voted instead to issue a proclamation stating that they did not have the power to do so, and that a special state convention would have to be called (see Kemp Hall, site #5Fc).

After seemingly secessionist acts such as agreeing to the burning of the railroad bridges north of Baltimore in April 1861, and opposing the landing of General Butler in Baltimore in May 1861, Governor Hicks turned, by September 1861, into a staunch Union supporter. He had been elected into office by the Nativist or "Know Nothing" party. After his term as governor was over he was elected to the U.S. Senate in 1862 and served until his death

Statue of Governor Hicks

in 1865. After his death the Maryland legislature appropriated funds to commission a statue of the former governor to be placed over his grave in Cambridge Cemetery (Cemetery Avenue and Academy Street).

9I. OLD TRINITY CHURCH CEMETERY

Return to Rt. 50, south, and turn right on Church Creek Road (Rt. 16). Go 5.3 miles southwest from Cambridge and the church is on the right.

Anna Ella Carroll is buried in the cemetery between the church and the river. Anna Ella Carroll was best known as an advisor to President Lincoln, although she had been a respected journalist for many years before the war. She wrote several treatises defending Lincoln's war-making powers and advising on military strategy. She devised the Tennessee campaign of the Union army, but her authorship was kept secret. Although it was well known that President Lincoln consulted with Anna on various military matters, she never received any official recognition for her role in the

Grave of Anna Ella Carroll

war. Her outrageous trespassing into matters formerly the exclusive territory of men made her a dynamic symbol for the women's movement. She was born in Somerset County, Maryland, and lived most of her life in Baltimore. Her epitaph reads: "Maryland's Most Distinguished Lady. A Great Humanitarian and Close Friend of Abraham Lincoln."

Other Civil War graves can be found in this lovely old cemetery of one of the oldest churches in continual operation in the country.

9J. BUCKTOWN—Birthplace of Harriet Tubman

From Rt. 50 in Cambridge turn right on Bucktown Road and travel 8 miles south to the intersection with Greenbriar Road, and a marker is located about 1.5 miles down Greenbriar Road. Tours of the town and of other sites connected with Harriet Tubman's life can be arranged by calling the Harriet Tubman Coalition, 410-228-0401.

A historic marker is placed near the site of Brodess Plantation where Harriet Tubman grew up. Harriet Tubman was called "Moses of her People" because of the 19 trips that she made from the Eastern Shore guiding more than 300 escaping slaves to freedom in the North. Born a slave on a plantation in the Bucktown area in about 1820, Harriet married John Tubman, a free black. She escaped to freedom by herself. Having gained knowledge of the route, this courageous woman continued to return to the Eastern Shore to lead groups of escaping slaves north until the Civil war broke out. She was aided by the Quaker Thomas Garrett, and knew Secretary Seward. John Brown referred to her as one of his soldiers.

During the Civil War Harriet Tubman worked as a nurse, scout and spy for the United States Army in South Carolina. She was sent to the aid of the U.S. Army in the South by Governor Andrew of Massachusetts and was employed by General Hunter, General Stevens, and General Sherman for scouting and spying and aiding in the communication with and transporting of "contrabands" (slaves in the South freed by Federal troops). When not employed in this work she was a nurse at the hospital for contrabands on Hilton Head Island, South Carolina.

9K. VIENNA

Take Rt. 50 fifteen miles southeast from Cambridge and turn right at Rt. 331. Go .5 mile and turn left and then right onto Water Street. The house is at the corner of Water and Church Street. Private residence.

Vienna, on the Nanticoke River, is one of those rare villages that time seems to have passed by. Not only does the town appear almost the same as it did in the 19th century, it also has not been "gentrified" like some of the other sea-towns on the Shore, and so retains its original ambiance of a not-too-affluent fishing community. Anchored on either end by two large, imposing houses, the main street facing the river is lined with modest two-story clapboard homes dating mainly from 1790 to 1850. Founded in 1706 the town was a customs collection point before the Revolutionary War. The British thought the town so important that it was raided both during the Revolutionary War and the War of 1812. A breastwork constructed to protect the town during the latter war can still be seen on the west side of town.

The house where Gov. Thomas Holliday Hicks lived from 1829 until 1840 at the corner of Church and Water Streets has been meticulously restored and is called "Governor's Ordinary" (see "Appleby"). The town of Vienna was a rendezvous site for smugglers in the early part of the war.

9L.   NANTICOKE RIVER
At the Rt. 50 bridge over the river 16 miles southeast of Cambridge.

The Nanticoke River with its wide mouth and numerous inlets was a favorite with smugglers, although all of the creeks and rivers on the eastern side of the Bay were probably used at one time or

Governor's Ordinary, Vienna

another by smugglers. Navigable to Vienna and beyond for some low-draft boats, the Nanticoke provided so many hiding places that we will probably never know just how much smuggling went on from there during the war. Supplies carried on these boats, bound for Virginia, came from many areas in the North. One boat captured by Potomac Flotilla commander Capt. Thomas Ward near Vienna had loaded its goods in Philadelphia. The boats carried everything from pig iron to medical supplies, and sometimes people—both spies and individuals wanting to go South for one reason or another. In the summer of 1862 Baltimore Belle Hetty Cary, who had been visiting friends in Baltimore from her exile in Richmond, used such a boat to get back to Virginia and almost didn't make it as the sloop she was a passenger on was chased and fired upon by a patrol boat as it neared the Virginia shore.

The smugglers' boats were usually sailing log canoes or doryboats, which lay very low in the water and were fast and maneuverable both in the bay and the shallow inlets and creeks. The boats would wait in hidden areas in the many marshes and streams during the day, and race across the Bay at night. The skill of the Eastern Shore captains and their knowledge of the intricate waterways of the Shore made them very difficult to capture if found on open water. Most of the captures of these boats were made when they were docked in hiding places during the day—and several were made around the Nanticoke (see site #9F for descriptions of boats).

Deal Island (formerly known as Devil's Island) at the mouth of the Nanticoke in Tangier Sound was so often visited by smugglers that at one time it was a Confederate supply and exchange station. At the beginning of the war a U.S. collector at Deal Island issued false licenses to Confederate boats, listing Maryland owners.

9M. SALISBURY

Salisbury is 32 miles southeast of Cambridge on Rt. 50. Camp Upton was located at the site of the Times building which stands next to the Wicomico River on the right side of the road after entering the city proper.

Camp Upton was established by General Lockwood in November 1861. It was here that 4,500 Union soldiers were gathered for the invasion of the Virginia Eastern Shore in November 1861. The troops went on to Newtown (Pocomoke City), the closest town to the Virginia border, and launched their invasion from there. The Confederates had been warned of their coming and had disappeared, so the march was without casualty all the way down to the southern tip of the Shore.

Salisbury being the terminus of the Delaware railroad at the time, the camp was kept garrisoned throughout the war. Companies of soldiers would make forays from here into the countryside looking for smugglers and contraband.

Dr. Isaac Costen House

9N. DR. ISAAC COSTEN HOUSE

206 Market Street, Pocomoke City. From Salisbury travel 29 miles south on Rt. 13. After crossing the Pocomoke River the house is three blocks on the right. The house is open by appointment by calling 410-957-0678.

    This fine old house was saved from demolition in 1974 by a dedicated group of citizens, The Spirit of Newtown Committee, which still runs the museum. Pocomoke City was known as Newtown during the Civil War. There was a Union camp outside the town on the banks of the river. Although the house was not built until 1870, it was the house of a well-known Civil War personage in the area, Dr. Isaac Costen, and contains furnishings of the period.

    Dr. Isaac Costen was a respected doctor who had saved many local people during the typhoid epidemic. Even though he was a known Confederate sympathizer he was accepted by the Union army to work at the hospital at Camp Upton in Salisbury and Camp Halleck on Clarke Avenue in Pocomoke City. For several years he and a local bay captain made many trips across the Chesapeake Bay to Virginia in the 40-foot sailing vessel *Fairfield* carrying medical supplies and mail. They would go down the Pocomoke River, hug the shoreline of the bay as far south as Exmore, then dash across to the Rappahannock River. Finally they were sighted and given chase by a Union barge, just barely escaping. His cover blown, Dr. Costen had no choice but to stay in Virginia for the last year of the war, putting his medical skills to practice for the Confederate army. After the war Dr. Costen returned to Pocomoke City, married a local girl and became the first mayor of the town in 1888.

9O. POCOMOKE SWAMP

From Pocomoke City travel northeast on Rt. 364 about 6 miles and the swamp is on the east side of the road.

This swamp has concealed Tories during the Revolutionary War, slaves stolen by Patty Cannon in the early 19th century, escaping slaves before the Civil War, and army deserters and draft evaders during the war. Those who knew the swamp could easily elude pursuers; those who did not know its maze of twisting waterways, forests of cypress trees, and pools of quicksand soon perished.

9P. SNOW HILL

Continue about 6 more miles and turn right on Rt. 12 to go 1 mile to the town.

Snow Hill was a port on the Pocomoke River and was a hotbed of smugglers at the beginning of the war. Goods would come from the North via boat to Chincoteague Bay or via train to Salisbury, then travel overland to Snow Hill were they were secreted down the Pocomoke River and across the Chesapeake Bay to Virginia. In November 1861 an end came to most smuggling in that area when the 4th Wisconsin Regiment, as a part of the general sweep of the Eastern Shore by Federal troops, entered Snow Hill and not only demanded that all of the arms in the area be turned in, but that the citizens of the town repair a bridge which the troops had just passed over with great difficulty. Union troops were known to have camped at Gallows Hill on the southwest side of town.

But the troops did not stay, and the smugglers returned, so the local citizens took matters into their own hands. George W. P. Smith, editor of the Snow Hill Shield, assembled a Union company known as "Smith's Independent Cavalry" on October 15, 1862, to serve for three years. The company served mainly on the Eastern Shore, with some time spent at Point Lookout, Relay, and Barnesville, Maryland, and was never involved in any military action. It was disbanded June 30, 1865.

SUGGESTED READING

Bradford, Sarah. *Harriet Tubman: The Moses of her People.* New York: Citadel Press, 1994 (reprinted from the second edition, 1886).

Douglass, Frederick. *My Bondage and Freedom.* New York: Arno Press, 1968.

Emory, Frederic. *Queen Anne's County, Maryland.* Baltimore: Maryland Historical Society, 1950.

Mills, Eric. *Chesapeake Bay in the Civil War.* Centreville, Md.: Tidewater Publishers, 1996.

Paul, William A. B. *Despot's Heel on Talbot.* Self-published, 1966.

Preston, Dickson J. *Talbot County, A History.* Centreville, Md.: Tidewater Publishers, 1983.

Touart, Paul Baker. *Along the Seaboard Side: The Architectural History of Worcester County, Maryland.* Worcester County, 1994.

Truitt, Dr. Reginald V., and Dr. Millard G. Les Collette. *Worcester County: America's Arcadia.* Snow Hill: Worcester County Historical Society, 1977.

Weeks, Christopher. *Between the Nanticoke and Choptank: An Architectural History of Dorchester County, Maryland.* Baltimore: The Johns Hopkins University Press, 1984.

Weeks, Christopher. *Where Land and Water Intertwine: An Architectural History of Talbot County, Maryland.* Baltimore: The Johns Hopkins University Press, 1984.

Wennersten, John R. *Maryland's Eastern Shore: A Journey in Time and Place.* Centreville, Va.: Tidewater Publishers, 1992.

FOR INFORMATION ON OTHER SITES, ACCOMMODATIONS, ETC.

Caroline County Office of Tourism
218 Market Street
Denton, MD 21629
410-479-0660

Cecil County Tourism Office
Office of Economic Development
129 East Main Street, Room 324
Elkton, MD 21921
800-CECIL-95, 410-996-5300

Dorchester County Tourism
203 Sunburst Highway
Cambridge, MD 21613
800-522-TOUR, 410-228-1000
www.shorenet.net/tourism

Kent County Tourism
400 S. Cross Street, Suite 1
Chestertown, MD 21620
410-778-0416
www.kentcounty.com

Queen Anne's County Office of
Tourism
425 Piney Narrows Road, Suite 3
Chester, MD 21619
410-604-2100
www.qac.org

Somerset County Tourism
P.O. Box 243
Princess Anne, MD 21853
800-521-9189, 410-651-2968
www.skipjack.net/le_shore

Talbot County Conference and
Visitors Bureau
210 Marlboro Avenue, Suite 3
Easton, MD 21601
410-822-4606
www.talbotchamber.org

Wicomico County Convention and
Visitors Bureau
8480 Ocean Highway
Delmar, MD 21875
800-332-TOUR,   410-548-4914
www.co.wicomico.md.us/tourism

Worcester County Tourism Office
105 Pearl Street
Snow Hill, MD 21863
800-852-0335, 410-632-3617
www.skipjack.net/le_shore

Harriet Tubman Coalition, Inc.
424 Race Street
Cambridge, MD 21613
410-228-0401

Kent County Historical Society
101 Church Alley
Chestertown, MD 21520
410-778-3499

Historical Society of Talbot County
25 S. Washington Street
Easton, MD 21601
410-822-0773

APPENDIX A

C & O CANAL SITES

mile

7	Clara Barton House, 4C	69.30	Antietam Village, 6D
14.30	Great Falls Tavern (Crommelin House), 4E	71.39	Boteler's Ford, 6E
		72.80	Ferry Hill Place, 6F
22.12	Rowser's Ford, 4L	75.73	Killiansburg Caves, 6G
31	Edward's Ferry, 4M	94.44	Falling Waters Ford, 6T
33-35	Harrison's Island, 4O	99.60	Williamsport, 6U
35.5	White's (Conrad's) Ferry, 4N	106.80	Dam #5, 6V
39.5	White's Ford, 4R	108.64	Four Locks, 6W
42.9	Monocacy aqueduct, 5A	110.42	McCoy's Ferry Ford, 6X
55.05	Brunswick (Berlin), 5M	112.40	Fort Frederick, 6Y
57.8x	Weverton Cotton Mills (access Lock #31), 6Aa	124.10	Hancock, 6AA
59.60	Sandy Hook, 6A	166.70	Old Town, 7B
60.67	B & O Railroad bridge to Harpers Ferry, 6Ab	175-184	Cumberland, 7C

APPENDIX B

CIVIL WAR MARYLANDERS OF NOTE

Abercrombie, (brev.) Brigadier General John Joseph, USA (1798-1877)

Born in Baltimore, Abercrombie was one of the senior members of the career military. He had served through many campaigns after graduating from West Point, including Florida and the war with Mexico, finally achieving the rank of colonel by the outbreak of the Civil War. He had a field command at the beginning of the war, serving at Falling Waters, Seven Pines, and Malvern Hill, but was assigned mainly garrison and administrative duties for the remainder of the war. He retired after the war to Long Island, New York. He is buried in Woodlands Cemetery in Philadelphia.

Andrews, Major Richard Snowden, CSA (1830-1903)

Although born in Washington, D.C., Baltimore architect Richard Snowden Andrews commanded a Maryland unit during the war and made his home in Baltimore afterwards. He commanded the 1st Maryland Artillery in 1861, the Artillery Battalion under General Jackson in 1862, and the Artillery Battalion under General Early in 1863. He was seriously wounded at Cedar Mountain and again at Second Winchester. He was dispatched to Europe in early 1864 to purchase supplies, and returned to Baltimore after the war.

Archer, Brigadier General James J., CSA (1817-1864)

Born in Bel Air, Harford County, Archer lived at "Rock Run" on the Susquehanna River in Harford County, Maryland. After graduating from The College of New Jersey (Princeton University) he practiced law, then joined the army to fight in Mexico. He began the Civil War as colonel of the 5th Texas, a unit he had organized, then became a brigadier general in command of the Tennessee Brigade. The brigade took part in actions at Beaver Dam Creek, Gaines' Mill, Frayser's Farm, Cedar Mountain, 2nd Manassas, the capture of Harper's Ferry, and Antietam. Archer was captured at the Battle of Gettysburg and imprisoned on Johnson's Island, Ohio. He was exchanged in August 1864 and put in command of the Tennessee Brigade (combined with Walker's brigade) once again, but died in October 1864 as a result of illness brought on by his imprisonment. He is buried in Hollywood Cemetery, Richmond, Virginia.

Atzerodt, George Andreas (alias Andrew Atwood) (1835-1865)

George Atzerodt was tried, convicted and hanged for his part in John Wilkes Booth's conspiracy to assassinate President Lincoln and others.

He was born in Prussia and immigrated to America with his family at the age of nine. They lived in Germantown, Maryland for about six years, then moved to Westmoreland County, Virginia. After his father's death George and his brother, John, operated a carriage painting business in Port Tobacco, Maryland. During the Civil War John worked in Baltimore as an assistant to the provost marshal, and George stayed at Port Tobacco doing some blockade running and courier work. In the conspiracy George was supposed to kill Vice-President Johnson, then meet with the other conspirators outside of Washington and lead them through Southern Maryland and across the Potomac to Virginia. On hearing of the Lincoln assassination he ditched the idea of attacking the vice-president and fled instead to the farm of his cousin, Hartman Richter, where he was arrested on the evening of April 19.

Bankhead, (brev.) Brigadier General Henry Cary, USA (1828-1894)

Bankhead was born in Baltimore, October 5, 1828. He joined the army as a young man and began his service during the Civil War as a captain in the 5th U.S. Infantry. He became a lieutenant colonel in the I Corps, Army of the Potomac, then the VI Corps, Army of the Potomac. He was breveted a brigadier general April 1, 1865, for "gallant and meritorious service in the Battle of Five Forks, Virginia." He retired as a major in 1879 and died in Bayonne, New Jersey January 9, 1894. He is buried in Green Mount Cemetery, Baltimore.

Beall, Colonel Lloyd James, CSMC (1808-1887)

This Marylander graduated from West Point in 1830 and served in the Seminole and Mexican Wars. In May 1861 he was appointed as the Confederate Marine Corps' first and only commandant. The small Marine Corps distinguished itself both on sea and land, most exceptionally at Dewry's Bluff and Saylor's Creek battles. After the war he settled in Richmond, Virginia.

Bennett, Captain John W., CSN (1822- ?)

Born in Talbot County, Bennett became a midshipman in the U.S. Navy in 1840, then attended the U.S. Naval Academy and was in the first class to graduate in 1846. He served in the Mexican War under commodores Conner and Perry and participated in the expedition to the East Indies in command of the flagship *Susquehanna*. He was serving at the Naval Observatory in Washington D.C. when the Civil War began, and joined the

CIVIL WAR MARYLANDERS OF NOTE

Confederate navy in the fall of 1861 where he was assigned the rank of lieutenant on the steamer *Nashville*. He commanded the gunboat *Gaine* in the Battle of Mobile Bay, which was disabled in the battle. He then commanded the steamer *Nashville* in the defense of Mobile.

Blair, Montgomery (1813-1883)

Born in Kentucky, Blair moved to Montgomery County, Maryland in 1853 where he built a house, "Falklands," next to his father's house, "Silver Spring." He attended West Point and participated in the Seminole War as a second lieutenant. As a lawyer in Washington, D.C. he defended Dred Scott in the famous case before the Supreme Court. As postmaster general in the Lincoln administration he organized the postal service to the army, introduced compulsory payment of postage by the sender, and designed the postal money-order system. After the war he opposed black suffrage and led the move of Union Party members to the Democratic Party to fight the black vote. He lost a bid for a seat in Congress in 1882.

Blumenberg, (brev.) Brigadier General Leopold, USA (1827-1894)

The only Jewish Maryland general in the Civil War, Leopold Blumenberg was born in Prussia and moved to Baltimore with his family in 1854. He helped raise the 5th Regiment, USA, made up of Maryland volunteers. He was commissioned a major in 1861 and was wounded at Antietam, where he was serving with the 5th Regiment, in the fall in 1862. After the war Blumenberg served as Baltimore's postmaster and also as a representative of the Internal Revenue Service. He is supposed to have been breveted a brigadier general by President Andrew Johnson, but it is unknown whether he actually received his commission. He is buried in Har Sinai Cemetery, Baltimore.

Bond, Major Frank A., CSA (1838-1923)

This Howard Countian helped to form the nucleus of the 1st Maryland Cavalry, CSA, in the spring of 1862 along with Ridgely Brown and James Griffith. At the end of the war he was adjutant general on the staff of General Leventhorpe, and after the war he became a brigadier general in the Maryland National Guard.

Booth, John Wilkes (1838-1865)

The infamous assassin of President Abraham Lincoln was born near Bel Air, Maryland. The son of actor Junius Brutus Booth, John vied with his brother, Edwin Booth, to attain fame in the acting business, touring in the south, midwest, and northwest. In 1859 he was a member of the local militia,

197

the Richmond Grays, and was present at the hanging of John Brown. During the war he continued as an actor playing in shows in both the North and South. In 1864 he stopped acting and concentrated on making contacts with the Confederate Secret Service, formulating a plan to kidnap President Lincoln and enlisting several others in his plot. After a kidnapping attempt on March 17, 1865, failed and Lee surrendered on April 9, 1865, the desperate Booth changed his plan to assassination. On April 14 he shot the President at Ford's Theatre in Washington, D.C. and made his escape, with cohort David Herold, through southern Maryland and into Virginia where he was trapped in a barn near Port Royal and killed in the gunfight that ensued on April 26, 1865. He is buried at Green Mount Cemetery, Baltimore.

Bowerman, (brev.) Brigadier General Richard Neville, USA (1831-1920)

Born in Baltimore, Bowerman was employed by the U.S. Customs Service before the war. He entered the army as a corporal, then became a captain with the 11th New York Infantry. He ended his military career as a lieutenant colonel with the 4th Maryland Infantry. He was breveted a brigadier general March 13, 1865, for "gallantry and good conduct at the Battle of Five Forks, Virginia." After the war he worked for the Consolidated Gas Company in Baltimore and died in that city. He died on August 9, 1920, and is buried in Green Mount Cemetery, Baltimore.

Bradford, Governor William Augustus (1806-1881)

Elected governor of Maryland in 1862 as a Unionist, Bradford had a son who was an officer in the Confederate army. As governor of an occupied state, he did not have much power. He protested in vain to Lincoln about the escape of Maryland slaves to the District of Columbia after the District passed an emancipation resolution early in 1862. With Montgomery Blair and former mayor of Baltimore, Thomas Swann, he helped form the Conservative Unionist party in May 1863, in opposition to Henry Winter Davis' Radical Unionist party. The new state constitution, passed in 1864 under his leadership, removed religious prohibitions on public office and established a state-supported public school system. He served as governor until 1866. He is buried in Green Mount Cemetery, Baltimore.

Breathed, Major James, CSA (1838-1870)

Fitzhugh Lee spoke of the "proverbial intrepidity of the reckless Breathed upon every battlefield of the Army of Northern Virginia." James Breathed was born in Morgan County, Virginia and graduated in medicine from the University of Maryland. During the Civil War he was a captain with the 1st Stuart Horse Artillery and joined with John Pelham to form the first horse artillery battery to serve with Stuart. He was promoted to major, in command of a battalion, in February 1864. Wounded at Yellow Tavern, he recovered to fight in the Shenandoah Valley Campaign of 1864. After the war he returned to the practice of medicine in Hancock, Maryland, and is buried at St. Thomas Cemetery there.

Brent, Brigadier General Joseph Lancaster, CSA (1826-1905)

Born in Charles County, Maryland, before the Civil War, Brent was an attorney in California after graduating from Georgetown University. During the war he was a major of artillery under General Magruder, then major and chief of artillery under Taylor in Louisiana. Appointed (though never actually commissioned) brigadier general of cavalry in October 1864, he led "Brent's Cavalry Brigade" which fought in the western arena. After the war he travelled much in Europe eventually settling in Baltimore where he practiced law until his death. He is buried in Green Mount Cemetery, Baltimore.

Brien, Lieutenant Colonel Luke Tiernan, CSA (1827-1912)

Gen. William H. F. Lee, on whose staff Brien served as adjutant general from April 1864 until the end of the war, had requested that he be commissioned a major, but it is not certain whether he ever received that commission. Brien was born in Urbana in Frederick County, but moved to Baltimore at age seven. He had a farm near Hagerstown when the Civil War began. He served as assistant adjutant general on the staff of Gen. J.E.B. Stuart from July 1861 until September 1862 when his health forced him into temporary retirement on the plantation of a friend in North Carolina. After the war he bought "Tyrone" in Urbana, the female seminary where Stuart had held a ball in September 1862. He died of tuberculosis and is buried in St. Ignatius Loyola Catholic Cemetery in Urbana.

Brown, Colonel Ridgely, CSA (1833-1864)

Ridgely Brown of Montgomery County enlisted as a private in the Confederate service June 1, 1861, and soon became a lieutenant of Company K, 1st Virginia Cavalry, which fought at the First Manassas. In 1862, with Frank Bond, James Griffith, and J. A. Pue, he helped to organize the nucleus of what was to become the 1st Maryland Cavalry, CSA. Brown was elected captain of Company A and eventually became a lieutenant colonel. His battalion was in the Valley and Peninsula Campaigns and he was wounded at Greenland Gap in April 1863, but was still able to fight at Gettysburg. He was killed in action at South Anna River on June 1, 1864. Colonel Brown's body was brought home to be buried on his family's estate, Elton, near Unity in Montgomery County. There is both a Sons of Confederate Veterans camp and a United Daughters chapter named in his honor.

Buchanan, Admiral Franklin, CSN (1800-1874)

Baltimorean Franklin Buchanan entered the U.S. Navy at the age of 14. He became part of the Eastern Shore society when he married Anne Catherine Lloyd in 1835 and built a home on the bank of the Miles River near Easton. He was co-founder and first superintendent of the Naval Academy in Annapolis. He served in the Mexican War and was captain of the Navy Yard when the Civil War broke out.

Thinking that Maryland was going to secede he resigned his commission, but later had second thoughts. When the U.S. Navy wouldn't take him back, he joined the Confederacy and was assigned as chief of the Bureau of Orders and Details. He was wounded while commanding the *Virginia* (*Merrimac*) at Hampton Roads. Promoted to admiral in 1862, he took command of the Mobile defenses where he was again wounded and captured.

After the war he served as a college president and was in the insurance business. He is buried in the Lloyd family burial ground at the Wye House on the Eastern Shore.

Buchanan, (brev.) Major General Robert Christie, USA (1811-1878)

Born in Baltimore, Buchanan attended West Point and participated in the Black Hawk War, the Seminole campaign in which he was promoted to captain, and the Mexican War. In 1862 he was given command of the "Regulars," a brigade of veteran army troops which served under Sykes in the battles of Seven Days, and under Fitz John Porter at Manassas. In 1864 he was made a colonel of the 1st Infantry. After the war he was commander of the Department of Louisiana. He retired in 1870 and is buried in Rock Creek Cemetery, Washington, D.C.

Carroll, Anna Ella (1815-1893)

Anna Ella Carroll was best known as an advisor to President Lincoln, although she had been a respected journalist for many years before the war. She wrote several treatises defending Lincoln's war-making powers and advising on military strategy. She devised the Tennessee campaign of the Union army, but her authorship was kept secret, and she never received official recognition for her role in the war. Her outrageous trespassing into matters formerly the exclusive territory of men made her a dynamic symbol for the women's movement. She was born in Somerset County, Maryland, and is buried at Old Trinity Cemetery near Cambridge, Maryland. Her epitaph reads: "Maryland's Most Distinguished Lady. A Great Humanitarian and Close Friend of Abraham Lincoln."

Cary, Hetty (1836-1892)

Touted as one of the most beautiful women in Baltimore, Hetty enjoyed being the center of the social scene of that city before the war. When war broke out she became a member of a group of high-society troublemakers called the "Monument Street Girls," wearing secessionist colors in defiance of the new laws, singing Southern songs, and harassing Federal troops. Her sister Jennie put the poem "Maryland" by James Ryder Randall to music, and the two sang the tune to Confederate troops in Virginia in July 1861 after they had come to the South to escape pending arrest in Baltimore. The song was an immediate hit and became the trademark tune for Marylanders in the Confederacy. On January 19, 1865, Hetty married Gen. John Pegram who was killed less than a month later. After the war she taught and toured in Europe and remarried in 1879.

Chatard, Commander Frederick, CSN (1807-?)

Chatard was born in Baltimore and entered the U.S. Navy in 1824. Trained as an artillery officer, he served in the Mediterranean with the flagship of Commodore John Rodgers, and in the Mexican War on the flagship of Commodore Shubrick. Promoted to commander he served in the Pacific on the *Saratoga*. On joining the Confederate navy he was assigned the command of batteries at Manassas, then at Evansport and Drewry's Bluff on the Potomac River. He was chief of heavy artillery under General Magruder on the Peninsula campaign and commander of CSS *Patrick Henry*. After the war he made his home in St. Louis.

Cooper, (brev.) Brigadier General James, USA (1810-1863)

General Cooper was born in Frederick on May 8, 1810. He was a lawyer by profession and settled in Gettysburg, Pennsylvania, where he was twice elected to the U.S. House of Representatives as a member of the Whig party. He served four terms in the Pennsylvania legislature, was a state's attorney, and was elected a U.S. senator in 1849. He was appointed a brigadier general in May 1861 and assigned by Lincoln to recruit troops in Maryland. He served briefly in the Shenandoah campaign and then was assigned as commander of Camp Chase prisoner of war camp in Columbus, Ohio where he died March 28, 1863. He is buried in Mt. Olivet Cemetery, Frederick, Maryland.

Covey, Dr. Edward Napoleon, CSA (1829-1896)
After attending school at his birthplace near St. Michael's, Talbot County, Covey received a medical degree from the University of Maryland. He served in the surgical department of the army of the west from 1855 to 1861. During the war he was a surgeon in the western arena and was captured in the spring of 1862 and exchanged that fall. In March 1863 he was made the Medical Director of Hospitals of North Carolina, and in the fall of that year was made medical inspector for hospitals in the South. After the surrender at Appomattox he escaped with Secretary of State Benjamin to London. After several years in England he returned to Talbot County. He died in Houston, Texas after answering a call for volunteers to fight a Yellow Fever epidemic.

Creswell, John (1828-1891)
John Creswell was adjutant general of Maryland during the Civil War, in charge of raising troops to meet the state's quotas. After the war he was prominent in Maryland politics, being elected to the U.S. House of Representatives and the Senate, and was postmaster general under President Grant. He was born in Cecil County where he lived all of his life and is buried in Elkton Presbyterian Cemetery.

Davidson, Commander Hunter, CSN (1826-1913)
Although born in Washington, D.C., Davidson was living in Maryland and was an instructor at the Naval Academy in Annapolis when the war broke out. He joined the Confederate navy and was a lieutenant on the CSS *Virginia* (*Merrimac*) during the battle with the USS *Monitor*. Hunter Davidson was known as a pioneer in the art of aquatic explosives. He headed the Confederacy's Submarine Battery Service and his electrical torpedoes sunk the USS *Commodore Jones* and damaged the USS *Commodore Barney* and several other enemy ships. These torpedoes were either floating mines or sunken bombs attached by wire to a detonation device on shore. He also designed a small torpedo boat, the *Squib*, with a torpedo attached to a long spar on the prow, in which he attacked and damaged the USS *Minnesota* at Hampton Roads.
He made his home on the Eastern Shore after the war when he was the first commander of the Oyster Navy, formed to hunt oyster pirates in the Chesapeake Bay. Accepting a position in Argentina he worked for that country until 1885 when he resettled in Villa Rica, Paraguay where he later died and is buried.

Deems, (brev.) Brigadier General James Monroe, USA (1818-1901)

James Deems was a music teacher and composer born in Baltimore January 5, 1818. He served as lieutenant colonel in the 1st Maryland Cavalry during the war, becoming assistant inspector of cavalry on the staff of General Sigel. He was breveted brigadier general March 13, 1865 for "gallant and meritorious services during the war." He is buried in Green Mount Cemetery, Baltimore.

Dement, Major William Fendlay, CSA (1826-?)

Dement was born near Cedar Point Neck, Charles County, Maryland. He was the lieutenant of a volunteer cavalry company before the war. He participated in the Baltimore Riot, being the one who directed the obstruction of the passage of the train cars with paving stones and sand. He was the commander of the 1st Maryland Artillery (Dement's) during the Battle of Antietam. He led a group of men across the Potomac River near Matthias Point in May 1861, and on joining the Confederate army recruited more men to form Dement's Battery of the 1st Maryland Artillery with Snowden Andrews as captain and Dement as first lieutenant. The battery saw action at Yorktown, Seven Days, Mechanicsville, Malvern Hill, Shenandoah Valley, Antietam, Gettysburg, Cold Harbor, Petersburg, and finally Sailor's Creek and Appomattox. After the war he worked for the Maryland Revenue Department.

Denison, (brev.) Brigadier General Andrew Woods, USA (1831-1877)

Colonel Denison lost an arm while leading the 8th Maryland in battle at Laurel Hill. He was wounded again near Petersburg and was breveted a brigadier general March 13, 1865, for valor at Wilderness and Spotsylvania, and major general for distinction at White Oak Road. He was postmaster of Baltimore after the war. He is buried in Green Mount Cemetery, Baltimore.

Dorsey, Lieutenant Colonel Gustavus, CSA (1838-1911)

Born in Montgomery County Gus Dorsey enlisted in Company K of the 1st Virginia Cavalry when it was first formed in the spring of 1861. A year later he was first lieutenant and transferred to the 1st Maryland Cavalry with Col. Ridgely Brown in command. Both units participated in numerous actions and when Colonel Brown fell, Dorsey was made lieutenant colonel of the company. He was wounded at Fredericksburg and at Fisher's Hill. After the war he returned to farming near Brookeville. He is buried in the family cemetery on Gregg Road.

Douglas, Major Henry Kyd, CSA (1838-1903)

Beginning the war as a private in the 2nd Virginia, Douglas had become a major and assistant adjutant general by 1863. He served on the staffs of Gen. Stonewall Jackson, Gen. Edward Johnson, General Gordon, and General Early. At the end of the war he commanded Walker's old Brigade in Ramseur's Division. He was wounded six times and arrested on his return home because he was still wearing his uniform. He wrote a book about his war experiences, *I Rode With Stonewall.* He was born at Ferry Hill in Washington County, Maryland and is buried at the Shepherdstown Cemetery in West Virginia across the Potomac River from his home.

Douglass, Frederick (1817-1895)

Frederick Douglass was born and grew up a slave on a plantation on the Eastern Shore of Maryland, spending some time in a household in Baltimore. Intelligent and defiant, he could not endure a life of slavery and escaped to the North as a young man. He became a brilliant orator and writer against slavery. His autobiography, *Narrative of the Life of Frederick Douglass,* an American Slave, inflamed abolitionists and inspired hope for the blacks as no other book had done. Later in life he became secretary of the Santo Domingo Commission, recorder of deeds in the District of Columbia, and minister to Haiti.

Elzy, Major General Arnold, CSA (1816-1871)

Born Arnold Elzy Jones at "Elmwood" in Somerset County December 18, 1816, he graduated from West Point and served in the Indian and Mexican Wars as a captain. He entered the Confederate army in April 1861 and was made colonel of the 1st Maryland Infantry. He was promoted brigadier general after the battle of First Manassas, was wounded in the fighting around Richmond, and was made a major general in December 1862. He was wounded at Port Republic and again at Gaines' Mill. Unfit for active service after his second wound he commanded the Department of Virginia from April 1863 to April 1864. He was then chief of artillery for the Army of Tennessee until the end of the war. After the war he lived on a farm in Anne Arundel County until his death February 21, 1871. He is buried at Green Mount Cemetery in Baltimore.

Emory, Major General William Hemsley, USA (1811-1887)

Born at "Poplar Grove" in Anne's City, Queen Anne's County, Maryland, Emory graduated from West Point in 1831 and began his career as a second lieutenant of artillery, but resigned after four years to become a first lieutenant in the Topographical Engineers. He did surveying in the northwest and southwest and served in the Mexican War. He held the rank of lieutenant colonel when the Civil War broke out and was made a brigadier general and served under McClellan in the Peninsula Campaign, under Nathaniel Banks in the Red River Campaign, and under Sheridan in the Shenandoah Valley Campaign. After the war he was promoted to major general and commanded the Department of West Virginia, then the Department of Washington, and finally the Department of the Gulf. He died in Washington, D.C. and is buried at Congressional Cemetery.

Evans, Brigadier General Andrew Wallace, USA (1829-1906)

Evans was an Elkton native who graduated from West Point and spent his entire military career, before, during, and after the Civil War, in the west. He retired in 1883 and is buried in the Elkton Presbyterian Cemetery.

Fleetwood, Sergeant Christian, USA (1840-1914)

Born to free black parents in Baltimore, Fleetwood attended Ashmun Institute (later Lincoln University) in preparation for a career as a merchant. When the Bureau of Colored Troops was established in 1863 he enlisted in the 4th Regiment Infantry, USCT. After training at Yorktown the 4th took part in the siege of Richmond and Petersburg beginning in the spring of 1864. In an attempt to break through Confederate lines at Chafin's Farm southeast of Richmond, the 4th and 6th Regiments, USCT, both Maryland units, were chosen to spearhead the attack on Newmarket Heights. Both regiments lost more than half its men during the attack. Sergeant Fleetwood carried the U.S. flag through a hail of bullets. Fleetwood, Pvt. Charles Viel, Sgt. James Harris, Pvt. William Barnes, and Sgt. Alfred Hilton (died of wounds) were Marylanders who received Medals of Honor for their heroism in that battle.

Fleetwood lived in Washington, D.C. after the war and worked for the government.

Forrest, Commandant French, CSN (1796-1866)

Born in St. Mary's County, Maryland, Forrest served in both the War of 1812 and the Mexican War. Soon after he joined the Confederacy, he was made commandant of the Norfolk Navy Yard and rebuilt the USS *Merrimac* as the CSS *Virginia*. In 1862 he was head of the Office of Orders and Details, and from the spring of 1863 to the spring of 1864, the flag officer of the James River Squadron. He is buried in Congressional Cemetery in Washington, D.C.

Freaner, Major George, CSA (1831-1878)

Major Freaner was aide-de-camp on the staff of Gen. J.E.B. Stuart until Stuart's death—at which time he became a member of the staff of Gen. Fitzhugh Lee. A native of Hagerstown, he was practicing law in that town when he was elected to the Maryland House of Delegates in 1859. He enlisted in the Confederate army in the fall of 1861 and was assistant adjutant of the 1st Virginia Cavalry, with Gen. J.E.B. Stuart, and with Gen. Fitz Lee. He was given commission as a major in November 1863, and assigned to the cavalry corps under Gen. R. E. Lee. From August 1864 to January 1865 he was assistant adjutant general and inspector general under Gen. Wade Hampton, and was again with Hampton at the end of the war. After the war he returned to his law practice in Hagerstown, was elected to the Maryland House of Delegates, and was a member of the board of commissioners appointed by the governor to accomplish Washington Cemetery for Confederates. He is buried in Rose Hill Cemetery, Hagerstown.

French, Major General William Henry, USA (1815-1881)

Born in Baltimore, French attended West Point and served in the Seminole War and the Mexican War. During the secession crisis he refused to surrender his garrison in Texas to the state and instead led his soldiers to a Federal post in Florida. Commanding a brigade of the II Corps he participated in the Peninsula Campaign and Antietam. He took over General Sickles' III Corps after the Battle of Gettysburg; he destroyed the Confederates' pontoon bridges over the Potomac, and delayed their retreat. After misdirecting his troops during the Mine Run campaign he was relieved of his command and given administrative posts for the rest of the war. He died in Washington, D.C. and is buried in Rock Creek Cemetery.

Gilmor, Lieutenant Colonel Harry, CSA (1845-1879)

Born at "Glen Ellen," Baltimore County, Harry Gilmor enlisted as a private in the Confederate army in Virginia at the beginning of the war. He helped organize the 2nd Maryland Cavalry and became their commander, leading them on daring raids throughout Virginia, Maryland, and Pennsylvania. One of his most famous raids was the capture of a train filled with Union supplies at Harpers Ferry in February 1862. In July 1864, as a part of Gen. Jubal Early's planned offensive against Washington Gilmor's cavalry threatened Baltimore, ranging north and west of the city.

By the end of the war Gilmor had attained the rank of lieutenant colonel. After the war he became police commissioner of the city of Baltimore and was very active in veterans' affairs until his death. There is a Sons of Confederate Veterans camp and a United Daughters of the Confederacy chapter named after him. He was the author of *Four Years in the Saddle*. He is buried at Loudon Park Cemetery in Baltimore.

Greenhow, Rose O'Neale (c.1815-1864)

Born in Montgomery County, Maryland, Rose O'Neale was a member of the high society of Washington, D.C. and a personal friend of James Buchanan and John C. Calhoun among others. She married Robert Greenhow in 1835 and they had four daughters. After her husband's sudden death in 1854 she bought a house at 398 Sixteenth Street in Washington, D.C.

Rose was enlisted as a spy for the Confederacy by Col. Thomas Jordan, who provided her with a cipher in the spring of 1861. During July of that year she provided General Beauregard, CSA, with troop numbers, movements, and plans before the First Battle of Manassas. Subsequent to that battle her home in Washington, D.C. became a rendezvous point for Confederate couriers until her arrest by detective Allan Pinkerton in late August 1861. After being imprisoned with her youngest daughter, Rose, she was tried and sent to the South in June 1862.

In 1863 she went to England to have her book, *My Imprisonment and the First Year of Abolition Rule at Washington*, published. Leaving her daughter, Rose, in a convent in France, she returned to the Confederacy with the proceeds from her book in the fall of 1864, only to be drowned during a storm when attempting to come ashore in a small boat from the British blockade runner, the *Condor*, on October 1, 1864, near Fort Fisher, North Carolina. She is buried in Oakdale Cemetery, Wilmington, North Carolina.

Hammond, Brigadier General William Alexander, USA (1828-1890)

Born in Annapolis, Maryland, Hammond received his medical degree from the University of the City of New York and became a surgeon for the U.S. Army. He had resigned his commission to become a professor at the University of Virginia and was teaching there when the Civil War broke out. Beginning his army career a second time he started at the bottom, but was made U.S. surgeon general in 1862. He created a general hospital service and was instrumental in the forming of an efficient ambulance corps. He clashed with Secretary of War Stanton on the direction of the medical corps, was court-martialed and dismissed from service in August 1864. Vindicated after the war, he was restored to brigadier general. He established the Army Medical Museum. He died in Washington, D.C. and is buried at Arlington National Cemetery.

Hardcastle, Colonel A. B., CSA (?-?)

Hardcastle was a private in the 2nd Dragoons, USA, in the spring of 1861 and accompanied Gen. Albert Sidney Johnston from California through New Mexico and Texas. In Mississippi he was made a major in command of a battalion of seven companies that had not been assigned to a regiment. This battalion opened the battle at Shiloh where he was wounded. At Corinth the battalion was reorganized as the 33rd (later 38th, and then 48th) Mississippi with Hardcastle in command as colonel, and participated in campaigns in Kentucky, Tennessee, Georgia, and the Carolinas. He was from Talbot County.

Herbert, Lieutenant Colonel James, CSA (1833-1884)

James Herbert was a native Marylander from Howard County. He became a merchant of grain, tobacco, and produce in Baltimore. During the war he was lieutenant colonel of the Independent Grays (Company D, 2nd Maryland). After the war he was elected colonel of the 5th Regiment, Maryland Guard, and was made brigadier general by the governor in 1871. General Herbert became a Police Commissioner in Baltimore after the war. He is buried in Loudon Park Cemetery, Baltimore, Maryland.

Hicks, Governor Thomas Holliday (1789-1865)

Thomas Holliday Hicks was governor of Maryland from 1858 to 1862. Soon after the election of Lincoln, Governor Hicks began to receive petitions to call a special session of the General Assembly to decide whether Maryland should secede from the Union. Hicks, who was elected to office on the Know-Nothing ticket, was pro-slavery and a strong states-rights man, but he knew the dangers of secession for a middle state like Maryland, which depended on the west and foreign shipping to supply its growing industries. He refused to call the General Assembly into special session and, even though they met anyway, Hicks went down in history as a Union supporter for this non-action. In April 1861 he had conspired with the mayor of Baltimore in the burning of the railroad bridges north of Baltimore to prevent Union troops from entering the city after the Baltimore riots, and in not allowing General Butler to land troops in Baltimore. After his governorship was over, Hicks became a U.S. senator and aligned himself with the conservative Unionists.

The erection of a monument over his grave was one of the last acts of the unconditional or radical Unionist party, in control of Maryland politics during the war. He is buried in Cambridge Cemetery, Cambridge.

Hollins, Commander George N., CSN (1799-1878)

George Hollins was on a ship captured by the British in 1814, just after becoming a midshipman at age fourteen. He then served in the Mediterranean and in the Mexican War. He became a lieutenant in 1829, a commander in 1841, and a captain in 1855. In the Confederate navy he commanded the naval station in New Orleans for a while, then spent most of his time patrolling the James River in Virginia, where he was wounded in the arm, and serving on numerous boards and courts. After the war he was a court officer in Baltimore. The most famous escapade of Hollins was the capture of the Chesapeake Bay steamer *St. Nicholas* at the beginning of the war. He is buried at Westminster Burying Grounds in Baltimore.

Horn, (brev.) Brigadier General James Watt, USA (1834-1897)

Born in Scotland, Horn became a carpenter and a military instructor after immigrating to America. During the Civil War he was captain of the 5th Maryland Infantry (USA) and then colonel of the 6th Maryland Infantry. After the war he was warden of the Maryland State Penitentiary and superintendent of the Cheltham Home for Colored Children. He died in Mitchellville, Maryland. He is buried in Loudon Park Cemetery, Baltimore, Maryland.

Johnson, Brigadier General Bradley Tyler, CSA (1829-1903)

Bradley Johnson, a native of Frederick, Maryland, graduated from The College of New Jersey (Princeton University) and was admitted to the Maryland bar in 1851. Before the war he was a lawyer, state's attorney, chairman of the state Democratic Committee, and delegate to the 1860 convention where, as a staunch supporter of Breckenridge, he was one of the leaders in dividing the party.

He took a major role in recruiting the 1st Maryland Infantry, CSA, and as major and then colonel of the unit he participated in First Manassas, the Valley Campaign, and the Seven Days battles. During the Second Bull Run Battle he commanded a brigade with distinction. After the 1st Maryland was dissolved he served in various duties until made brigadier general in command of William Jones' cavalry brigade in June 28, 1864, which participated in Gen. Jubal Early's raid on Washington, D.C. Johnson and his 2nd Maryland Cavalry threatened Baltimore and went as far as Beltsville.

After the war he served for four years in the Virginia Senate before moving to Baltimore, where he was the head of the Society of the Army and Navy of the Confederacy in Maryland and was prominent in founding the Maryland Old Line Home for Confederate veterans.

Johnson, Jane Claudia (1832-1899)

Jane Claudia Johnson was born in North Carolina, the daughter of Romulus M. Saunders, a distinguished Congressman and ambassador to Spain. When she was 16 she married Bradley T. Johnson, a young Maryland lawyer at the time, and they went to live in Frederick, Maryland.

When the war began she followed her husband to Virginia. When the 1st Maryland Infantry was formed with her husband at its head, the soldiers had no uniforms, guns, or equipment because Maryland had not joined the Confederacy. Jane Claudia went to North Carolina for help. In the short space of ten days she returned to the camp of the newly forming Maryland Line with a good supply of uniforms, arms, camp equipment, and food. She followed the regiment as long as it existed, caring for the sick and wounded, setting up hospitals, arranging for church services, organizing a traveling library, and generally boosting the morale of the men. She even did some courier work for the Confederate army.

In Baltimore, after the war, Jane Claudia helped found the Hospital for Women and was president of the Board of Visitors of the Maryland Line Confederate Home when it was founded. When she died the Confederate veterans took up a collection and erected a monument over her grave in Loudon Park Cemetery, Baltimore. It is the first monument erected to a woman in Maryland.

Judah, (brev.) Colonel Henry Moses, USA (1821-1866)

Born in Snow Hill on the Eastern Shore of Maryland Judah attended West Point and participated in the Mexican War. In 1862 he was made inspector general of the Army of Tennessee, and then inspector general of the Army of Ohio. In command of the 3rd Division of the XXIII Corps he was outmaneuvered by Confederate raider John Hunt Morgan on his Ohio Raid. Thereafter he was assigned to desk duty in the Department of the Cumberland. After the war he served in Plattsburg, New York, where he died.

Kelty, Captain Augustus H., USN (?-?)

Kelty enlisted in the U.S. Navy in 1821. A commander at the beginning of the war he was appointed to St. Louis, Missouri to help organize a flotilla. He commanded the gunboat USS *Mound City* which was sunk at Fort Pillow. The *Mound City* was raised and repaired and participated in the taking of Fort St. Charles on the White River, Arkansas. Commissioned as captain in 1862 he commanded the ironclad USS *Roanoke*. He was later commissioned a rear admiral.

Kenly, (brev.) Major General John Reese, USA (1818-1891)

A lawyer before the Civil War, Baltimorean John Kenly had seen battle before as a major of volunteers during the Mexican War. He began his Civil War career as a colonel of the 1st Maryland Infantry, serving garrison duty along the Potomac. His regiment fought the 1st Maryland, CSA, at Front Royal, Virginia on May 23, 1862, and he was severely wounded and captured. Back in service after being exchanged, he was promoted to brigadier general and went on to command the Maryland brigade in western Maryland, and then the District of Eastern Shore. After the war he was breveted a major general and presented with a sword by the city of Baltimore. He is buried in Green Mount Cemetery, Baltimore.

Lanier, Sidney (1843-1874)

Poet and musician Sidney Lanier taught at Johns Hopkins University in Baltimore after the war. He had been a Confederate soldier, serving with the 2nd Georgia. He was confined for many months in Point Lookout Prisoner of War Camp, where he contracted the tuberculosis which caused his death sixteen years later. His poetry was much loved in both the North and the South. A simple boulder marks his grave at Green Mount Cemetery, Baltimore, and inscribed on it are the words "I am lit with the sun."

Lee, Commodore Samuel Phillips, USN (1812-1897)

Born on Sully plantation in Virginia in the midst of wealth and plenty, Lee's mother, Jane Fitzgerald Lee, died when he was only four; and his father, Francis Lightfoot Lee, son of the signer of the Declaration of Independence, Richard Henry Lee, died when he was barely eight, leaving no legacy but debts. Phillips Lee, along with his two brothers and two sisters, was raised by relatives, and at the age of 14 he entered the U.S. Navy. In 1848 he married Elizabeth Blair, daughter of Francis Preston Blair. Phillips Lee acquitted himself well as commander of the *Washington* during the Mexican War. By 1859 he had saved enough money to build a house next to the Blair House—in Washington, D.C.—which is joined to that house by a common wall, but he and his wife spent most of their time at the family estate, Silver Spring, in Montgomery County, Maryland.

At the outbreak of the Civil War Phillips Lee was in command of the sloop *Vandalia* off the coast of Africa. After successfully participating in several campaigns, Lee was promoted to captain, in command of the *Oneida* in July 1862. As acting rear admiral under Admiral Farragut in the Mississippi campaign he helped to capture the forts guarding New Orleans in the spring of 1862, and was then given command of the North Atlantic Blockading Squadron. Late in 1864 he returned to the Mississippi to help with the capture

211

of Vicksburg. He was made a rear admiral after the war and retired to farming at Silver Spring. He is buried at Arlington National Cemetery.

Linthicum, Captain Charles Frederick, CSA (1838-1864)
Rev. Charles Linthicum was born in Frederick County and entered the Methodist ministry. During the Civil War he served first as chaplain for the 8th Virginia Infantry. He was one of the volunteers who accompanied Elija White to capture 325 Union soldiers on the banks of the Potomac River after the Battle of Ball's Bluff (site #40). In December 1862 he was appointed adjutant general on the staff of Brig. Gen. Richard B. Garnett and subsequently on the staff of Brig. Gen. Eppa Hunton. He was very popular among the men of the regiment and brigade, acting as both a chaplain and leader. At Gettysburg he had his horse shot out from under him, but comforted the wounded and at the same time regrouped the able men into a line of defense. He was killed at Cold Harbor on June 3, 1864.

Little, Brigadier General Lewis Henry, CSA (1817-1862)
Born in Baltimore March 19, 1817, Little was the son of a noted Congressman. He had fought in the Mexican War and so was commissioned a major of artillery when he joined the Confederate cause in May 1861. Soon he was promoted to colonel under General Price and distinguished himself at the Battle of Elkhorn, after which he was promoted to general. During the Battle of Iuka, September 19, 1862, he was conversing on horseback with three other generals when a ball from the Federal lines passed under the arm of one of the others and hit Little in the forehead, killing him instantly. He is buried in Green Mount Cemetery, Baltimore.

MacKall, Brigadier General William Whall, CSA (1817-1891)
This West Point graduate was born at his family home, "Wilna," in Cecil County, Maryland. After fighting in the Seminole Wars and the Mexican War he resigned his commission to join the Confederacy and was appointed lieutenant colonel in the adjutant general's office. Soon after being promoted to brigadier general in 1862 he was captured and later exchanged. He then served under Gen. Braxton Bragg and Gen. Joseph E. Johnston. After the war he resided in Virginia and is buried on his farm, "Lewinsville," near McLean.

Marshall, Colonel Charles, CSA (1830-?)
Born in Virginia and educated at the University of Virginia, Marshall became a lawyer in Baltimore in 1852 after a stint at teaching mathematics at the University of Indiana. He joined the Confederate service when Virginia seceded and was appointed major and aide-de-camp to Gen. Robert E. Lee in

March 1862. He was promoted to lieutenant colonel in 1863. He was charged with the duty of preparing the official reports of the Army of Northern Virginia. He was the only member of General Lee's staff who accompanied him to the conference with General Grant at Appomattox Courthouse on April 9, 1865, and it was he who drew up the letter of acceptance of the terms of surrender. He also prepared General Lee's general order containing his farewell address. After the war he returned to practice law in Baltimore.

McKaig, Colonel William Wallace, Jr., CSA (1842-1870)
Born in Cumberland May 5, 1842, McKaig was the son of the first mayor of that city, prominent lawyer William McKaig. He was a first lieutenant in Company A, 2nd Maryland Cavalry. After the war he became a colonel in the Maryland National Guard. He was an industrialist, heir to his father's foundry, and a member of the Cumberland City Council. He was shot and killed on the streets of Cumberland by Crawford Black, the brother of Myra Black, a woman McKaig had had an affair with and who was carrying his child. He is buried in Rose Hill Cemetery, Cumberland.

Mudd, Dr. Samuel (1833-1883)
The case of Dr. Mudd's involvement in the Lincoln assassination plot is still a subject of debate. Not having practiced medicine for years, Dr. Mudd was approached, on his farm near Bryantown, by the escaping John Wilkes Booth to repair his leg, which he did. Convicted by a military court of conspiracy, Mudd was sent to Fort Jefferson prison in Dry Tortugas, Florida where he voluntarily treated sick prisoners and guards. After several petitions to the courts, he was released by a pardon by President Andrew Johnson on February 8, 1869. He spent the rest of his life on his farm in southern Maryland and is buried in St. Mary's Catholic Cemetery, Bryantown.

Norris, Colonel William, CSA (1820-1896)
After graduating from Yale Law School in 1840 Norris went to New Orleans to practice law. He returned to his home in Reisterstown in 1851 and became president of the Baltimore Mechanical Bakery. He offered his services to the Confederacy when war broke out and became head of the Signal Corps when it was formed in April 1862. He was also head of the Confederate Secret Service and set up a "Secret Line" from New York to Baltimore to Washington to the South. There is a Sons of Confederate Veterans Camp named for him. He is buried in All Saints Episcopal Cemetery, Reisterstown.

Owens, Private Benjamin Welch, CSA (1836-1917)
Private Owens was posthumously awarded the Confederate Medal

of Honor on June 5, 1993, for his heroism at the Battle of Stephenson's Depot. Born in Anne Arundel County, Owens was in Baltimore on April 19, 1861 and participated in the rioting. He was arrested and was not acquitted until May 1863, at which time he immediately went to Virginia and enlisted in the 1st Maryland Artillery, CSA. Although later fighting at Gettysburg, the Battle of Stephenson's Depot on June 15, 1863, was his first taste of fire. He manned the remaining cannon after all the rest of his company were killed or wounded and continued firing until help came. Without that cannon the Confederate line would have been overrun.

After the war he was a deputy clerk at the county court in Annapolis until he retired to the Confederate Soldiers Home in Pikesville. He is buried at Loudon Park Cemetery in Baltimore.

Parker, Commander Foxhall Alexander, USN (1821-1879)

Born in New York City, Parker became a midshipman in the U.S. Navy in 1839, and was made lieutenant in 1850. He was a veteran of West India, East India, and Pacific squadrons before the Civil War. He was made the executive officer of the U.S. Navy Yard in 1861, and manned Fort Ellsworth in Alexandria, Virginia. He commanded the ship *Mahska*, and was Commander of the Potomac Flotilla from 1864 to 1865. He continued his naval career after the war, serving in Europe and at home. He authored several books on naval tactics. He was a brother of William H. Parker, CSN.

Peter, Lieutenant Walter Gibson "Gip," CSA (1842-1863)

Gip Peter was the last child born to Maj. George Peter and his third wife, Sara, at Montanverde near Darnestown in Montgomery County, Maryland. After acting as a courier for several units Peter was made a lieutenant in a small company of cavalry forming under the command of Captain Elijah Viers White in Leesburg, Virginia. In February 1862 he was made a lieutenant in Company L, Tennessee Light Artillery under the command of his cousin, Col. William Orton Williams. He was acting as an aide to his cousin when both became unassigned in early June 1863. The pair were captured in Union uniforms behind enemy lines on June 8, 1863, and hanged as spies on June 9, 1863, at Fort Granger near Franklin, Tennessee. Both men claimed that they were not spies and neither were recognized as spies by the Confederate authorities. Gip Peter is buried at Oak Hill Cemetery in Washington, D.C.

Purviance, Commodore Hugh Y., USN (?-?)

Having entered the service in 1818 Purviance commanded the frigate *St. Lawrence* at the beginning of the war, which captured several ships in the southern Atlantic blockade and sank the Confederate privateer *Petrel*. He was commissioned a commodore in 1862 and was lighthouse inspector from 1863 to the end of the war. He was later made a rear admiral.

Randall, James Ryder (1839-1908)
    The Baltimorean Randall was teaching in Louisiana when he was inspired by the Baltimore Riots of April 1861 to write the poem "Maryland," which was later put to music by Jennie Cary and became Maryland's state song, "Maryland, My Maryland," in 1939. He was the son of Christopher Randall, the founder of Randallstown, Maryland and a graduate of Georgetown University. He tried to enlist in the Southern army, but was refused on medical grounds. After the war Randall was a journalist and poet.

Rhett, Colonel Thomas Smith, CSA (1827-1893)
    Rhett was a Baltimore bank clerk from South Carolina, but he had graduated from West Point and was assigned as captain of artillery when he offered his services to the South in the fall of 1861. He was made a colonel of artillery in 1862 and commanded the defenses of Richmond until the fall of 1863 when he was sent to Europe to purchase arms. He finished the war in the ordinance department and then returned to his previous work in Baltimore.

Ringgold, Rear Admiral Cadwallader, USN (1806-1867)
    The Baltimorean Ringgold was a career navy man, achieving the rank of lieutenant by age 27. He was a captain at the beginning of the Civil War, becoming a commodore in 1862, and a rear admiral by the end of the war. He died April 29, 1867, and is buried in Green Mount Cemetery, Baltimore.

Rodgers, Commodore John, USN (1812-1882)
    Born in Havre de Grace, Maryland, Rodgers was the son of the U.S. naval hero of the same name. He had cruised the world before being appointed commander in 1855. At the beginning of the war he was busy converting steamers into gunboats for service on the Mississippi River, before assuming command of the USS *Flag* and participating in DuPont's Port Royal Expedition and taking part in the surrenders of Forts Walker and Beauregard on the east coast. He then commanded the ironclad USS *Galena* in the James River during the Peninsula Campaign. As captain of the USS *Weehawken* in Atlantic blockade duty he defeated the ironclad CSS *Atlanta*.
    He continued his illustrious naval service after the war and became

superintendent of the Naval Observatory in 1872. He died in Washington, D.C. ten years later, the oldest active rear admiral, and is buried at Arlington National Cemetery.

Ryan, Father Abram Joseph (1838-1886)

The famous Confederate poet-priest was born and raised in Hagerstown, Maryland before his family moved to Missouri. Ordained a priest in Philadelphia he abandoned his teaching to join the Confederate army in 1862 where he acted as a chaplain. His most well-known poems are "In Memoriam," written on the death of his brother, and "The Conquered Banner."

Sands, Captain Benjamin Franklin, USN (1812-1883)

Sands was born in Baltimore and appointed midshipman in 1828. He went on to a long and illustrious career in the navy, becoming a rear admiral in 1871. He was a commander in 1855 when, as head of the navy's Bureau of Construction, he invented a device for deep-water sounding. He supervised the evacuation of the U.S. Navy Yard in Norfolk in 1861, and then was assigned coastal duty in the Pacific. In 1862 he was made a captain and head of the blockade of North Carolina where he commanded the USS *Dacotah*, and the USS *Fort Jackson*. He participated in the attack on Fort Fisher in January 1865. He died in retirement in Washington, D.C.

Semmes, Admiral and Brigadier General Raphael, CSN (1809-1877)

Born in Charles County, Maryland, Semmes began his career in the navy as a midshipman in 1826 and fought in the Mexican War. In 1861 he was appointed commander in charge of the Confederate Lighthouse Service. In 1862 he had a steamer, the *Sumter*, converted to a cruiser, and with her captured 17 merchant ships. With the CSS *Alabama* he captured 55 more ships and sank the U.S. warship *Hatteras*. When in Cherbourg, France for repairs the *Alabama* was sunk by the USS *Kearsage* in June 1864. In February 1865 he took command of the James River squadron and was made a brigadier general after he had to destroy the squadron to avoid its capture.

After the war he lived in Maryland for a few years, then returned to his home before the war in Mobile, Alabama.

Stanton, (brev.) Brigadier General David Leroy, USA (1840-1919)

Stanton was a merchant in Baltimore who became a colonel in the 1st Maryland Infantry during the Civil War. He was breveted brigadier general for "gallant conduct in the Battle of Five Forks, Virginia." He returned to Baltimore after the war where he was a U.S. pension attorney. He is buried in Loudon Park National Cemetery, Baltimore.

Steuart, Brigadier General George Hume, CSA (1828-1903)

Born near Baltimore, Steuart served on the western frontier after graduating from West Point. He joined the Confederate army as a captain of cavalry and then became a lieutenant with the 1st Maryland, CSA. In March 1862, he was commissioned a brigadier general under the command of General Ewell. He was wounded at Cross Keys and captured at Spotsylvania. After the war he became a farmer in Maryland and for many years was the head of the Maryland Division, United Confederate Veterans. He is buried in Green Mount Cemetery, Baltimore.

Stokes, Brigadier James Hughes, USA (1815-1890)

Born in Hagerstown, Maryland, Stokes moved to Baltimore at a young age. After graduating from West Point he was assigned duty in the west where he stayed to enter the railroad business. In 1862 he recruited a battery in Chicago and re-entered military service, commanding a division of artillery by November 1863. He then became a quartermaster inspector with the rank of lieutenant colonel. In July 1865, he was appointed brigadier general. After the war he was engaged in the real estate business in Chicago and New York.

Sullivane, Colonel Clement, CSA (1838-1920)

Sullivane was born in Mississippi but was brought to Cambridge, Maryland as an infant to be raised by his grandparents after his parents had died. He became a lawyer in Cambridge but "went South" to join the Confederate army when the war broke out. He first enlisted in the 10th Mississippi, but transferred to Company B of the 21st Virginia, mainly Marylanders, when that company formed. He was in charge of part of the retreat from Richmond on April 2-3, 1865, and supervised the burning of the Mayo Bridge after all personnel had crossed. He was captured at Saylor's Creek April 16, 1865. He is buried in Christ Church Cemetery on High Street, Cambridge, Dorchester County.

Surratt, Mary Elizabeth Jenkins (1823-1865)

Mary Jenkins, born in Prince George's County, Maryland was raised a Catholic. She married John Surratt in the 1830s and helped to tend a tavern built by him in 1852 in what is now Clinton, Maryland until his death in 1862. She moved to Washington, D.C. in 1864 where she ran a boarding house. The tavern was a stop on the secret Confederate mail line for which her son, John, became a courier. John Wilkes Booth and other Lincoln assassination conspirators stayed at both the tavern and the boarding house and Mary delivered some field glasses for Booth to pick up at her old tavern on the day of the assassination. On this evidence she was convicted by a military court of conspiracy and hanged on July 7, 1865.

Swann, Governor Thomas (1809-1883)

Swann was the Know-Nothing Party mayor of Baltimore just before the war, and became governor of Maryland in 1866 as a Conservative Unionist who quickly changed to Conservative Democrat, following the lead of Montgomery Blair, after the war, and was instrumental in regaining the vote for the Southern sympathizers and Maryland Confederates after the war. After serving as governor he was elected to the U.S. Senate. He is buried in Green Mount Cemetery, Baltimore.

Taney, Chief Justice Roger Brooke (1777-1864)

Roger Brooke Taney was born in Calvert County and lived in Frederick for 22 years—from the time of his graduation from Dickinson College and post-graduate work in Annapolis until 1823—working as a lawyer. As attorney general, Roger Brooke Taney was well-known for his defense of President Jackson's withdrawal of government deposits from the United States Bank. In 1836 Taney was approved as chief justice of the U.S. Supreme Court. As chief justice his most memorable act was the handing down of the Dred Scott decision in which he declared that a slave could not escape his condition by moving into free territory. This decision dismissed the Missouri Compromise as unconstitutional and was one of the major arguments that precipitated the Civil War.

In May 1861, while still chief justice but in his capacity as judge on the Federal circuit court of Maryland, he issued a writ of *habeas corpus* on behalf of John Merryman, arrested by Federal authorities for his part in burning the railroad bridges to Baltimore after the April riot. By this act Taney challenged the authority of President Lincoln to impose martial law on Maryland. He is buried in St. John's Catholic Cemetery, Frederick.

Thomas, Brigadier General Allen, CSA (1830-1907)

Born in Howard County, Thomas graduated from the College of New Jersey (Princeton University) and practiced law in Maryland before he moved to Louisiana in 1852. There he raised a battalion of infantry which would become the 29th Louisiana Infantry. In 1862 he was made colonel of that regiment which fought and surrendered at Vicksburg. Exchanged and returned to service, he was assigned to reorganize parolees west of the Mississippi River. In 1864 he was promoted to brigadier general in Maj. Gen. Richard Taylor's department. He took over Maj. Gen. Camille Polignac's division in 1865. After the war he was a professor of agriculture at Louisiana State University. From 1894-97 he was the American consul in Venezuela. He is buried in Donaldsonville, Louisiana.

CIVIL WAR MARYLANDERS OF NOTE

Tilghman, Brigadier General Lloyd, CSA (1816-1863)
Born at "Rich Neck Manor," Talbot County, Tilghman was from an old Eastern Shore family. After graduating from West Point he served in the Mexican War, and then was the engineer for several railroads, settling in Kentucky. During the Civil War he was inspector of Forts Henry and Donelson in Tennessee and commanded Fort Henry, which he surrendered in February 1862. After being exchanged, he assumed command of Maj. Gen. William Wing Loring's division and led the unit at Corinth, Holly Springs, and in the Vicksburg campaign. During the Battle of Champion's Hill, May 16, 1863, he was killed by a shell fragment. He is buried in Woodlawn Cemetery in New York City.

Trimble, Major General Isaac R., CSA (1802-1888)
Trimble was a native of Culpeper County, Virginia who had graduated from West Point in 1822. He served as a lieutenant of artillery until 1832 when he resigned to become an engineer for the Eastern and Southern Railway construction, living in Maryland. He was commissioned a colonel of engineering in the Confederate forces and constructed the defenses of Norfolk. He served as a brigadier general in the Valley campaign under Ewell. He was wounded at Second Manassas and returned just in time to participate in the Battle of Gettysburg, where he lost a leg and was captured. He made his home in Baltimore after the war where he was involved in veterans' activities. He is buried in Green Mount Cemetery, Baltimore.

Townsend, George Alfred (1841-1914)
Although born in Georgetown, Delaware, Townsend spent part of his childhood years on the Eastern Shore of Maryland, and made Maryland his home after the Civil War. He was a correspondent for the *New York Herald* at the beginning of the war, and became a well-known columnist after the war, taking the pen name of "GATH." A prolific writer, Townsend authored plays, poems, articles, and several novels. One of his most famous novels was *Katy of Catoctin*, a story about the Civil War in Maryland. At his home on South Mountain near Burkittsville, Maryland, he constructed the War Correspondents Arch, a monumental tribute to reporters of the Civil War.

Tubman, Harriet (c.1820-1913)
During the Civil War Harriet Tubman worked as a nurse, scout and spy for the United States Army in South Carolina. She was sent to the aid of the U.S. army in the South by Governor Andrew of Massachusetts and was employed by General Hunter, General Stevens, and General Sherman for scouting and spying and aiding in the communication with and transporting

219

of "contrabands." When not employed in this work she was a nurse at the "contraband" hospital on Hilton Head Island.

Tubman is better known as the "Moses of her People," having led more than 300 slaves to freedom on the "Underground Railroad," without ever losing a passenger. She was born a slave by the name of Araminta Ross on the Brodess plantation just south of Cambridge, on Maryland's Eastern Shore. When she was about 29 years of age she escaped to freedom by herself, and then returned about 19 times to bring others to freedom. After the war she returned to her farm near Auburn, New York.

Tyler, Brigadier General Robert Charles, CSA (1833-1865)

Born in Baltimore this adventurous mercenary soldier joined Company D of the 15th Tennessee Infantry in 1861 and by that fall had been elected captain. In December 1861 he was lieutenant colonel of the regiment and led it in the Battle of Shiloh where he was wounded. As a colonel he led the regiment in several more battles in 1863. He led the combined 15th and 37th Tennessee Infantry at Chickamauga and Missionary Ridge where he lost a leg. In February 1864 he was made a brigadier general. He was killed while defending his post at West Point, Georgia on April 16, 1865.

Vandever, (brev.) Major General William, USA (1817-1893)

Although born in Baltimore Vandever moved to the midwest when he was twenty-two, where he practiced law and was elected to Congress. In 1861 he became a colonel in the army and led a brigade at Pea Ridge. He was promoted to brigadier general and participated in the Vicksburg Campaign and the Carolina Campaign, returning to his law practice after the war. He later moved to Ventura, California and was again elected to Congress.

Vickers, Major General George, USA (1801-1879)

George Vickers was admitted to the Maryland bar in 1832 and practiced law in Chestertown. He served as a delegate to the Whig National Convention in 1852. During the Civil War he was a general of the Maryland militia. After the war he was a member of the Maryland Senate from 1866 to 1868 when he was elected to fill the vacant Maryland seat in the U.S. Senate. He is buried in Chester Cemetery, Chestertown.

Waddell, Lieutenant Commanding James Iredell (1824-1886)

Although born in Pittsboro, North Carolina, Waddell considered Annapolis his home after graduating from the Naval Academy in 1847. On hearing of the outbreak of war he resigned his commission on the USS *John Adams* in St. Helena on November 20, 1861. After marrying his sweetheart,

Ann, he proceeded to Virginia where he was commissioned first lieutenant. In October 1864 he was given command of the *Sea King*, renamed the CSS *Shenandoah* and ordered to harass the Union merchant and whaling ships. Sailing around the world he had a total of 36 prizes when he finally learned of the end of the war in August 1865. He sailed his ship to Britain, whence she had come, and surrendered on November 6, 1865, being the last command to surrender. After the war he spent the last years of his life in Annapolis in command of the Maryland Oyster Patrol.

Wallace, Colonel James, USA (1818-1887)

Born in Dorchester County in 1818, Wallace became a lawyer and was elected to the Maryland House of Delegates in 1852. In 1861, at the request of Governor Hicks, he raised the 1st Eastern Shore Volunteer Infantry Regiment. This regiment served mainly on the Eastern Shore throughout the war, but was engaged in the Battle of Gettysburg where it fought against the 2nd Maryland Infantry Regiment, CSA, on Culp's Hill. There are monuments to each regiment on the hill in Gettysburg. He is buried in Cambridge Cemetery, Cambridge in Dorchester County.

Ward, Commodore James Harmon, USN (1806-1861)

Born in Hartford, Connecticut, Ward became the U.S. Naval Academy's first executive officer in 1852, teaching from his own book, *An Elementary Course of Instruction on Ordinance and Gunnery* (1845), and living in Annapolis. In 1861 he was a commander in command of the USS *North Carolina* when he conceived of a plan to form a "flying flotilla" to protect the Chesapeake Bay and its tributaries. In the beginning the flotilla consisted of three steamers and two schooners. Its first action was in providing gun support for the invasion of Alexandria in May 1861, then in bombarding the Confederate batteries at Aquia Creek. During the attack on Confederate batteries at Matthias Point on the Potomac, Commodore Ward, on board the USS *Thomas Freeborn*, was mortally wounded, being the first U.S. Navy officer to be killed in the Civil War.

White, Colonel Elijah Veirs "Lige," CSA (1832-1907)

Born at his family's estate, Stoney Castle in Poolesville, Montgomery County, Maryland, White moved to his own farm across the Potomac River in Virginia with his new wife in 1857. After successfully capturing 325 of the enemy at the Battle of Ball's Bluff with a small force of about 35 men, he formed a cavalry unit of which he was captain. By October

1862 this unit had become so large that it was made the 35th Virginia Cavalry with White, now a major, commanding. In December 1862 he took 96 of his men on a raid into Poolesville, Maryland, capturing horses, arms, and supplies. By February 1863 the unit had grown to six companies and White was made a lieutenant colonel. The 35th Virginia participated in raids on the B & O Railroad, the Battle of Brandy Station, and the Battle of Gettysburg from day one. At the end of 1863 the brigade was made part of the 1st Cavalry Division, the Laurel Brigade, and nicknamed the "Commanches." It continued through the Wilderness, Spotsylvania, Petersburg, and the Battle of Trevalian Station. Though never given the rank of brigadier, White commanded the Laurel Brigade through the last months of the war.

After the war he became a merchant, county sheriff, and Baptist preacher. He is buried in Leesburg, Virginia.

Wilkins, Colonel Edward D., USA (1813-1878)

Wilkins was commander of the 2nd Eastern Shore Volunteer Infantry consisting of eight companies organized in Chestertown from October to December 1861. Companies A, B, C, D, and E were from Kent County; Company F from Baltimore; Companies G and H were from Harford County. They served on the Eastern Shore and in the Shenandoah Valley campaign. He is buried in Chester Cemetery, Chestertown, Maryland.

Winder, Brigadier General Charles Sidney, CSA (1829-1862)

Winder was born in Talbot County on October 18, 1829. He graduated from the U.S. Military Academy in 1850 and was promoted captain in 1855. He joined the Confederacy in April 1861 and was appointed a major of artillery. In July of the same year he was commissioned a colonel of the 6th South Carolina Infantry. He became a brigadier general in command of the "Stonewall Brigade" in Jackson's division in March 1862. After participating in several campaigns he was mortally wounded at Cedar Mountain on August 9, 1862. He is buried in the cemetery of Old Wye Episcopal Church, Talbot County, Maryland.

Winder, Brigadier General John Henry, CSA (1800-1865)

Born at "Rewston" in Somerset County, Maryland, Winder graduated from West Point in 1820. He then served in the Mexican War and rose to the rank of major. When he joined the Confederate army in April 1861, he was made provost marshal of Richmond, a command which made him unpopular among the citizens. In 1864 he was assigned the duties of commissary general of prisoners east of the Mississippi. The Federal government's refusal to effect an exchange of prisoners at that point, compounded by the lack of provisions, made his task almost impossible and brought him much criticism from the North. He died of anxiety and exhaustion in Florence, South Carolina, February 2, 1865. He is buried in Green Mount Cemetery, Baltimore.

Wood, Colonel John Taylor, CSA (First Lieutenant, CSN) (c.1803-1904)

One of the few men to hold a dual rank in both the navy and army, Wood was born in Iowa territory, but was living in Maryland and teaching at the Naval Academy in Annapolis at the beginning of the war. A graduate of the Naval Academy, he was the nephew of Jefferson Davis. He was serving on the CSS *Virginia* during the battle with the USS *Monitor*, and led the crew in manning the heavy artillery at Drewry's Bluff, aiding in the Confederate victory. During the fall of 1862 he led two small-draft boats with a crew of about 15 on several daring raids, capturing the schooner *Frances Elmore* and the merchant ship *Alleghanian*. In the summer and fall of 1863 they captured the USS *Reliance* and the USS *Satellite* at the same time, then the schooner *Golden Rod* and the anchor-sweepers *Two Brothers* and *Coquette*. He was with Jefferson Davis when General Lee surrendered and escaped with him to Georgia where he was captured with Davis. But Wood escaped and made his way to Florida where, with John C. Breckenridge and four others, he sailed to Cuba in a lifeboat, nearly losing his life in a storm. After the war he settled in Canada with his wife and children.

Zarvona, Colonel Richard Thomas, CSA, Zarvona's Zouaves (?-1875)

Born in St. Mary's County, Maryland, as Richard Thomas, this young man left the Military Academy at West Point to go to Italy to fight with Garibaldi. At that time he changed his last name to Zarvona. At the beginning of the Civil War he returned home and formed Zarvona's Maryland Zouaves, CSA. He joined with Captain Hollins in the capture of the *St. Nicholas* on June 28, 1861, but a week later was arrested and imprisoned at Fort Lafayette in New York until 1863. He then went back to Europe and was a soldier in the Franco-Prussian War. He later returned to southern Maryland, died about 1870, and is buried in the family burial grounds at Deep Falls, St. Mary's County.

CIVIL WAR MARYLANDERS OF NOTE

FOR ADDITIONAL INFORMATION

Goldsborough, W. W. *The Maryland Line in the Confederate Army 1861-1865.* Gaithersburg, Md.: Butternut Press, 1983 (reprinted from 1900).

Hartzler, Daniel D. *Marylanders in the Confederacy.* Silver Spring, Md.: Family Line Publications, 1986.

Hartzler, Daniel D. *Medical Doctors of Maryland in the CSA.* Silver Spring, Md.: Family Line Publications, 1979.

Toomey, Daniel Carroll. *Marylanders at Gettysburg.* Baltimore, Md.: Toomey Press, 1994.

Warner, Ezra J. *Generals in Blue* and *Generals in Gray.* Louisiana State, 1959.

224

APPENDIX C

ROUTE MAPS

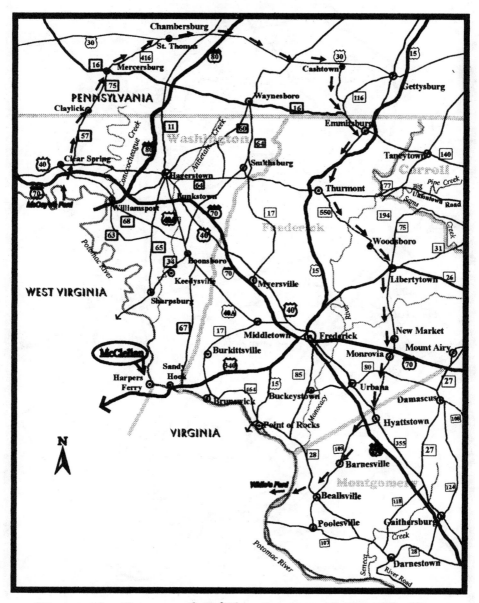

Stuart's Second Ride Around McClellan
October 10-12, 1862

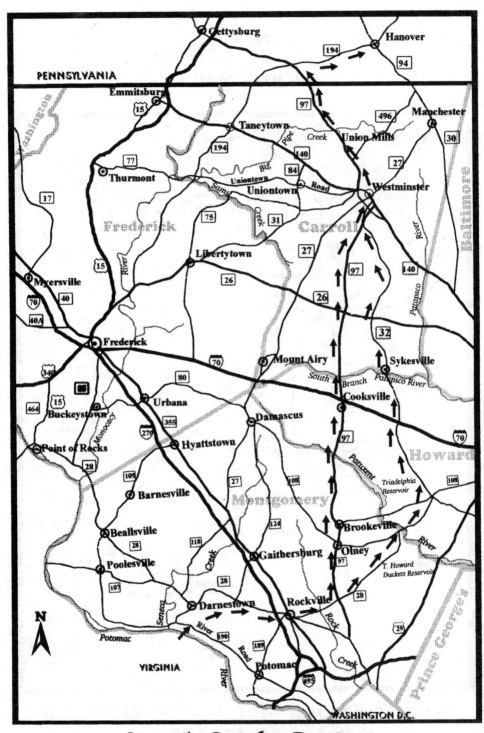

Stuart's Cavalry Route
on June 27-July 1, 1863

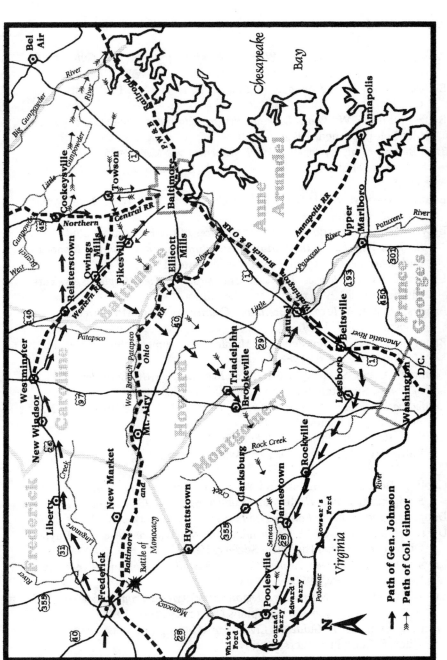

Confederate Cavalry Raid of July 1864

BIBLIOGRAPHY

Adams, Charles S. *The Civil War in Frederick County, Maryland*. Self-published, 1995.

Adams, Charles S. *The Civil War in Washington County: A Guide to 66 Points of Interest*. Self-published, Shepherdstown, W.V., 1996.

Beirne, Francis F. *The Amiable Baltimoreans*. New York: E. P. Dutton and Co., 1951.

Beitzell, Edwin W. *Point Lookout Prison Camp for Confederates*. Abell, Md. Self-published, 1972.

The Biographical Cyclopedia of Representative Men of Maryland and Baltimore. Baltimore, Md.: National Biographical Publishing Co., 1879.

Boatner, Mark Mayo III. *The Civil War Dictionary*. New York: David McKay Co., Inc., 1987.

Bowie, Oden. *Description of the Burial Places of the Remains of Confederate Soldiers Who Fell in the Battles of Antietam, South Mountain, Monocacy and Others*. Hagerstown: Free Press, no date [1868].

Bradford, Sarah. *Harriet Tubman: The Moses of Her People*. New York: Citadel Press, 1994 (reprint of 1886 edition).

Brooks, Neal A. *A History of Baltimore County*. Towson, Md.: Friends of the Towson Library, 1979.

Brugger, Robert J. *Maryland: A Middle Temperament*. Baltimore: Johns Hopkins Univ. Press, 1988.

Clemmer, Gregg S. *Valor in Gray: The Recipients of the Confederate Medal of Honor*. Staunton, Va.: The Hearthside Publishing Co., 1996.

Confederate Military History, Extended Edition, Vol. II. Wilmington, N.C.: Broadfoot Publishing Co., 1987.

Cooling, Benjamin Franklin. *Jubal Early's Raid on Washington: 1864*. Baltimore: The Nautical and Aviation Publishing Co. of America, 1989.

Cooling, Benjamin Franklin, and Walton H. Owen II. *Mr. Lincoln's Forts*. Shippensburg, Pa.: White Mane Publishing Co., 1988.

Douglass, Frederick. *My Bondage and Freedom*. New York: Arno Press, 1968.

Dyer, Frederick H., ed. *A Compendium of the War of Rebellion*. Dayton, Ohio: The National Historical Society, 1979.

Emory, Frederic. *Queen Anne's County, Maryland*. Baltimore: Maryland Historical Society, 1950.

Evitts, William J. *A Matter of Allegiances: Maryland From 1850 To 1861*. Baltimore, Md.: The Johns Hopkins University Press, 1974.

Forman, Stephen. *A Guide to Civil War Washington*. Washington, D.C.: Elliott & Clark Publishers, 1995.

Hahn, Thomas F. *Towpath Guide to the C & O Canal* (4 sections). Shepherdstown, W.V.: the American Canal and Transportation Center, 1974.

Hartzler, Daniel D. *Marylanders in the Confederacy*. Silver Spring, Md.: Family Line Publications, 1986.

Hartzler, Daniel D. *Medical Doctors of Maryland in the CSA*. Silver Spring, Md.: Family Line Publications, 1979.

Hiebert, Eldon, and Richard K. MacMaster. *A Grateful Remembrance: The Story of Montgomery County*. Rockville, Md.: Montgomery County Government, 1976.

Holien, Kim Bernard. *Battle at Ball's Bluff*. Self-published, 1985.

Holly, David C. *Tidewater by Steamboat: A Saga of the Chesapeake Bay*. Baltimore: Johns Hopkins Univ. Press, 1991.

Hoye, Captain Charles E. "General Jones' Raid Through Garrett County, Maryland," in the Garrett County Historical Society file, reprinted from the *Oakland (Maryland) Republican*.

Hoye, Captain Charles E. "The War in This Section," *The Glades Star*, Civil War Centennial Issue, vol. 3, #5 (June 1961), published by the Garrett County Historical Society.

Hunt, Roger D., and Jack R. Brown. *Brevet Brigadier Generals in Blue*. Gaithersburg, Md.: Old Soldiers Books, 1990.

Jacobs, Charles T. *Civil War Guide to Montgomery County, Maryland*. Montgomery County Historical Society, 1983 (revised 1996).

Jacobs, Timothy, ed. *The History of the Baltimore and Ohio: America's First Railroad*. New York: Crescent Books, 1989.

Keller, S. Roger. *Events of the Civil War in Washington County, Maryland*. Shippensburg, Pa.: Burd Street Press, 1995.

Klapthor, Margaret Brown, and Paul Dennis Brown. *The History of Charles County, Maryland*. La Plata, Md.: Charles County Tercentenary, Inc., 1958.

Klein, Fredrick S. *Just South of Gettysburg*. Westminster, Md.: Historical Soc. of Carroll Cnty, 1963.

Klein, Fredrick S. "Meade's Pipe Creek Plan," Maryland Historical Magazine, 57 (1962): 133-49.

Leach, Isabelle. "Dr. Isaac Costen: From Blockade Runner to Mayor." Costen House, Spirit of Newtown Committee, Pocomoke City, Md.

Manakee, Harold R. *Maryland in the Civil War*. Baltimore: Maryland Historical Society, 1961.

Maryland Civil War Centennial Commission. *Maryland Remembers: A Guide to Historic Places and People of the Civil War in Maryland*. Hagerstown, Md., 1961.

Massey, Mary Elizabeth. *Women in the Civil War.* Lincoln, Nebr.: University of Nebraska Press, 1966.

Mills, Eric. *Chesapeake Bay in the Civil War.* Centreville, Md.: Tidewater Publishers, 1996.

Nesbitt, Mark. *Rebel Rivers: A Guide to Civil War Sites on the Potomac, Rappahannock, York, and James.* Mechanicsville, Pa.: Stackpole Books, 1993.

Paul, William A. B. *Despot's Heel on Talbot.* Self-published, 1966.

Portrait and Biographical Record of the Eastern Shore of Maryland, New York: Chapman Publishing Co., 1898.

Posey, Calvert, and Judith L. *A History of the Role Charles County Played in the Civil War.* Self-published (no date).

Preston, Dickson J. *Talbot County, A History.* Centreville, Md.: Tidewater Publishers, 1983.

Priest, John Michael. *Before Antietam: The Battle for South Mountain.* Shippensburg, Pa.: White Mane Publishing Co., 1995.

Robinson, Felix G., ed. *Tableland Trails,* vol. II, #4 (summer, 1963).

Rusk, William Sener. *Art in Baltimore: Monuments and Memorials.* Baltimore: Norman Remington Co., 1929.

Scharf, J. Thomas. *History of Baltimore City and County.* Baltimore: Regional Publishing Company, 1971 (reprint of 1881 edition).

Scharf, J. Thomas. *History of Western Maryland.* Baltimore: Regional Publishing Company, 1968 (reprint of 1882 edition).

Schlosnagle, Stephen, and the Garrett County Bicentennial Commission. *Garrett County: A History of Maryland's Tableland.* Parsons, W.V.: McLain Printing Co, 1978.

Scott, Harold L., Sr. *The Civil War Hospitals at Cumberland and Clarysville, Maryland.* Cumberland, Md., self-published.

Shields, Jerry. *Gath's Literary Work and Folk and Other Selected Writings of George Alfred Townsend.* Wilmington, Del.: Delaware Heritage Press, 1996.

Shriver, Frank R. *Walking in Baltimore: An Intimate Guide to the Old City.* Baltimore: Johns Hopkins Univ. Press, 1995.

Sifakis, Stewart. *Who Was Who in the Civil War.* New York: Facts on File Publications, 1988.

Soderberg, Susan. *A History of Germantown, Maryland.* Self-published, 1988.

Soderberg, Susan Cooke. *Lest We Forget: A Guide to Civil War Monuments in Maryland.* Shippensburg, Pa.: White Mane Publishing Co., 1995.

Steers, Edward, Jr. *His Name is Still Mudd: The Case Against Dr. Samuel Alexander Mudd.* Gettysburg, Pa.: Thomas Publications, 1997.

230

BIBLIOGRAPHY

Steers, Edward, Jr., and Joan L. Chaconas. *The Escape & Capture of John Wilkes Booth*. Marker Tours, revised May 1989.

Stegmaier, Harry I., et al. *Allegany County: A History*. Parsons, W.V.: McLain Printing Company, 1976.

Stotelmyer, Steven R. *The Bivouacs of the Dead*. Baltimore, Md.: Toomey Press, 1992.

Summers, Festus P. *The Baltimore and Ohio in the Civil War*. Gettysburg, Pa.: Stan Clark Military Books, 1992 (reprint of 1939 edition).

Thomas, James W., and T. J. C. Williams. *History of Allegany County*. Cumberland, Md.: L.R. Titsworth & Co., 1923.

Tidwell, William A. *April '65: Confederate Covert Action in the American Civil War*. Kent, Ohio: Kent State Univ. Press, 1995.

Tidwell, William A., James O. Hall, and David Winfred Gaddy. *Come Retribution: Confederate Secret Service and the Assassination of Lincoln*. Oxford: University Press of Mississippi, 1988.

Toomey, Daniel Carroll. *The Civil War in Maryland*. Baltimore, Md.: Toomey Press, 1988.

Toomey, Daniel Carroll. *A History of Relay, Maryland and the Thomas Viaduct*. Baltimore, Md.: Toomey Press, 1984.

Toomey, Daniel Carroll. *Marylanders at Gettysburg*. Baltimore, Md.: Toomey Press, 1994.

Touart, Paul Baker. *Along the Seaboard Side: The Architectural History of Worcester County, Maryland*. Worcester County, 1994.

Truitt, Dr. Reginald V., and Dr. Millard G. Les Collette. *Worcester County: America's Arcadia*. Snow Hill: Worcester County Historical Soc., 1977.

Warren, Nancy M., et al. *Carroll County, Maryland: A History*. Westminster: Carroll County Bicentennial Committee, 1976.

Warner, Ezra J. *Generals in Blue*. Louisiana State, 1959.

Warner, Ezra J. *Generals in Gray*. Louisiana State, 1959.

Weeks, Christopher. *Between the Nanticoke and Choptank: An Architectural History of Dorchester County, Maryland*. Baltimore: The Johns Hopkins Univ. Press, 1984.

Weeks, Christopher. *When Land and Water Intertwine: An Architectural History of Talbot County, Maryland*. Baltimore: The Johns Hopkins Univ. Press, 1984.

Wennersten, John R. *Maryland's Eastern Shore: A Journey in Time and Place*. Centreville, Va.: Tidewater Publishers, 1992.

Who Was Who. Historical Volume. Chicago: A. N. Marquis Co., 1963.

Williams, Thomas J. C. *A History of Washington County*. Hagerstown: J. M. Runk and L. R. Titsworth, Publishers, 1906.

BIBLIOGRAPHY

Williams, Thomas J. C. *A History of Frederick County*. Hagerstown: L. R. Titsworth, Publisher, 1910.

Williams, Thomas J. C. *A History of Western Maryland*. Baltimore: Regional Publishing Co., 1906, Vols. I & II.

Wilson, Jane B. *The Very Quiet Baltimoreans*. Shippensburg, Pa.: White Mane Publishing Co., 1991.

Worthington, Glenn H. *Fighting for Time: The Battle That Saved Washington*. Shippensburg, Pa.: White Mane Publishing Co., 1988 (orig. 1932).

INDEX

INDEX

Stuart's
Oct. 1862: xxi, 41, 56, 71,
73, 77, 127, 128, 225
June, 1863: xxii, 41, 43,
44, 45, 47, 56, 61, 63,
66 , 226
McNeill's Rangers, 129, 140, 144,
145, 146
Mosby's Rangers, 64, 66, 69, 98
Voss, Col. Arno, CSA, 105

W

Waddell, Capt. James, CSN, 24, 26, 184, 220
Walker, Maj. Gen. John E., CSA, 79, 104,
107, 195, 204
Wallace, Col. James, USA, 172, 173, 183,
221
Wallace, Maj. Gen. Lew, USA, xxii, 4, 5, 83,
137
Wallis, Severn Teackle, 8, 16
War Correspondents Arch, 96-97
Ward, Commodore James, USN, 24, 28,
162, 221
Ward, Capt. Thomas, USA, 188
Washington, D.C., attack on, 55, 57, 60, 64-
66, 68-70, 72, 82-83, 88-89
Washington Branch of the B & O Railroad,
xix, 5, 18
Washington Cemetery, Hagerstown, 118
Washington County, 101-129
Washington Monument, Baltimore, 15
Washington Monument, South Mountain,
95
Watts Branch Skirmish, 60
Weaver, Dr. Jacob, 49
Weaver, Harrison, 49
Weaver House, Uniontown, 49
Weems steamboat line, 165, 167
West Virginia, statehood, xvii, 133
Westminster, Md., xviii, xxii, 15, 41, 42, 43,
44-45, 46, 63
Weverton Cotton Mills, 103
Wheeling, Va. (W. Va.), xvii, xviii, 13, 14,
32, 101, 133, 137, 138
White, Col. Elijah V. ("Lige"), CSA, 56, 63,
66, 67, 68, 69, 70, 212, 221
White, Levi, 5
White's (Conrad's) Ferry, 68, 81, 194
White's Ford, xxi, 56, 68, 70, 71, 72, 73, 78,
81, 127, 194

Wicomico County, 176, 189
Wilkins, Col. Edward D., USA, 172, 222
Williams, Brig. Gen. Alpheus, USA, 122
Williams, Jerome, 161
Williamsport, Md., xix, xxi, xxii, 66, 77, 102,
105, 113, 114, 119, 120, 122, 123, 124
Winans steam gun, 32
Winans, Ross, 8, 32
Winchester, Va., xix, xxii, 123, 134, 138
Winder, Brig. Gen. Charles Sidney, CSA,
175, 222
Winder, Brig. Gen. John Henry, CSA, 176,
222
Wisconsin military units
4th Wisconsin Infantry, 191
Wood, Col. John Taylor, CSA, 24, 162, 223
Worcester County, 176, 190-191
Worthington House, 83
Wright, Brig. Gen. Horatio, USA, 67, 72, 116
writ of *habeas corpus*, 7, 26, 218
Wye House, 175, 178, 200

Y

Yeocomico River, Va., 162
Youghioheny River, 145

Z

Zarvona, Col. Richard Thomas, CSA, 162,
167, 223
Zion Episcopal Church, Urbana, 82
Zion Evangelical Church, Hagerstown, 120
Zion Lutheran Church, Middletown, 93

246